101 Weapons of
Spiritual
Warfare

101 WEAPONS OF SPIRITUAL WARFARE

ISBN 978-978-920-071-9
July 2013

Published by

THE BATTLE CRY CHRISTIAN MINISTRIES
322, Herbert Macaulay Way, Yaba, Lagos.
P. O. Box 12272, Ikeja, Lagos.
08033044239, 01-8044415

All Scripture quotations are from the
King James version of the Bible.
Unless otherwise stated.

Cover page illustration by
Pastor (Mrs.) Shade Olukoya

DR. D. K. OLUKOYA

APPRECIATION

I salute my wonderful wife, Pastor Shade, for her invaluable support in the ministry. I appreciate her unquantifiable support in the book ministry as the cover designer, art editor and art advisor.

– CONTENTS –

INTRODUCTION

Never in the history of the world has there been an era of war, both physical and spiritual, like this era. This is a tougher era of warfare. More people are under bondage now, more than in any other period of human history. There are cases of deep bondage, uncommon attacks against the family and horrendous occurrences in the lives of individuals. The devil has wreaked a lot of havoc upon humanity. The Bible has described, in vivid terms, the activities of satanic agents.
Psalm 74:20

Have respect unto the covenant: for the dark places of the earth are full of the habitations of cruelty.

You do not need to go too far to have a feel of the horrific events that are going on in the habitations of cruelty. Beloved, the devil has painted the world in cruel or harsh colours. We cannot afford to fold our arms or bury our heads in the sand like the proverbial ostrich. The world is looking up to the militant church to rescue the perishing and the bewitched. To be quite honest with you, globally, the Church has converted the Mountain of Fire and Miracles Ministries to an intensive care hospital. Many rush to our deliverance programmes in search of urgent help.

God is aware of the high spate of demonic hostilities. Hence, the Holy Ghost has vomited the prophetic revelations in this book in order to place us in good stead for a unique role in this end times. This manual is the first of its kind. This manual exceeds the entire nuclear weapons which have been put together by nations of the world. God has just launched an array of weapons that have never been researched into and presented in our entire history.

This is the apex of deliverance. We are at the threshold of a revival of spiritual warfare. The sweeping and the far reaching effect shall be best described as awesome!

Your friend in the school of prayer and deliverance,

Dr. D.K. Olukoya

take charge now!

WEAPON

1

THE STARS

► *WHEN DEALING WITH MURDEROUS PURSUERS.*
► *WHEN DEALING WITH STRONGMEN HAVING FEARFUL CREDENTIALS.*
► *WHEN YOU ARE DEALING WITH HOUSE HOLD WITCHCRAFT.*
► *WHEN YOU ARE BATTLING THE SPIRIT OF DEATH AND HELL.*
► *FOR VICTIMS OF STAR HUNTERS.*
► *DEALING WITH DRAWERS OF POWERS FROM THE HEAVENLIES.*

The numbers of weapons in God's armory are simply awesome. There is a level of mastery you would attain in spiritual warfare when you learn to make use of advanced weapons. God has reserved unique weapons for a special squad in his army. Tested and proven deliverance ministers and experts in spiritual warfare make use of weapons that are unique. No wonder the Psalmist described a class of warriors whose hands are taught to war and fingers to fight. **Psalm 144:1**

> ***Blessed be the LORD my strength, which teacheth my hands to war, and my fingers to fight:***

AN ADVANCED SCHOOL

Beloved, I have a burden for believers in this generation. A lot of children of God are yet to include spiritual warfare in their curriculum. Only very few can actually say that their hands have been taught to do warfare and their fingers to fight the battles of life. When you begin to make use of the types of weapons analyzed in this manual. You will begin to confess like David. **2Sam. 22:35**

> ***He teacheth my hands to war; so that a bow of steel is broken by mine arms.***

I want you to meditate on the above verse once again. The phrase "teacheth my hands to war" actually suggests that we should come up with an advanced school of spiritual warfare where seasoned warriors and deliverance ministers are taught to use spiritual weapons like the sword or the battle axe. The church should no longer fold her hands. We must not close our eyes and allow the enemy to do reckless damage in our environment.

WAR COLLEGE

Towards this end, we shall devote a lot of energy to teaching those who want to win the end time battle and be used of God to undo heavy burdens and lead God's children into the realm of total deliverance. The church has stayed for too long a time without being battle ready. Global occurrences have confirmed the fact that this is the era of intense warfare. Men and women are going into bondage in their droves. We must go back to the Bible and re-discover the essence of warfare. **Judges 5:20**

> ***They fought from heaven; the stars in their courses fought against Sisera.***

Beloved, how many modern Christians understand what the Bible means when it says that stars fought against Sisera. The mystery of the weapon of the stars is deep. There are many levels of spiritual warfare weapons. Unknown to many people, God has placed soldiers in strategic places in the universe. The phrase, "The stars in their courses" means the stars in their realm.

WAR BULLETS

Beloved, stars have bullets. Stars are weapons of spiritual warfare. Stars are loaded with spiritual bombs. Sisera did not know that stars would be used as a weapon to fight against him. The mystery of co-operative warfare is that God has placed weapons in strategic places to deal with the enemy. You can imagine the force of the constellation of stars, when God decides to use them as weapons of destabilizing and damaging the enemy.

Beloved, there is a realm of spiritual warfare we must attain in this end times. The stars are not just there to adorn the sky. They are God's soldiers. Stars are God's weapons for oppressing and disgracing the enemy. When you invoke the stars, enemies are in trouble.

PRAYER POINTS

1. Any evil thing programmed into the sun and moon against my life, be dismantled, in the name of Jesus.

2. You spiritual wickedness in the heavenlies militating against my star, I bring the hook of the Lord against you and frustrate your activities, in the name of Jesus.

3. Any evil thing written in the cycle of the moon against me, be blotted out, in the name of Jesus.

4. Let every satanic checkpoint mounted against me in the heavenlies be dismantled by the word of the Lord, in the name of Jesus.

5. Every evil altar prepared against my breakthrough in the heavenlies, and in the sea, be dismantled by fire, in the name of Jesus.

6. Every arrangement that sorcerers and witches have prepared against me, be overthrown, in the name of Jesus.

7. I send lightening, thunder and the hook of the Lord against the evil queen in the heavenlies militating against me, in the name of Jesus

WEAPON

2

THE SPEAR OF THE LORD

▶ TO BE USED DURING INTENSIVE WARFARE.
▶ TO TACKLE STUBBORN PURSUERS AND PERSECUTORS.
▶ TO BE USED WHEN PEOPLE ARE ASKING "WHERE IS YOUR GOD?".
▶ TO SEND JUDGMENT TO THE CAMP OF WICKED ENEMIES.
▶ TO FORCE THE ENEMY TO TAKE A BOW.
▶ TO BE USED WHEN YOU FACE RECURRENT DREAM BATTLES.
▶ TO BE USED WHEN YOU ARE FACING MULTIPLE ENEMIES.

The weapons of spiritual warfare are created for diverse purposes. Distinct from human weapons and superior to the weapons of the kingdom of darkness, weapons of spiritual warfare have been meticulously manufactured by God to enable us score hundred percent victory in the battles of life.
Going to the field of battle without weapons that have been proven and tested will expose the fighter to danger, and if possible, death or destruction. God has spared no effort in creating error free weapons so that we would be able to conquer the enemy swiftly, decisively and completely. If human beings can spend billions to research, discover and produce physical weapons of warfare, how much more the Ancient of days who has all power, ability and resources to produce first class spiritual warfare equipment and weapons?

A MIGHTY WEAPON

The Bible makes it crystal clear that the weapons of our warfare are not carnal but mighty through God to destroy and disgrace all types of enemies that may come our way. **2Cor. 10:4**

> ***(For the weapons of our warfare are not carnal, but mighty through God to the pulling down of strong holds;)***

Other verses in this chapter contain a preliminary list of weapons. But there are other terrible weapons tucked in here and there in the scriptures. The weapons are supposed to be discovered and utilised by serious students in the school of spiritual warfare. Just as gold cannot be found lying on the surface of the ground, they must be explored, refined and utilised if profit must be derived from them. In the same vein, rare spiritual warfare weapons cannot be found lying here and there. It takes an earnest researcher to dig deep into the body of spiritual warfare scriptures and begin to make use of them.

A TOUGH RESEARCH

To be quite honest with you beloved, this book contains one of the toughest researches which God has ever led me into in close to forty years of deep research into uncommon areas in the scriptures. The more I discover these rare weapons, the more my heart goes out to Christian believers who have been tossed here and there by wicked powers. How can you say that you are an end time believer and you know close to nothing about spiritual warfare? How can you claim that your hands have been taught to war and fingers to fight when you know nothing concerning powerful weapons of spiritual warfare?

What I have said so far is to prepare your mind for the wonders of this particular weapon; the weapon is what I have called the weapon of the **"Spear of the Lord".**

CLASSES OF ENEMIES

There are classes of enemies that cannot be handled with ordinary weapons. They must be tackled decisively through the use of high class weapons of spiritual warfare. The spear of the Lord is one weapon that has swallowed the blood of the enemy. It is a weapon that can be used to disembowel wicked personalities. It is one weapon that can be used to send Goliath to an early grave. It is one weapon that can be used to subject wicked powers to sorrow and mourning. It is a tough weapon that the enemy cannot withstand.

When the heavens draw out the spear, no evil power can trespass, no persecutor can move forward and no attacker can come anywhere near you. When the spear of the Almighty is drawn, the battle line is drawn. The drawing out of the divine spear reveals the Almighty as the Captain of your salvation.

DIVINE INTERVENTION

The spear is a symbol of divine intervention. It represents the might of the Almighty. When the spear is drawn, evil powers are made to see the strength of the arm of the Lord, the rage of His fury and the resolve of heaven to make your life a no go area for dark powers. **Psalms 35:3**

> ***Draw out also the spear, and stop the way against them that persecute me: say unto my soul, I am thy salvation.***

The spear of the Lord is the spear of judgment. The Lord's spear is the spear of vengeance. The spear of the Lord is thirsty for the blood of your oppressors. The spear of the Lord is a weapon that is needed to orchestrate the burial of the powers that will not let you go. The spear of the Lord is what will draw Pharaoh and all his officers into the arena of their graveyard. The spear of the Lord is a weapon that you need to disgrace your oppressors and scatter your enemies.

A GALLANT EXIT

The spear of the Lord is a weapon that is needed to grant you a gallant exit from the prison of darkness. The spear of the Lord is a weapon of unchallengeable victory. When you stretch out the spear of the Lord towards a particular department of your life, victory is won. The spear of the Lord is a weapon of conquest and uncommon victory over the kingdom of darkness. **Joshua 8:18**

> ***And the LORD said unto Joshua, Stretch out the spear that is in thy hand toward Ai; for I will give it into thine hand. And Joshua stretched out the spear that he had in his hand toward the city.***

REGAL AUTHORITY

It is unfortunate, however, when the spear of the Lord is not even known not to talk of being utilised by members of the Lord's army. It is a tragedy beloved, that in this generation, the weapon of the spear of the Lord has not been discovered. Only very few know how to invoke the spear of the Lord and draw it against the territory of the enemy. When the Lord's spear is not utilised, the enemy will continue to have a field day; witches and wizards will continue to swallow the virtues of God's people. **Judges 5:8**

> ***They chose new gods; then was war in the gates: was there a shield or spear seen among forty thousand in Israel?***

The spear is a symbol of regal authority. It is also referred to as a javelin. **1 Sam 18:11**

> ***"And Saul cast the javelin; for he said, I will smite David even to the wall with it. And David avoided out of his presence twice."***

SMITE THE ENEMY

With the javelin or the spear of the Lord, you can smite your enemy. The enemy cannot flee unless you smite him. God has created the spear to orchestrate the destruction of enemies that will not stop pursuing you. If you have been in and out of battles, if you have become a perpetual victim of bondage and if you want to experience total deliverance, you must use the weapon of the spear or javelin.

The spear of the Lord is loaded with the regal power of the Lord. No power of the enemy, no agent of darkness, no stubborn pursuer can withstand the onslaught of the Lord's spear. This is one weapon that will put paid to all forms of satanic harassment. This weapon will enable you to sing your song and dance your dance.

Prayer Points that send the spear of the Lord to the territory of the enemy will usher you into resounding victory and complete deliverance.

PRAYER POINTS

1. Spear of the Lord, locate and destroy every enemy of my destiny.
2. O heavens, bombard every evil gathering assigned against me with the spear of the Lord
3. My father, locate every hidden enemy of my soul with your spear
4. Where is the spear of the God of Elijah? Pursue my pursuers in the name of Jesus
5. Every power shooting me from the dark, receive the spear of the Lord in Jesus name
6. O spear of the Lord, arise in the thunder of your power and paralyse my oppressors in Jesus name
7. Drinkers of blood and eaters of flesh, hear the word of the Lord, receive the spear of heaven
8. O spear of the Lord, arise, send confusion into the camps of my enemies, in the name of Jesus.
9. O heavens, bombard every evil gathering assigned against me with the spear of the Lord, in the name of Jesus.
10. My Father, locate every hidden enemy of my soul with Your spear, in the name of Jesus.

11. Let the spear of the God of Elijah pursue my pursuers, in the name of Jesus.
12. Drinkers of blood and eaters of flesh, hear the word of the Lord, receive the spear of heaven, in the name of Jesus.
13. Let the spear of the Lord arise and fight for me, in the name of Jesus,
14. Every power shooting at me from the dark, receive the spear of the Lord, in the name of Jesus.
15. O spear of the Lord, arise in the thunder of Your power and paralyse my oppressors, in the name of Jesus.

WEAPON 3

THE MYSTERY OF THE FLYING ROLLS

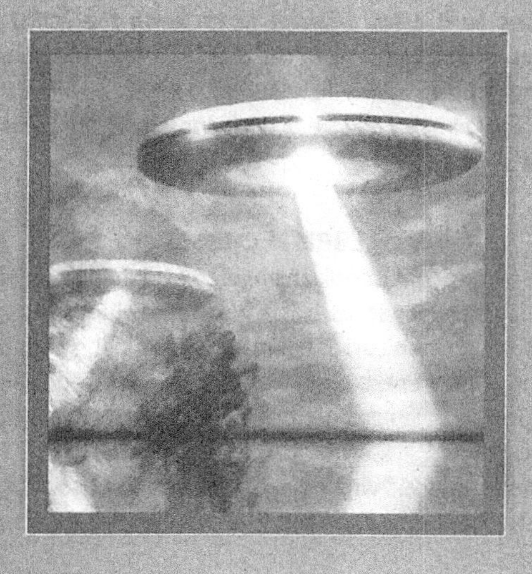

► *TO RECOVER STOLEN MATERIALS.*
► *A WEAPON TO ENFORCE RESTORATION.*
► *FOR VICTORY OVER HOUSE HOLD WICKEDNESS.*
► *TO DISGRACE FAMILIAR SPIRITS.*
► *TO TACKLE THE ARROW OF DEATH.*
► *TO DEAL WITH COMPETITORS THAT ARE USING FETISH POWER AGAINST YOU.*

This is one weapon that is conveyed by angels that have no mercy. It is called mystery of the flying rolls. This is no doubt a unique weapon that has elaborate functions. It is described below. **Zechariah 5:1-4**

> ***"Then I turned, and lifted up mine eyes, and looked, and behold a flying roll. And he said unto me, What seest thou? And I answered, I see a flying roll; the length thereof is twenty cubits, and the breadth thereof ten cubits. Then said he unto me, This is the curse that goeth forth over the face of the whole earth: for every one that stealeth shall be cut off as on this side according to it; and every one that sweareth shall be cut off as on that side according to it. I will bring it forth, saith the LORD of hosts, and it shall enter into the house of the thief, and into the house of him that sweareth falsely by my name: and it shall remain in the midst of his house, and shall consume it with the timber thereof and the stones thereof".***

TERRIBLE CURSES

This weapon is so deep that it took an angel to explain the mystery behind it. It is a weapon that is unusually long. It is a weapon of judgment. It functions as a divine curse; on it is written curses against evil doers. It is capable of catching up with and arresting God's enemy universally. It can be used against enemies who have violated God's commandment like "touch not my anointed and do my prophets no harm".

One of the mysteries of the flying roll is that divine curses written on it cannot be escaped by any human being or power. The fact that this weapon flies describes the speed of God's judgment. It also reminds us of the fact that it can catch up with any enemy anywhere in the world. The fact that the curses are written on both sides emphasizes its ability to catch up with satanic agents wherever they are hiding.

A MYSTERIOUS WEAPON

The beauty of this weapon is that head or tail, dark agents, familiar spirits or household wickedness will lose. This weapon is completely shrouded in mystery. The flight of the roll shows that God's move against the enemy is mysterious. This weapon has been created by the Almighty to cut the enemy off.
This is the weapon that God uses when He is angry with the wicked. It is a weapon that consumes without leaving any remnant. When this weapon lands upon the head of the enemy it can vomit instant death, leprosy, paralysis, death or the wiping away of the army of darkness.

AN UNSUAL WEAPON

The flying roll is not a weapon that God brings out on an ordinary day. It is a weapon that is used when God wants to deal with multiple enemies. It is a weapon of judgment without mercy. It is a weapon that can be used to send evil arrows to sender. It is the weapon to use when the battle cry is 'enough is enough'. It is the weapon to use when you want to stop evil powers before they stop you and you want to make agents of darkness to fall into the pit which they constructed for you.
This is a weapon that suits wicked Pharaoh and stubborn Herod. It is the best weapon to use against powers that have vowed that your destiny will never see the light of day. When you use this weapon, your victory is final and your enemies will be buried in shame. This is the weapon to use when you want to blind the enemy and make evil powers to become blindfolded and begin to destroy themselves. The weapon of the mystery of the flying roll unfortunately, has been lying unused in God's armory. This is the time to bring it out.

PRAYER POINTS

1. Let heavens release the flying rolls to enforce the release of every good thing stolen from me, in the name of Jesus.
2. O flying rolls, be released against the destiny robbers assigned

against my life, in the name of Jesus.

2. Every destiny robber assigned against my life, I come against you with the flying roll in the name of Jesus
3. Let the mystery of the flying roll defend my portion, in the name of Jesus.
4. I invoke the power of the flying roll to arrest my arrester in the name of Jesus.
5. In the heavenlies, on earth, in the water, let the flying roll recover my stolen possession, in the name of Jesus.
6. Flying roll from heaven, confuse every cover assigned against my destiny, in the name of Jesus.
7. Power of the flying roll arise in your mysterious power and scatter my oppressors, in the name of Jesus.
8. O heavens, release the flying roll to enforce the release of every good thing stolen from me, in the name of Jesus.

WEAPON

4

THE HISS OF THE LORD

▶ TO BE USED WHEN YOU WANT TO SUMMON DIVINE POWER FROM HEAVEN.
▶ SUITABLE FOR USE WHEN YOU NEED ANGELIC ASSISTANCE.
▶ TO STOP WICKED POWERS BEFORE THEY STOP YOU.
▶ TO FIGHT ANCESTRAL BATTLES.
▶ TO BE USED FOR OVERCOMING BATTLES IN THE FAMILY.
▶ TO BE USED WHEN YOU WANT TO OBTAIN YOUR FOREIGN BENEFITS.
▶ TO BE USED WHEN YOU ARE FIGHTING CRITICAL BATTLES IN THE AREA OF DELIVERANCE.

This is a method which God has created to enable us deal with the enemy and bury all manner of satanic agents in shame and disgrace. God uses the weapon of hiss to silence the enemy and put an end to all that is done contrary to the plan and purpose of God for your life.
Beside the fact that God uses the hiss as a weapon of judgment, He also uses it as a weapon of granting his children swift victory. **Isaiah 5:26**

> ***And he will lift up an ensign to the nations from far, and will hiss unto them from the end of the earth: and, behold, they shall come with speed swiftly:***

A DIVINE SUMMON

With one powerful hiss from the Lord divine soldiers shall respond as if they are responding to the whistle of warfare. The divine hiss functions as a weapon of issuing summons to violent warriors, who are empowered to fight and demolish the camp of the enemy. **Isaiah 7:18**

> ***And it shall come to pass in that day, that the LORD shall hiss for the fly that is in the uttermost part of the rivers of Egypt, and for the bee that is in the land of Assyria.***

Here we discover that the hiss does not function alone as a weapon. Wherever the hiss sounds, some flies and bees shall invade the enemy like an avalanche. Beloved, God has given us all kinds of strange weapons which we are yet to learn how to utilize. When a hiss is released by God, the enemy is in trouble.

DIVINE SOLDIERS IN WAITING

The word hiss is very symbolic. It is taken from the practice of bee keepers. They draw out the bees in their farm through a hiss and lead them back into the farm through a hiss. In other words, there are soldiers in waiting. They function like bees and are ready to sting the enemies of your breakthroughs and deliverance. The sound of a hiss is all you need to provoke the armies of God and cause them to demolish every power that has been assigned against your destiny.

The hiss of the Lord symbolizes a battle cry. It is a divine signal that is rare. But, the moment the sound comes up, Holy Ghost fire will consume unto desolation, all evil forces gathering together with the intention of keeping you in captivity perpetually. They will be disgraced and destroyed.

A CALL TO ARMS

The hiss of the Lord is a call to arms. The hiss of the Lord is a trumpet that symbolizes the fact that tragedy has been flagged off in the camp of every power opposing you. You need the weapon of the hiss of the Lord when you desire swift and decisive victory.

The hiss of the Lord is the weapon to use when you want to summon aggressive soldiers from heaven. You need this weapon when you want to dribble the enemy. This weapon will prove effective when simple weapons fail. This weapon will lead you into testimonies that will embarrass the enemy.

PRAYER POINTS

1. My father, hiss at my oppressors after the order of Herod who was eaten by worms.
2. Let the hiss of the Lord clothe my stubborn pursuers with shame.
3. Every whispering familiar spirit, be silenced by the hiss of the Lord.
4. Every witch who speaks or mutters, be silenced by the hiss of the Lord.
5. Opportunity wasters, I waste you by the hiss of the Lord.
6. My father, disappoint the devices of the crafty by the hiss of heaven.

WEAPON

5

HUNTERS AND FISHERS OF THE LORD

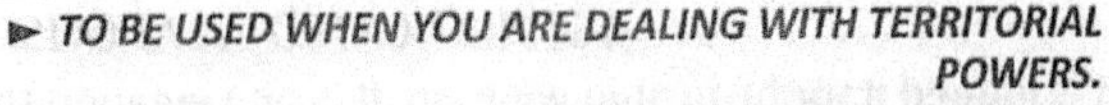

► ***TO BE USED WHEN YOU ARE DEALING WITH TERRITORIAL POWERS.***

► ***TO BE USED WHEN YOU ARE DEALING WITH MARINE POWERS.***

► ***TO BE USED FOR DEALING WITH THE POWER OF YOUR FATHER'S HOUSE.***

► ***TO BE USED WHEN EVIL POWERS ARE BEHIND SERIOUS SET BACKS IN YOUR LIFE.***

► ***TO BE USED WHEN YOU ARE DEALING WITH TERRITORIAL DEMONS.***

► ***TO BE USED WHEN YOU ARE A VICTIM OF COLLECTIVE CAPTIVITY.***

► ***TO BE USED WHEN YOU ARE FIGHTING AGAINST HIDDEN ENEMIES.***

► ***TO BE USED WHEN YOU ARE GOING THROUGH COMPLEX BATTLES.***

Spiritual warfare is a mystery. This explains why the Bible declares that: Ephesians 6:12

> ***For we wrestle not against flesh and blood, but against principalities, against powers, against the rulers of the darkness of this world, against spiritual wickedness in high places.***

There are lots of deep lessons to learn from this passage. The powers we contend with have been duly classified in the scriptures.

TOUGH WEAPONS

To deal with principalities you need tough spiritual warfare weapons. To be delivered from bondage that has been orchestrated by wicked powers and rulers of the dark kingdom, you need uncommon weapons. You cannot just wrestle against flesh and blood. Beloved, when you want to deal with wicked spirits in high places, you must make use of superior weapons. If only we can become deeply aware of the reality of spiritual warfare we will learn how to make use of uncommon weapons.

If the devil has become so smart as to create an intelligent hierarchy in his kingdom, we must pray that our fingers should be taught to fight and our hands to war. The weapon we are looking at, here, is a serious one. It is a weapon that no power can withstand. It is one of the toughest weapons in the armory of the Almighty. Even if the enemy tries to hide underground, this weapon will fetch the enemy from there and give him a large dose of God's judgment.

SOPHISTICATED WEAPONS

It is indeed a sophisticated weapon. It is one weapon that frightens the enemy. When this weapon is used, the enemy is captured. With the use of this weapon we shall make a public show of the enemy. When you use this weapon, the enemy will not be able to stand and fight another day. We are referring to the weapon of the hunters and fishers of the Lord.

This is an intelligence arm of God's army. This prayer point is useful for men and women who have been dribbled by the enemy. It is the best weapon for those who are constantly attacked and harassed by invisible powers. You need to make use of this weapon and attack enemies who have gone into the field of your destiny and have sown tares among your wheat.

DIVINE INSTRUCTIONS

This is the best weapon to use when you are contending with the powers that have put your entire lineage under the bondage of slavery. This weapon is the one you must use when you have gone through multiple deliverance sessions and wicked captivity has not allowed you to be delivered. This, without doubt, is one of the toughest spiritual battles. **Jer. 16:16**

> ***Behold, I will send for many fishers, saith the LORD, and they shall fish them; and after will I send for many hunters, and they shall hunt them from every mountain, and from every hill, and out of the holes of the rocks.***

TOUGH HOOKS

Stubborn powers that hide in the dark, launch attacks against you, only to disappear again will meet their waterloo when you begin to use this weapon. Hunters and fishers of the Lord are terrible weapons that will drive the nail into the enemy's coffin. You need to command God's fishes to fish out witchcraft forces and the powers of your father's house and deal with them accordingly. Hunters and fishers of the Lord make use of tough hooks. **Amos 4:2**

> ***The Lord GOD hath sworn by his holiness, that, lo, the days shall come upon you, that he will take you away with hooks, and your posterity with fishhooks.***

They also make use of divine nets. **Habakkuk 1:15**

> ***They take up all of them with the angle, they catch them in their net, and gather them in their drag: therefore they rejoice and are glad.***

Either you are dealing with marine powers in the sea or forest demons in the bush, this is the weapon to use.

PRAYER POINTS

1. Every cleverly concealed enemy, be exposed and be disgraced by the fishers and hunters of the Lord, in the name of Jesus.
2. O fishers and hunters of the Lord, raid every satanic archive and recover my stolen blessings, in the name of Jesus.
3. Every sensitive enemy, I bring you down by the power of the fishers and hunters of the Lord, in the name of Jesus.
4. Every marine power fishing and hunting for my virtue, I destroy your power by the fishers and hunters of the Lord, in the name of Jesus.
5. Every masquerading spiritual entity hiding to cleverly oppress me, I call on the fishers and hunters of the Lord to pull you down, in the name of Jesus..
6. I invoke the power of the fishers and hunters of the Lord against the troublers of my Israel, in the name of Jesus.
7. Every strong man hiding to oppress me, I paralyse you by the fishers and hunters of the Lord, in the name of Jesus.
8. Those powers of Beelzebub of my fathers house, I fish you out and destroy you by the fishers and hunters of the Lord, in the name of Jesus.

WEAPON

6

NET OF THE LORD

▶ TO ENABLE YOU FIGHT YOUR BATTLES IN A PROPHETIC MANNER.
▶ TO BE USED WHEN MULTIPLE SATANIC AGENTS HAVE INVADED YOUR LIFE AND FAMILY.
▶ TO ENABLE YOU CAPTURE POWERS THAT HAVE DESIGNED AN EVIL AGENDA TO CAPTURE YOU.
▶ IT CAN BE USED AS WEAPON AGAINST FLYING BIRDS. AND DEMONS THAT OPERATE FROM THE AIR.
▶ YOU CAN USE THIS WEAPON TO INVOKE THE WRATH OF GOD UPON POWERS THAT SPONSOR TERRIBLE WITCHCRAFT AGENDA AGAINST YOUR LIFE.
▶ YOU CAN USE THIS WEAPON WHEN YOU WANT TO SILENCE EVERY EVIL VOICE SPEAKING AGAINST YOU.

As long as you are not ready to languish in ignorance, the enemy shall not overcome you. There is no weapon you will ever need to fight your battles and obtain victory that cannot be found in the word of God. We serve a God who is a man of war, and specializes in making use of diverse weapons. He can make use of fire, lightening thunder, stones, the atmosphere, the rain, mysterious blasts and complex weapons.

God has manufactured and made ready for our use specific weapons that are tailor made to enable us obtain victory in our areas of challenges. When you use the right weapon, victory, liberty, deliverance and breakthroughs will be yours. The beauty of spiritual warfare is that God has not created any power he cannot tame or arrest.

POWERFUL WEAPONS

God has lots of weapons and warfare manuals for every battle mankind will ever fight. The survival strategy for this end time is to locate the right weapon and fight all manner of battles emanating from the kingdom of darkness.

Prophetic warfare thrives on your ability to come against the enemy with a suitable weapon. As long as you are making use of the right weapon, there is no need to struggle before you overcome the enemy. The use of right weapon unleashes upon you the anointing of ease which will make you an overcomer in every spiritual warfare session.

THE NET

The net of the Lord is a weapon given unto us by God for specific areas of warfare. When God wants to capture stubborn run-away enemies he will use the weapon of the divine net.

Ezekiel 12:13

> ***My net also will I spread upon him, and he shall be taken in my snare: and I will bring him to Babylon to the land of the Chaldeans; yet shall he not see it, though he shall die there.***

Ezekiel 17:20

> ***And I will spread my net upon him, and he shall be taken in my snare, and I will bring him to Babylon, and will plead with him there for his trespass that he hath trespassed against me.***

Hosea 7:12

> ***When they shall go, I will spread my net upon them; I will bring them down as the fowls of the heaven; I will chastise them, as their congregation hath heard.***

ARRESTING THE ARRESTER

The net is an instrument for subjecting the enemy to the same captivity which he has schemed for God's people. It is wonderful to behold a great company of people who have been arrested through the use of the divine net. This is a weapon that God uses when he sets out to capture a network of evil powers. This is a weapon of mass destruction. It is a weapon that has continued to baffle the enemy as a result of its ability to overshadow and capture a mass of enemies who believe that they can escape the anger of the Almighty.

When God decides that the enemy's cup of iniquity has become full and it is time to capture and subject the enemy to shameful defeat. He spreads a net. Of course, when the net is spread it will capture an entire company of agents of the pit of hell. This is the weapon you need to make use of when you have discovered that it is time for God to round off the enemy in a net and throw them into the fire of God's judgment.

PRAYER POINTS

1. My Father, attack my attackers with the net of fire, in the name of Jesus.
2. O heavens, fish out every strange power in charge of my case by your net, in the name of Jesus.
3. O heavens, command your net to possess my possessions, in the name of Jesus.
4. My Father, use Your net of fire to restore my stolen stars, in the name of Jesus.
5. O net of the Lord, hear the word of the Lord, pursue my pursuers, in the name of Jesus.
6. Holy Ghost and blood of Jesus defend me by your net of fire, in the name of Jesus.
7. O Lord, dispatch Your violent angels with their net to disgrace my disgrace, in the name of Jesus.

WEAPON 7

INDIGNATION OF GOD

▶TO BE USED WHEN YOU WANT TO INVOKE GOD'S ANGER UPON ASSOCIATIONS OF SATANIC AGENTS.
▶ IT CAN BE USED TO DESTABILIZE THE MISSION OF STUBBORN PURSUERS.
▶ IT IS A POWERFUL WEAPON TO BE USED TO DISGRACE AND PARALYSE SATANIC AGENTS SENT TO STEAL YOUR GLORY AND SWALLOW YOUR VIRTUE.
▶ IT IS A POWERFUL WEAPON FOR EVERY POWER THAT HAS VOWED THAT YOU WILL NOT BE DELIVERED.
▶ IT IS A WEAPON TO BE USED WHEN YOU ARE DEALING WITH POWERS THAT BITE WITHOUT ANY REMNANT.

One of the toughest weapons which God has made available for effective spiritual warfare is the weapon of the indignation of God. There is a special weapon earmarked for seasons of victory. This is a fitting weapon for the enemy that will not let you go. The indignation of God is a weapon that the Almighty rarely brings out. This particular weapon has been designed to express to the fullest, the anger and fury of God. It is the weapon that shows no mercy. When this weapon is in use, there is no looking back.

AN ERUPTION

The purpose of this weapon is to totally consume and finish the enemy. This weapon has been manufactured with the intent of showing the enemy the eruption of God's anger like liquid fire in a volcano. The indignation of God is a weapon that pours out the entire content of God's anger against the enemy.
When the weapon of indignation is taken out of God's armory the enemy camp is in trouble. This weapon will not be taken back until it is fully birthed with the blood of Pharaoh and all his soldiers. This is a weapon that shows the finality and severity of God's judgment. **Ezekiel 22:31**

> ***Therefore have I poured out mine indignation upon them; I have consumed them with the fire of my wrath: their own way have I recompensed upon their heads, saith the Lord GOD.***

A DESTRUCTIVE WEAPON

The nature of this weapon is that it is poured out like poisonous powder to wipe out the traces of the agents of darkness. This is a weapon we can use when the Church is harassed and the anointed is insulted. It can be used when dark angels dare touch the anointed or do God's prophet any harm. The weapon of indignation of God stands for the pouring out of God's fury. **Ezekiel 22:22**

> ***As silver is melted in the midst of the furnace, so shall ye be melted in the midst thereof; and ye shall know that I the LORD have poured out my fury upon you.***

A DESTRUCTIVE STORM

When the weapon of indignation of God is used, heaven releases a destructive storm of calamity and tragedy. This weapon comes out of the breath of the Almighty when his anger is provoked. It is a deeply spiritual weapon. It is also a reward that fits the wicked. **Ezekiel 20:8**

> ***But they rebelled against me, and would not hearken unto me: they did not every man cast away the abominations of their eyes, neither did they forsake the idols of Egypt: then I said, I will pour out my fury upon them, to accomplish my anger against them in the midst of the land of Egypt.***

When the president of a powerful nation pours out his military might against another nation, atomic bombs could be used, nuclear warheads could be discharged and fighter jets could drop killer bombs upon the head of the populace. But that is how far the wrath of man can go. But when the Almighty pours out His fury, the result can be compared with what happens when silver is melted in hot furnace.

This tough weapon may be what your enemy needs to leave you alone or let you go. The wicked powers of your father's house cannot be cajoled or appeased to leave you alone. The weapon of indignation of God is the language they understand. Use this weapon today and your enemies will feel the full wrath of God's anger. Evil powers will tremble and let you go.

PRAYER POINTS

1. Father, arise in Your indignation and pursue my pursuer, in the name of Jesus
2. Let the power of your indignation put every digger of holes against my life into their holes, in the name of Jesus.

3. O indignation of the most high God, arise and frustrate my enemies, in the name of Jesus.
4. Let the fire of divine indignation arrest my arresters and contend with those who contend with me, in the name of Jesus.
5. O God, arise in Your indignation and put to shame every power of the oppressor, in the name of Jesus.
6. O indignation of the Most High God, arise and possess my possessions for me, in the name of Jesus.

WEAPON

8

NORTH WIND THAT DRIVES AWAY RAIN

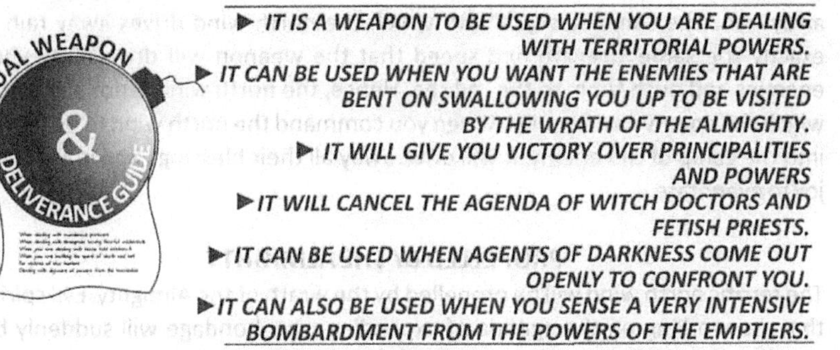

► ***IT IS A WEAPON TO BE USED WHEN YOU ARE DEALING WITH TERRITORIAL POWERS.***

► ***IT CAN BE USED WHEN YOU WANT THE ENEMIES THAT ARE BENT ON SWALLOWING YOU UP TO BE VISITED BY THE WRATH OF THE ALMIGHTY.***

► ***IT WILL GIVE YOU VICTORY OVER PRINCIPALITIES AND POWERS***

► ***IT WILL CANCEL THE AGENDA OF WITCH DOCTORS AND FETISH PRIESTS.***

► ***IT CAN BE USED WHEN AGENTS OF DARKNESS COME OUT OPENLY TO CONFRONT YOU.***

► ***IT CAN ALSO BE USED WHEN YOU SENSE A VERY INTENSIVE BOMBARDMENT FROM THE POWERS OF THE EMPTIERS.***

By the act of God's creative power there is no entity he cannot convert to a weapon of spiritual warfare. When warfare becomes tough God's network can convert anything He has created to a weapon of warfare. The amazing thing about the weapon of God is that each of them is custom made to fulfil a particular goal or purpose. By and large, what you achieve in life, the victory you win and deliverance you obtain rest solely on the way you are able to make use of divine warfare weapons. No doubt, life is tough and there are lots of challenging situations, but the use of specific spiritual warfare weapons is capable of reducing complex problems to extremely easy ones.
There is no problem mankind would ever have that has not been taken care of by God through the provision of appropriate weapons or solutions. Hence, we do not need to go outside the sphere of God's armoury to look for another weapon. The weapon we are looking at in this section is a very complex one. **Prov. 25:23**

> ***"The north wind driveth away rain: so doth an angry countenance a backbiting tongue."***

A TERRIFIC WEAPON

The north wind is a terrific weapon. When a particular wind emanates from the north figuratively it is coming from the abode of the Almighty. This is a spiritual warfare weapon that portrays the terrible majesty of God. **Job 37:22**

> ***"Fair weather cometh out of the north: with God is terrible majesty.***

The north wind is a messenger of God's terrible majesty. When it comes, it drives away rain. The same strength with which the north wind drives away rain is exactly the same strength and speed that the weapon will drive away your enemies and push them to the red sea. Hence, the north wind is not a weapon which the enemy can toy with. When you command the north wind to be blown into the camp of the enemy, it will drive away all their blessings and make their joy to evaporate.

PROPELLED BY THE ALMIGHTY

The terrific north wind will be propelled by the wrath of the Almighty. Evil spirits that are working on the agenda of expanding your bondage will suddenly be dispersed and blown into the pit of darkness. Just as the north wind comes in its fury, this weapon will achieve a divine invasion that will completely bind the enemy with hot fetters and chains of iron.

The weapon of the north wind is the best weapon to use when you discover that the evil powers that buried your destiny are nowhere to be found. You need this weapon when you are confronted by fetish and occult powers. You also need this weapon when you discover that the rope of bondage that is binding you is in several folds. The weapon of the north wind is needed when you are contending with principalities and powers. You need to make use of this weapon when powers behind false religions are attacking you.

This weapon is appropriate when a particular community is being disturbed by witches and wizards. The weapon of the north wind will change your situation when you are dealing with deep bondage. Command the north wind to visit the habitation of darkness and you will witness amazing results.

PRAYER POINTS

1. Father, I provoke the North wind that drives away rain of affliction, in the name of Jesus.
2. Let the power of the North wind arise and cause confusion in the camp of my enemies, in the name of Jesus.
3. Thou power of the North wind, drive away every rain of sorrows, in the name of Jesus.
4. Thou power of North wind, disgrace every plantation of darkness and blow them away, in the name of Jesus.
5. Thou power of the North wind, quench the power of Satanic rain fighting against my destiny, in the name of Jesus.

6. Thou power of the North wind, arrest every rain of darkness falling in the garden of my destiny, in the name of Jesus.
7. Oh North wind, arise and confuse the camp of my enemies, in the name of Jesus.

WEAPON

9

MYSTERIES OF THE EVENING TIDE

▶ ***THIS WEAPON CAN BE USED TO TERMINATE POWERS THAT ARE BENT ON TERMINATING YOUR DESTINY.***

▶ ***IT CAN BE USED TO ARREST DEMONIC ROBBERS.***

▶ ***IT IS A WEAPON FOR SPOILING THE POWERS THAT ARE SPOILING YOUR DESTINY.***

▶ ***IT IS A WEAPON FOR FIGHTING MYSTERIOUS BATTLES***

▶ ***IT IS A POWERFUL WEAPON FOR DEALING WITH THE POWERS OF WITCHCRAFT.***

▶ ***IT CAN BE USED WHEN YOU WANT THE GOD OF SUDDENLY TO APPEAR AND REVOKE EVERY EVIL AGENDA OF DARKNESS.***

▶ ***THIS WEAPON IS USEFUL WHEN YOU WANT TO INVOKE SUDDEN DESTRUCTIONS UPON POWERS THAT ARE BENT ON SWALLOWING YOUR DESTINY.***

Beloved, God is aware of the extent that the enemy has gone to attack God's people in this end times. God has, therefore, brought out strange weapons in order to put an end to the era of shameful defeat by the enemy.

The Bible has rightly predicted that perilous times shall come in the end times.

2Tim. 3:1

> ***"This know also, that in the last days perilous times shall come.***
>
> ***Perilous times are seasons of uncommon aggressive warfare. The devil has changed his gear to the toughest one because he knows that he has a short time."***

Rev. 12:12

> ***"Therefore rejoice, ye heavens, and ye that dwell in them. Woe to the inhabiters of the earth and of the sea! for the devil is come down unto you, having great wrath, because he knoweth that he hath but a short time."***

PERILOUS TIMES

The situation is so tough that the Bible declared "woe" upon these who live in the world. The devil has come with great wrath. Therefore, those who display ignorance concerning spiritual warfare will continue to be casualties on the field of battle. If you are current with news of strange happenings all over the world you would agree with me that we are in an era that is characterized by the greatest level of spiritual warfare.

With the strange things that the enemy has started doing all over the world, what kind of weapon do we need? We must begin to learn how to use strange weapons for this strange era. This weapon is subtle but powerful. It is a mysterious weapon. It is a weapon that has been described as the portion of the enemies of God's people. **Isaiah 17:14**

> ***"And behold at eveningtide trouble; and before the morning he is not. This is the portion of them that spoil us, and the lot of them that rob us."***

A WEAPON OF VENGEANCE

This weapon is so loaded with God's mysterious power that it is capable of wiping off the enemy. It is a weapon that God has earmarked for finishing the enemy. There are some enemies you are not supposed to allow to live. Witchcraft enemies are not supposed to be allowed to live. **Exod. 22:18**

> ***"Thou shalt not suffer a witch to live."***

The weapon of the mystery of the evening tide is a weapon you must use when you determine that the enemy must perish. One of the characteristics of this weapon is that it constitutes terror, or trouble to the enemy. The purpose of this weapon is the cutting off of the enemies of God's people. When you make use of this weapon you must not be shocked when you hear news of sudden death of wicked witches that have almost swallowed half of members of your family.

GOD KILLS

One of the mysteries of spiritual warfare is that God has weapons for dealing with every cadre of the enemy. To be quite honest with you beloved, God is a killer. **1Sam. 2:6**

> ***"The LORD killeth, and maketh alive: he bringeth down to the grave, and bringeth up."***

God is ready to unleash sudden destruction upon wicked powers. **1Thes. 5:3**

"For when they shall say, Peace and safety; then sudden destruction cometh upon them, as travail upon a woman with child; and they shall not escape."

This weapon has been decided by God to dish out a fitting portion to those who secretly or openly torment God's people. This weapon functions in a mysterious way. When you make use of prayer points that carry the mysteries of the evening tide, your enemies are in trouble. One night God will visit them and by the following day they shall be buried in shame after the order of the evening tide.

PRAYER POINTS

1. Let the mystery of the even tide send panic and fear into the camp of my enemy, in the name of Jesus.
2. Let the mystery of the even tide appear and surround every evil association against me to discomfit them in the name of Jesus.
3. Let the mystery of the even tide contend with those who contend with me, in the name of Jesus.
4. Let the mystery of the even tide begin to disgrace every witchcraft plantation, in the name of Jesus.
5. Let the mystery of the even tide begin to strike unto death every strong man attached to the morning, to the afternoon and to the evening of my life, in the name of Jesus.
6. Let the mystery of the even tide do great and marvellous wonders in my life and also destroy every plantation of wickedness, in the name of Jesus.
7. Let the mystery of the even tide arise in its mysterious power to reverse every plantation of darkness, in the name of Jesus.
8. Let the mystery of the even tide arise and fight all my battles for me, in the name of Jesus.

WEAPON 10

PESTILENCE

▶ ***IT IS A POWERFUL WEAPON TO BE USED WHEN YOU WANT THE CAMP OF THE ENEMY TO WITNESS MULTIPLE CAUSALITIES.***

▶ ***TO ARREST FAMILIAR SPIRITS AND LOCAL WITCHES AND WIZARDS.***

▶ ***TO DETHRONE EVERY EVIL KING.***

▶ ***TO ENABLE YOU DESCEND ON POWERS THAT HAVE VOWED THAT YOUR DESTINY WILL REMAIN BURIED FOR LIFE.***

▶ ***TO PARALYSE NIGHT CATERERS AND PUT AN END TO THEIR WICKED ACTIVITIES.***

I have stated, time and again, that the only language which the enemy understands is the language of holy violence.

Aggressive powers need to be handled aggressively. Terrible powers can only shift grounds when terrible weapons land on their head. Beloved, there is no denying the fact that the enemy has switched to an abnormal gear. These days, witches fly in broad day light. Mothers, chew their children, and members of the political class are made to pound day old babies in the mortar just to obtain power. Witch-doctors go on air to advertise their power and display their wares. There is a proliferation of black and white witches. The atmosphere has been polluted and communities are bewitched by powerful fetish priests and occult masters. Demonic activities have reached a bizarre dimension. God is in search of violent end-time soldiers who will rise up gallantly and turn the tables.

INTENSIVE WARFARE

Beloved, the answer is that we must march into the armoury of the Almighty and bring out tough weapons of spiritual warfare. There are people who may never experience total deliverance until they take further steps in spiritual warfare and begin to handle strange battles with strange weapons.

To succeed in this dimension, we must learn how to make use of the weapon of pestilence. When we want to handle a particular weapon, we must examine the credentials of the manufacturer. The Bible says in **Exodus 15:3**

"The LORD is a man of war: the LORD is his name."

God is the greatest warrior that this world has ever known. **Psalm 24:8**

"Who is this King of glory? The LORD strong and mighty, the LORD mighty in battle."

Beloved, the truth is that God does not make weapons and abandon them. He is a warrior. **Rev. 19:11**

"And I saw heaven opened, and behold a white horse; and he that sat upon him was called Faithful and True, and in righteousness he doth judge and make war."

Any weapon that has been manufactured by God is for a purpose. God does not joke with His weapons. He knows the particular goal that His weapons will accomplish. The weapon of pestilence is a weapon of destruction.
Exodus 5:3

"And they said, The God of the Hebrews hath met with us: let us go, we pray thee, three days' journey into the desert, and sacrifice unto the LORD our God; lest he fall upon us with pestilence, or with the sword."

CASUALTIES GALORE

Pestilence is not a weapon that can descend upon the enemy and there will be no noticeable casualty. In one instance, in the scripture, God sent pestilence and seventy thousand people died. **1Chornicles 21:14**

"So the LORD sent pestilence upon Israel: and there fell of Israel seventy thousand men."

The Bible describes a category of pestilence as noisome. In other words, this kind of pestilence will create negative waves. **Psalm 91:3**

"Surely he shall deliver thee from the snare of the fowler, and from the noisome pestilence."

A VEHICLE OF DESTRUCTION

The purpose of pestilence is to destroy. It is a vehicle for conveying divine judgment. Those who are attacked by this weapon will reap destruction. This weapon must be used to attack the spirit of Pharaoh. It is a fitting weapon for the power of Herod. You need to make use of this weapon when you are swimming against the tide and powers that bite without remnant, and they are almost swallowing you up. When pestilence descends upon the enemy evil powers will let you go. Demons that have swallowed your virtue will vomit it, your victory will remain unchallenged and your testimony will be overwhelming.

PRAYER POINTS

1. Let the power of pestilence arise and swallow my swallowers, in the name of Jesus.
2. Thou power of pestilence, arise and fight against every yoke of the enemy, in the name of Jesus.
3. Thou power of pestilence, pursue my pursuers, in the name of Jesus.
4. Thou power of pestilence, torment and oppress my oppressors, in the name of Jesus.
5. Thou power of pestilence, eat into the bones and the marrows of wickedness, in the name of Jesus
6. Thou power of pestilence, move in your mysterious power and disappoint the devices of the crafty, in the name of Jesus.

WEAPON 11

PLAGUE

► ***THIS WEAPON IS NEEDED WHEN YOU WANT GOD TO DEFEND HIS INTEREST IN YOUR LIFE.***

► ***WHEN YOU WANT TO ENFORCE DIVINE JUDGMENT UPON ROBBERS OF DESTINY.***

► ***WHEN YOU WANT TO DEAL DECISIVELY WITH THE POWERS OF YOUR FATHER'S HOUSE.***

► ***WHEN YOU WANT TO PRAY YOUR WAY OUT OF EVERY EVIL CAGE.***

► ***WHEN YOU WANT THE POWER THAT HAS SWALLOWED YOUR GOODNESS TO VOMIT IT BY FIRE.***

► ***WHEN YOU WANT THE POWERS THAT ARE KEEPING YOU IN BONDAGE TO RELEASE YOU INSTANTLY.***

When God acts decisively on the field of battle, no power can withstand Him. There are tough battles that must be fought with tough weapons. The reason why many people struggle with problems that resist prayer is because they have not tackled the enemy with tough weapons. We are fighting an enemy that has grown thick skin and will not easily respond when minimal or elementary efforts are made. There are methods that will not suffice on the field of deliverance. There is no way you can confront the enemy that has fortified himself with a weak pat on the back.

To defeat the enemy who has a track record of surfacing and putting up new appearances from time to time; you need weapons that will announce your desperation. You need weapons that will portray the might of God and the aggression of the Most High. You must, therefore, make use of a weapon that will spread calamity and casualties throughout the length and breadth of the camp of the enemy. One of such weapons is the weapon of the plague. There is what is referred to as the weapon of the plague.

A REGIME OF PLAGUES

When God decides to plague your enemy with a great plague, that is the end of the discussion. No power can collide with great plagues and remain the same. When great plagues from the Almighty fall upon the powers that are holding you captive they will be ground to powder. When the camps of the enemy receive the visitation of great plagues no power will remain alive to tell the story. When God rolls out the regime of plagues, nobody will be able to contend with the terror.

When pestilence is poured upon the head of unrepentant Pharaoh, tragedy will litter his camp. When God introduces a plague, the manifestations are diverse.

Your enemies will become God's enemies. Those who have been trying to destroy you will knock their heads on the rock of ages.

STRANGE TRAGEDIES

God can go any length to defend His interest in your life. When God decides to send a plague into Pharaoh's court anything can happen. The enemy will begin to witness strange tragedies and mysterious occurrences. When this begins to happen, Pharaoh will open the door and allow you to come out of the house of bondage. **Ex 10:7-11**

> ***"And Pharaoh's servants said unto him, How long shall this man be a snare unto us? let the men go, that they may serve the LORD their God: knowest thou not yet that Egypt is destroyed? And Moses and Aaron were brought again unto Pharaoh: and he said unto them, Go, serve the LORD your God: but who are they that shall go? And Moses said, We will go with our young and with our old, with our sons and with our daughters, with our flocks and with our herds will we go; for we must hold a feast unto the LORD. And he said unto them, Let the LORD be so with you, as I will let you go, and your little ones: look to it; for evil is before you. Not so: go now ye that are men, and serve the LORD; for that ye did desire. And they were driven out from Pharaoh's presence."***

Psalm 105:14

> ***"He suffered no man to do them wrong: yea, he reproved kings for their sakes;"***

A plague comes as a result of terrible judgment. Some enemies will not allow you to go until they begin to suffer great plagues. When the effect of the plague begins to bite the enemy, those who are fighting against you will be subjected to carrying out useless assignments that will force them to release you. The weapon of divine plague is a weapon you must use if you want your victory to be quick and decisive.

PRAYER POINTS

1. God, arise and send your plagues after the order of Egypt to the lives of my stubborn pursuers, in the name of Jesus.
2. Father, release Your plagues upon every enemy that does not want to let me go, in the name of Jesus.
3. Father, release Your plagues upon every coven discussing my matter, in the name of Jesus.
4. Father, release Your plagues upon every evil association gathered to suppress me, in the name of Jesus.
5. Father, release Your plagues upon all who are sitting on my breakthroughs, in the name of Jesus.
6. Father, release Your plagues upon all those whom the kingdom of darkness has assigned to make my destiny sink, in the name of Jesus.

WEAPON

12

FAN OF THE LORD

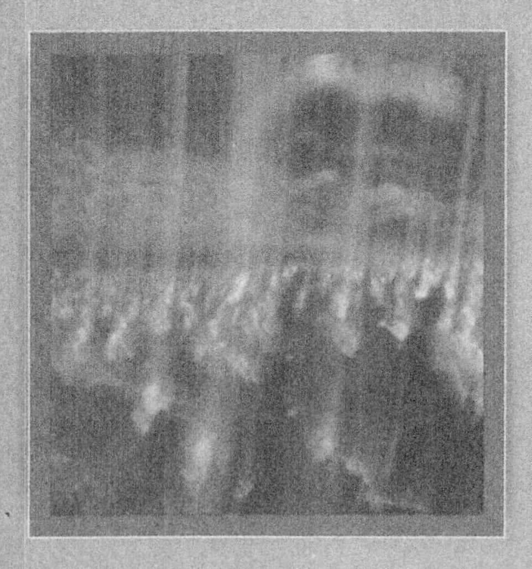

► ***WHEN YOU WANT TO SCATTER EVIL GATHERINGS WHERE EVIL POWERS GATHER TOGETHER AGAINST YOUR LIFE.***
► ***WHEN YOU WANT TO VIOLENTLY ATTACK YOUR ATTACKERS.***
► ***WHEN YOU WANT TO DEAL WITH THE POWERS OF THE EMPTIERS.***
► ***WHEN YOU WANT TO VOMIT FIRE UPON SATANIC AGENTS.***
► ***WHEN YOU WANT TO SEND EVIL ARROWS BACK TO SENDER.***
► ***WHEN YOU WANT TO PUT THE SPIRIT OF DEATH AND HELL UNDER BONDAGE.***

God has destined us to win unchallengeable victory in spiritual warfare. To ensure that uncommon victory is ours, He has created and given us certain strange weapons. There is no way we will not achieve victory if these powerful weapons are used.

Our God is the greatest warrior. Hence, His weapons are superior to any form of weapon used by the enemy. The secret of spiritual warfare is this; as long as you continue to use the right weapons for the right battle or warfare wherever the battle is fought you are the number one person whose name would be listed as people who have achieved victory. The weapon we are considering here, is the weapon of the fan of the Lord.

THE WEAPON THAT SCATTERS

There is a fan of the Lord that blows the enemy unto destruction. The working of this weapon is strange. When the enemy wages war against you or when plans are made to perpetuate your bondage or fortify a cage in order to hold you captive the Lord comes with this strange weapon. Beloved, it works in a very strange manner. **Isaiah 41:16**

> ***"Thou shalt fan them, and the wind shall carry them away, and the whirlwind shall scatter them: and thou shalt rejoice in the LORD, and shalt glory in the Holy One of Israel."***

The onslaught of the enemy is carried out in this manner. A divine fan starts to blow against the enemy and a violent wind begins to carry them away. Then, a divine whirl-wind is ushered in to finish the work by scattering them unto desolation. With the full operation of this weapon, the powers that have fought against you will not be able to come together and launch another attack having being scattered by the divine whirl-wind. God uses the fan as a weapon of emptying the camp of the enemy. **Jer. 51:2**

> ***"And will send unto Babylon fanners, that shall fan her, and shall empty her land: for in the day of trouble they shall be against her round about."***

DIVINE FANNERS

God blows the enemy away like chaff. The fan of the Lord will also spread calamity throughout the enemy's camp. **Jer. 15:7**

> ***"And I will fan them with a fan in the gates of the land; I will bereave them of children, I will destroy my people, since they return not from their ways."***

God knows what befits the powers that are holding you under bondage. The Almighty has declared *"And I will fan them with a fan"*. The fan of the Lord is a fitting weapon for stubborn pursuers. When the enemy refuses to turn back and you issue a cry of vengeance against him, your prayer will become the fan of the Lord and you shall destroy them.

THE DESTRUCTIVE WEAPON

You need to use this weapon when a network of evil powers is behind your bondage or battles. The fan of the Lord will come like a whirl-wind and blow off all the enemies no matter how numerous they are. When you declare saying; Oh thou fan of the Lord, blow away the association of dark agents that are behind my attacks. They will be blown away and their agenda will be frustrated.

The fan of the Lord is violent. The fan of the Lord is destructive. The fan of the Lord is deadly. No power from the pit of hell can withstand it. When you begin to use the weapon of the fan of the Lord you will discover that your prayers will become a terror to the kingdom of darkness.

Use this weapon today and you shall experience resounding victory.

PRAYER POINTS

1. Let the fan of the Holy Ghost blow against every evil wind working against my life, in the name of Jesus
2. Let the wind that carries fire emanate from the fan of the Lord and scatter the camp of the oppressor, in the name of Jesus.
3. Thou fan of the Lord, blow away every satanic plantation in the garden of my life, in the name of Jesus.
4. Thou fan of the Lord, blow away every yoke of the oppressor militating against my life, in the name of Jesus.

WEAPON 13

RAVENOUS BIRDS

- ***IT IS A POWERFUL WEAPON FOR DEALING WITH BIRDS OF DARKNESS.***
- ***WHEN YOU WANT ANGELS THAT HAVE NO MERCY TO VISIT THE CAMP OF STUBBORN PURSUERS AND THE POWER OF THE EMPTIERS.***
- ***WHEN YOU WANT TO DISGRACE THE POWERS OF YOUR FATHER'S HOUSE.***
- ***WHEN YOU WANT TO IMPRISON VAGABOND SPIRITS.***
- ***WHEN YOU WANT TO EXPERIENCE UNCHALLENGEABLE VICTORY.***
- ***WHEN YOU WANT TO OBTAIN TOTAL DELIVERANCE.***

Deliverance Ministers and those who are involved with spiritual warfare are aware of the fact that the devil has used evil birds to cause havoc in the lives of men and women. These birds perform all manners of destructive activities. However, what has not been known to believers is the fact that God has created some birds to cause commotion in the camp of the enemy. God knows how to confront the enemy. God knows how to tackle the enemy fire for fire and send wicked arrows back to sender. God often dispatches, into the gathering of evil forces, what the Bible describes as a ravenous bird. **Isaiah 46:11**

> ***"Calling a ravenous bird from the east, the man that executeth my counsel from a far country: yea, I have spoken it, I will also bring it to pass; I have purposed it, I will also do it."***

TOTAL VICTORY

A raven is a bird that consumes everything around it. Beloved, when the cup of the enemy's iniquity is full the weapon God uses is a ravenous bird. The characteristic of the ravenous bird includes swiftness, fierceness and total victory over the enemy. **Ezekiel 39:4**

> ***"Thou shalt fall upon the mountains of Israel, thou, and all thy bands, and the people that is with thee: I will give thee unto the ravenous birds of every sort, and to the beasts of the field to be devoured."***

Beloved, you can speak to all kinds of ravenous birds and command them to devour stubborn pursuers and unrepentant Pharaoh. **Ezekiel 39:1**

> ***"Therefore, thou son of man, prophesy against Gog, and say, Thus saith the Lord GOD; Behold, I am against thee, O Gog, the chief prince of Meshech and Tubal:"***

POWER TO BURY THE PURSUER

You need this weapon when you want to achieve the burial of the powers that have vowed that they will not rest until you are buried. **Ezekiel 39:13**

> ***"Yea, all the people of the land shall bury them; and it shall be to them a renown the day that I shall be glorified, saith the Lord GOD."***

Beloved, there is no mercy on the field of spiritual warfare. The enemy that has programmed terrible bondage in order to finish you does not deserve your pity. When you are on the battle field you either attack the enemy or he attacks you. Beloved, you must destroy them before they destroy you. Ravenous birds constitute the best weapons to use when you are involved in a do or die battle. When activities are going on in a witchcraft coven against you and your family you cannot afford to fold your hands. You simply need to pack a bunch of ravenous birds and dump them into the coven. Within a few days they shall all be buried.

The powers that have vowed that you will have no rest must not be allowed to rest. You must issue a death sentence against them by commanding a ravenous bird to enter their midst and feed on them. This weapon will give you uncommon victory and deliverance. Use it today and your story will change.

PRAYER POINTS

1. Father, let the mystery of the ravenous birds trouble the troublers of my Israel, in the name of Jesus.
2. Oh ravenous birds, arise in anger, attack any satanic bird assigned against me, in the name of Jesus.
3. Father, let the ravenous birds pick up every vulture of darkness assigned against my destiny, in the name of Jesus.

4. Father, let the weapon of the ravenous bird move into every complex situation terrorizing my destiny, in the name of Jesus.
5. O company of ravenous birds, move in an uncommon way and attack every enemy of my progress, in the name of Jesus.
6. Let heavens command ravenous birds to fight my battles for me, in the name of Jesus.
7. Every satanic bird assigned against my destiny, be destroyed by the ravenous bird in the name of Jesus
8. Oh ravenous birds, from heaven, eat up all eaters of flesh, in Jesus name.

WEAPON 14

RAZOR OF THE LORD

▶ WHEN YOU WANT TO DEAL WITH WICKED POWERS IN A DEVASTATING MANNER.
▶ WHEN YOU WANT TO DISGRACE BOASTING POWERS.
▶ WHEN YOU WANT TO ARREST THE TIDE OF THE ARROW OF SHAME AND DISGRACE.
▶ IT IS A SUITABLE WEAPON FOR BRUISING THE HEAD OF THE SERPENT.
▶ IT IS A POWERFUL DELIVERANCE WEAPON.
▶ THIS WEAPON WILL TAKE YOU OUT OF THE VALLEY OF DEFEAT AND PLACE YOU ON THE MOUNTAIN OF VICTORY.

God has created and given unto us lots of tough weapons of warfare. One of the weapons He has created for high level spiritual warfare is the weapon called razor of the Lord. It is a sharp weapon for dealing with the enemy. **Isaiah 7:20**

> ***"In the same day shall the Lord shave with a razor that is hired, namely, by them beyond the river, by the king of Assyria, the head, and the hair of the feet: and it shall also consume the beard."***

Here, the Bible refers to a razor that is hired. It is a weapon that is employed by God as an instrument of His wrath. God can employ any weapon and use it to devastate the enemy. When the Lord chooses the razor as the right weapon for a particular battle or a stubborn enemy it shows that God wants to deal with that enemy or put an end to that battle.

TOTAL DEMOLITION

A serious look at this passage shows that the purpose of this weapon is to ensure far-reaching, devastating effects. To shave with the hired razor the head, the feet and the beard means to bulldoze and demolish the entire network of the powers that have put you under bondage and subjected your destiny to destruction and confusion.

This weapon has been created to destroy the honour of the enemy. In those days, to pluck a man's beard was an attempt to disgrace the man. It is a weapon that will serve the purpose of destroying and consuming the host of darkness. This weapon is useful when you discover that enemies are constantly attacking you in the dream. You can also use this weapon when you discover that the

enemy is busy passing your case from one department to another in the dark kingdom. This weapon is useful when you want to unleash shame upon the enemies that are trying to push you into the valley of shame and disgrace.
2Sam. 10:4-6

> ***"Wherefore Hanun took David's servants, and shaved off the one half of their beards, and cut off their garments in the middle, even to their buttocks, and sent them away. When they told it unto David, he sent to meet them, because the men were greatly ashamed: and the king said, Tarry at Jericho until your beards be grown, and then return. And when the children of Ammon saw that they stank before David, the children of Ammon sent and hired the Syrians of Bethrehob, and the Syrians of Zoba, twenty thousand footmen, and of king Maacah a thousand men, and of Ishtob twelve thousand men."***

YOUR WEAPON OF VICTORY

This weapon is the answer when you are looking for ways of stopping the enemy before he stops you. You need this weapon when the enemy has vowed to rubbish your destiny and bury your name in shame. You need to use this weapon when the enemy has placed you inside a cage and locked it with multiple padlocks. This weapon will prove effective for those who have suffered as a result of wicked arrows.

This is a weapon you need to invoke in prayer when you want your deliverance to be quick, complete and permanent. The razor of the Lord must be used to wound and bruise the head of the serpent when serpentine and marine enemies are fighting desperately to subject you to terrible bondage. The razor of the Lord will inflict wounds that will paralyze house-hold wickedness. It will also terminate evil terminators and invoke a decree of death upon the head of stubborn witches and wizards. The sharp razor of the Lord will enable you to fight and cut your way to the realm of deliverance. The razor of the Lord is one weapon that will pour the wrath of the Almighty upon the enemy.

PRAYER POINTS

1. O razor of the Lord, cut through every wall of blockage assigned to frustrate me, in the name of Jesus.

2. O razor of the Lord, cut into the body of the enemy and extract from them anything they have swallowed from me, in the name of Jesus.
3. O razor of the Lord, arise in great anger, fight for me in the morning, fight for me in the noon and fight for me at night, in the name of Jesus.
4. O razor of the Lord, discipline every witchcraft coven assigned to trouble my life, in the name of Jesus.
5. O razor of the Lord, remove from my days every cobweb power, in the name of Jesus.
6. O razor of the Lord, cut to pieces every net of darkness assigned to cage my finances, cage my home, or cage my marriage, in the name of Jesus.
7. O razor of the Lord, move in great speed and disgrace my Goliath in Jesus name.

WEAPON 15

THE REBUKE OF THE LORD

▶ *THIS WEAPON CAN BE USED TO DEAL WITH PRINCIPALITIES AND POWERS.*
▶ *IT IS A WEAPON THAT CAN BE USED TO ARREST STUBBORN DEMONS AND FORCE THEM TO SUBMIT.*
▶ *IT IS A POWERFUL WEAPON TO BE USED WHEN YOU ARE FIGHTING ENOUGH IS ENOUGH BATTLES.*
▶ *IT CAN BE USED WHEN YOU ARE BEING ATTACKED BY HIGH RANKING DEMONS AND EVIL PRINCIPALITIES.*
▶ *IT IS A WEAPON THAT WILL CANCEL DEMONIC INCANTATIONS.*
▶ *YOU CAN USE THIS WEAPON WHEN YOU WANT EVIL POWERS TO DO REPEATED SOMERSAULTS AND DIE.*
▶ *IT IS USEFUL WHEN YOU ARE FIGHTING ANCESTRAL BATTLES.*

The weapon we are going to examine in this section is a very powerful weapon. One of the weapons we can make use of in our battles is the weapon that comes out of the mouth of the Lord. The voice of the Lord drives the sound of terror to the ears of the enemy. When God speaks thunder strikes the enemy. When God declares judgment, the enemy shivers. The voices of the Lord will capture satanic arrows and make them go back to sender. The rebuke of the Lord will invoke destruction upon the enemy. **Psalm 104:7**

> ***"At thy rebuke they fled; at the voice of thy thunder they hasted away."***

When God rebukes, the enemy flees. When the Almighty rebukes, the association of witches and wizards scatter. When you declare the Lord rebuke thee; stubborn pursuers will flee. The rebuke of the Lord can be likened to an atomic bomb. It will vomit fire upon the head of the powers behind your bondage. The rebuke of the Lord comes with terrible judgment. When God rebukes, the power of your father's house will let you go. The rebuke of the Lord will heap coals of fire upon the enemy's head.

A POWER DELIVERANCE WEAPON

At the rebuke of the Almighty your captives shall flee. Your enemies shall quickly set you free no matter how tough the battle is. No matter how deep bondage appears the rebuke of the Lord will set you free. Even the captives of the terrible shall be released. This weapon is loaded with the anointing that will make the enemy to be thrown into panic and release your instantly. God has given us this weapon so that powers that are operating here and there will discover that your case is different.

ENOUGH IS ENOUGH

The rebuke of the Lord must sound in the camp of the enemy. A single rebuke from the Almighty will force Pharaoh to declare that he is ready to let you go. If you are tired of being a constant victim of satanic attacks you must activate the rebuke of the Lord. If you are tired of being insulted by elemental powers, simply make use of the weapon of the rebuke of Lord. The result is that satan will tremble, evil powers will somersault and die and the enemy will never toy with you again. Enough is enough battles are best fought with this weapon. The rebuke of the Lord is a weapon the enemy cannot withstand. Unfortunately, this weapon has been lying fallow in the armoury of the Lord.

When you invoke divine rebuke upon the enemy the result will completely drive demonic soldiers away from the field of battle.

PRAYER POINTS

1. Father, rebuke every storm contending with my life, in the name of Jesus.
2. Father, rebuke every association contending with my destiny, in the name of Jesus.
3. Father, let the rebuke of the Lord go forth and arrest all my arresters and put to shame every power mocking my prayers, in the name of Jesus.
4. O God, arise and rebuke every satanic angel assigned against my destiny, in the name of Jesus.
5. Let the rebuke of the Lord work to defend my interest, in the name of Jesus.
6. Every principality that is against my destiny, let the rebuke of the Lord trouble them, in the name of Jesus.

WEAPON 16

FIERY SERPENTS AND SCORPIONS

- ***USE THIS WEAPON WHEN YOU WANT TO FIGHT AGAINST WICKED POWERS.***
- ***IT IS A WEAPON YOU CAN USE WHEN YOU ARE UNDER SERIOUS SATANIC THREATS.***
- ***WHEN YOU WANT TO USE THE WEAPON OF JUDGEMENT TO PUNISH THOSE WHO ARE AN ON EVIL ASSIGNMENT AGAINST YOUR LIFE.***
- ***IT CAN BE USED WHEN THE BATTLE BECOMES HOT.***
- ***IT IS A POWERFUL WEAPON TO BE USED DURING SEASONS OF SATANIC INVASION.***
- ***IT IS AN EFFECTIVE WEAPON WHEN YOU WANT EVIL ARROWS TO GO BACK TO SENDERS.***
- ***IT CAN BE USED WHEN YOU WANT TO DEAL WITH STUBBORN PURSUERS.***
- ***YOU CAN COMMAND THIS WEAPON TO INVADE WITCHCRAFT COVENS WHEN YOUR MATTER IS BEING TABLED.***

Serpents and scorpions have been known to be deadly and destructive. They are often viewed as agents of destruction. In the Old Testament when people get bitten by serpents they face the threat of tragic instant death. The dread of fiery serpents and scorpions has instilled horror in the heart of many people. The devil has used serpents and scorpions as weapons of attack against many people. But it is deeply mysterious that what the devil has been doing is to create counterfeits of original weapons that God has created. What the enemy has copied is a fake version of the original. But, God is the authentic manufacturer of the weapon of fiery serpents and scorpions. God has created fiery serpent and scorpions to deal with the enemy. **Deut. 8:15**

> ***"Who led thee through that great and terrible wilderness, wherein were fiery serpents, and scorpions, and drought, where there was no water; who brought thee forth water out of the rock of flint;"***

METHODS OF DELIVERANCE

Do you know that God can actually send fiery serpents as a means of delivering His people? **Numbers 21:6**

> ***"And the LORD sent fiery serpents among the people, and they bit the people; and much people of Israel died."***

You can go to the armoury of the Almighty and bring out fiery serpents which will be dispersed to the camp of the enemy. God has endowed some serpents with deadly virus. Beloved, enough of having bad dreams of being pursued and bitten by serpents. It is now your turn to dispatch serpents into areas where enemies are gathered to destroy your destiny and swallow your life.

GOD'S RESERVED ARMY

You can actually command fiery serpents to bite the demonic agents assigned to destroy you and put you in the land of bondage. You can command such fiery serpents to plant their teeth in the bodies of your enemies and inject them with deadly venoms. You can also command divine scorpions to arise and sting stubborn pursuers to death. You can invoke a company of scorpions from God's reserved army to arise and fight your battles until victory is won.

Fiery serpents and scorpions have been reserved for the season of judgment. Now is the time to declare, enough is enough. You need to identify terrible enemies and release fiery serpents and scorpions to their arena. When evil powers are saying that your deliverance shall not become a reality you can command fiery serpents to bite them. You can also command deadly scorpions to sting them. Stubborn powers will not listen to your pleas and entreaties.

VIOLENT WEAPONS

The only weapon that can grind them to a halt is the use of violence and deadly weapons. God wants to launch His end time soldiers into a season of offensive warfare. Rather than remain on the defensive you must move to the realm of the offensive and make use of the weapon of fiery serpents and scorpions. These weapons are useful because they are endowed with deadly powers.

The devil cannot stand such weapons. If you have an eye on swift and decisive victory you must make use of this particular weapon. With this weapon in your hands, you can rightly declare that your hands are taught to war and fingers to fight.

PRAYER POINTS

1. Let the fiery serpents of the Lord move with violence into the camps of the serpent and scorpions troubling my life, in the name of Jesus.

2. Let the serpents and scorpions of the Lord swallow up the serpents and the scorpions of the enemy, in the name of Jesus.
3. Let the serpents and scorpions of the Lord move into every coven troubling my life and trouble my troublers, in the name of Jesus.
4. Let the fiery serpents and scorpions of the Lord introduce fire into the camp of my oppressor, in the name of Jesus.
5. Let the fiery serpent and scorpions of the Lord trouble every power that has made it a full time work to trouble my destiny, in the name of Jesus.
6. Every serpent and scorpion assigned to trouble me, let the fiery serpents and scorpions of the Lord trouble them today, in the name of Jesus.
7. You fiery serpents and scorpions of the Lord arise in great rage and move to the camp of my enemies, in the name of Jesus.

WEAPON 17

EVIL BEAST

- ***THIS WEAPON CAN BE USED WHEN YOU WANT STRANGERS TO BE FRIGHTENED OUT OF THEIR HIDDEN PLACES.***
- ***THIS WEAPON CAN BE INVOKED TO DEVOUR THE POWERS BEHIND YOUR BONDAGE.***
- ***IT IS AN INSTRUMENT OF VENGEANCE.***
- ***IT IS A WEAPON OF DELIVERANCE.***
- ***IT IS USEFUL WHEN YOU WANT TO BULLDOZE SATANIC ROAD BLOCKS.***

One of the fearful weapons that God has given seasoned students in the school of spiritual warfare is the weapon of evil beasts. It may surprise you that evil beasts are also at the beck and call of the Almighty. God can use them to achieve His divine goals.

When a battle gets hot or complex God has the prerogative of using complex weapons. God has the right to dispatch evil beasts into the camp of the enemy to tear them to pieces and consume them. We need this kind of weapon when we want to achieve unchallengeable victory.

INSTRUMENTS OF VENGEANCE

Evil beasts are instruments of divine vengeance. The power that puts people under bondage, household witchcraft and anti-breakthrough powers can only continue their evil activities when we fail to make use of serious spiritual warfare weapons. When God wants to deal with your enemies there are four weapons He often makes use of. They are listed below;

Ezekiel 14:21

> ***"For thus saith the Lord GOD; How much more when I send my four sore judgments upon Jerusalem, the sword, and the famine, and the noisome beast, and the pestilence, to cut off from it man and beast?"***

THE NOISOME BEAST

One of these weapons is described as noisome beast. When this messenger of judgment is sent to the camp of dark forces, the messenger will roar like a lion. The noise of the beast will signal the beginning of judgment. Beasts are part of the toughest weapons used in warfare by the Almighty. To break the backbone of unrepentant Pharaoh, you need to pray and send wild beasts to execute judgment. **Job 39:15**

> ***"And forgetteth that the foot may crush them, or that the wild beast may break them."***

THE RESERVED ARMY

When wild beasts are dispatched, they demolish and break to pieces the stronghold of darkness. You need not wonder why God uses wild beasts to accomplish His purpose. It is simply because they belong to God. They are part of His reserved army. **Psalm 50:10**

> ***"For every beast of the forest is mine, and the cattle upon a thousand hills."***

Evil beasts act as devourers when God wants to deal with stubborn foundational powers. **Psalm 80:13**

> ***"The boar out of the wood doth waste it, and the wild beast of the field doth devour it."***

DEVOURING BEASTS

These beasts will waste and devour the captains of the armies of the dark kingdom. The beast in question is deadly and destructive according to **Isaiah 35:9.**

> ***"No lion shall be there, nor any ravenous beast shall go up there on, it shall not be found there; but the redeemed shall walk there:"***

STRANGE BEASTS

You must learn how to invoke ravenous beasts against the powers that will not let you go.

The Bible gives us a picture of the characteristics of these beasts. **Daniel 7:26**

> ***"But the judgment shall sit, and they shall take away his dominion, to consume and to destroy it unto the end."***

They are endowed with fearful looking teeth that are capable of devouring everything in the camp of the enemy. The moment the powers that are threatening you are threatened by the beast that has four heads, they will release you and let you go.
You can imagine what will happen when a beast that has three ribs in the mouth between its teeth will do when such a beast confronts the powers that are trying to destroy you. The beast will simply devour them.

I have good news for you. The power that bites without any remnant will meet their match when they come face to face with the evil beasts.

God is a wonderful warrior. When He discovers that satanic beasts are sent to devour you, He will send beasts from His own heavenly army to swallow the satanic beasts. This is exactly what happened in Pharaoh's court; when Moses' rod became a serpent and swallowed the magician's serpent. God is the only one who has the power to swallow the battles that are confronting you and put satanic warriors out of business.

THE LION
Beloved, you need not fear the enemy, when the enemy comes like a roaring lion; the Lion of the tribe of Judah will tear it to shreds. **Hosea 13:8**

> ***"I will meet them as a bear that is bereaved of her whelps, and will rend the caul of their heart, and there will I devour them like a lion: the wild beast shall tear them."***

When you do not know what weapon to use, simply command evil beasts from the Lord to invade the enemy's territory and watch what happens!

PRAYER POINTS

1. Father, release Your evil beasts to comb the corners of the earth and attack my oppressors, in the name of Jesus.
2. Evil beasts from the Lord, rage and vomit fire and torment upon the camp of the enemy, in the name of Jesus.
3. Evil beasts from the Lord, torment my tormentors, harass those

who harass me, silence those who have tried to silence me, in the name of Jesus.

4. Evil beasts from the Lord roar in great anger and pursue my pursuers
5. Evil beasts from the Lord, tear to pieces every evil beast assigned against me, in the name of Jesus.
6. Evil beasts from the Lord, move in great rage into the waters, into the forest and into the bottom of the earth and pursue my pursuers, in the name of Jesus.

WEAPON

18

FIRE OF GOD

▶ ***THIS IS AN ALL-PURPOSE WEAPON.***
▶ ***IT IS SUITABLE FOR THE ENTIRE GAMUT OF THE BATTLE OF LIFE.***
▶ ***IT CAN BE USED TO COMBAT STUBBORN PURSUERS.***
▶ ***IT IS A POWERFUL WEAPON THAT CAN BE USED TO SUBDUE MARINE WITCHCRAFT.***
▶ ***IT SHOULD BE APPLIED ON ANCESTRAL AND FOUNDATIONAL BONDAGE.***
▶ ***YOU CAN ASK THE FIRE OF GOD TO CONSUME EVERY HABITATION OF CRUELTY MILITATING AGAINST YOUR LIFE.***

This is one of the most terrible weapons given to us by God in order to enjoy resounding victory. The fire of God is an uncommon weapon. When this weapon is used God throws, as it were, the totality of His strength into our battles. The Bible makes it clear, time and again, that God is a consuming fire. **Deut. 4:24**

"For the LORD thy God is a consuming fire, even a jealous God."

Deut. 9:3

"Understand therefore this day, that the LORD thy God is he which goeth over before thee; as a consuming fire he shall destroy them, and he shall bring them down before thy face: so shalt thou drive them out, and destroy them quickly, as the LORD hath said unto thee."

Heb. 12:29

"For our God is a consuming fire."

THE WEAPON OF FIRE

When God goes into battle, He comes with fire as His weapon of war. In the spiritual realm fire is more potent than any gun that can be used on the field of battle. When God throws balls of fire into the camp of the enemy, the enemy is in trouble. The forces of darkness will abandon their inferior weapons and flee.

The fire of God is an irresistible warfare weapon. It consumes the horse and its rider. It will burn to ashes the ranks and files of the army of darkness. The weapon of fire has been created by God to consume and exterminate the power of the enemy. The consuming fire of God does not deal half way with the enemy. This weapon spreads terror and tragedy in the enemy's camp like a wildfire.

Note the scripture: **Deut. 9:3**

> ***"Understand therefore this day, that the LORD thy God is he which goeth over before thee; as a consuming fire he shall destroy them, and he shall bring them down before thy face: so shalt thou drive them out, and destroy them quickly, as the LORD hath said unto thee."***

THE CONSUMING FIRE

As a consuming fire, He shall destroy them. The function of the consuming fire of God is total destruction. Most of the time, it is the remnants of the enemies forces that forment trouble among God's children. But, when you make use of the weapon of the consuming fire, you will completely wipe out wicked powers in such a way that the memory of them will be gone.

When God gets involved with your warfare or when the Almighty decides to carry out your deliverance, He often makes use of the weapon of fire. The Bible makes it clear that when God is on the move fire accompanies him. **Psalm 18:12-13**

> ***"At the brightness that was before him his thick clouds passed, hail stones and coals of fire. The LORD also thundered in the heavens, and the Highest gave his voice; hail stones and coals of fire."***

The Bible states categorically that fire announces the presence of God. **Psalm 18:8**

> ***"There went up a smoke out of his nostrils, and fire out of his mouth devoured: coals were kindled by it."***

Psalm 50:3

> **"Our God shall come, and shall not keep silence: a fire shall devour before him, and it shall be very tempestuous round about him."**

No wonder the Psalmist invoked burning coals of fire upon the enemy. **Psalm 140:10**

> **"Let burning coals fall upon them: let them be cast into the fire; into deep pits, that they rise not up again."**

God cares about His children. That is why the Bible says that he who touches us touches the apple of God's eyes. Any power that confronts you is preparing his obituary. The Bible says; **Psalm 11:6**

> "Upon the wicked he shall rain snares, fire and brimstone, and an horrible tempest: this shall be the portion of their cup."

THE RAIN OF FIRE

Here, we are told that God can rain fire upon the territory of the enemy; God did it in the book of Genesis. **Gen. 19:24**

> ***"Then the LORD rained upon Sodom and upon Gomorrah brimstone and fire from the LORD out of heaven;"***

God is ever ready to pour liquid fire upon the head of any power confronting His children. **Ezekiel 38:22**

> ***"And I will plead against him with pestilence and with blood; and I will rain upon him, and upon his bands, and upon the many people that are with him, an overflowing rain, and great hailstones, fire, and brimstone."***

To deal with the enemy when the battle gets heated up, you can rain fire upon your stubborn pursuers. **Psalm 11:6**

> **"Upon the wicked he shall rain snares, fire and brimstone, and an horrible tempest: this shall be the portion of their cup."**

ACIDIC PRAYERS

There are certain prayer points that are so acidic that immediately you make use of them the fire of God will begin to burn the powers that have held you in captivity. The weapon of the fire of God must be used for tough battles. You must make use of this weapon when the powers that have captured you have vowed that they will never let you go. This weapon is needed when you want to be free from the activities of marine witchcraft. You need this weapon when you want to put an end to foundational bondage.

The weapon of the fire of God will grant you immunity and make eaters of flesh and drinkers of blood become so confused that they will begin to eat their own flesh and drink their own blood. For unchallengeable victory, this is the weapon you must use.

PRAYER POINTS

1. Father, You are a consuming fire, arise in your fire and trouble every troubler of my life, in the name of Jesus.
2. Oh fire of God, fall upon every satanic prophet troubling my life, in the name of Jesus.
3. Where is the Lord God of Elijah? Arise in Your fire and fight for me, in the name of Jesus.
4. Fire of God arise, burn to ashes every plantation of darkness, in the name of Jesus.
5. Oh fire of God, arise and shake down every citadel of darkness and burn them to ashes, in the name of Jesus
6. By fire by force, let my portion be released, in the name of Jesus.
7. Oh God that answereth by fire, answer my prayers by fire, in the name of Jesus.
8. Oh God, arise in Your fire of judgement, torment my tormentors, in the name of Jesus.
9. Every rage of the enemy, be quenched by the fire of God, in the name of Jesus.
10. O fire of God, arise, burn to ashes every coven of darkness, in the name of Jesus.
11. Fire of God, arise in the thunder of Your power and disgrace every power trying to disgrace me, in the mighty name of Lord Jesus.
12. The God that answereth by fire, answer all my prayers by fire, in the name of Jesus.

WEAPON 19

THE HOOK OF GOD

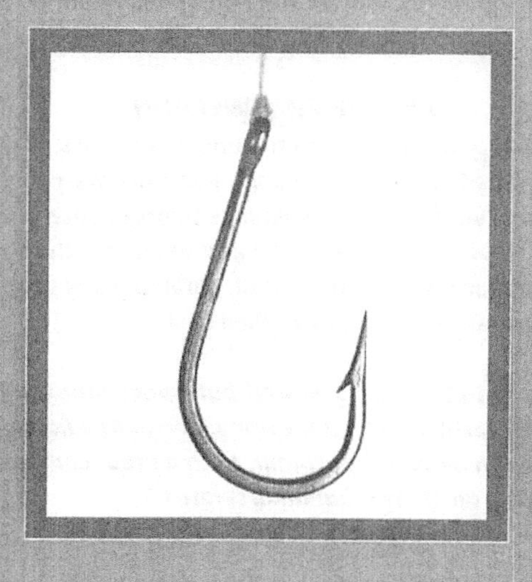

▶ ***THIS WEAPON IS SUITABLE FOR DEALING WITH ANTI-DESTINY POWERS.***

▶ ***IT MUST BE USED WHEN YOU WANT TO ARREST YOUR ARRESTERS.***

▶ ***THIS WEAPON WILL ENABLE YOU TO SACK THE POWERS OF YOUR FATHER'S HOUSE.***

▶ ***IT WILL ENABLE YOU HAND-CUFF SATANIC SOLDIERS AND IMPRISON THEM.***

▶ ***YOU CAN USE THIS WEAPON WHEN YOU ARE DEALING WITH CAMOUFLAGING ENEMIES.***

▶ ***IT CAN BE USED WHEN YOU WANT TO DEAL WITH WICKED SATANIC AGENTS.***

This is a terrible weapon of deliverance and spiritual warfare. This weapon is needed by victims of marine bondage. When marine spirits are holding you captive you need to command the hook of the Lord to fetch them out and stop them from troubling the water of your destiny.

Divine hooks are powerful weapons created to locate the mouth of the fish that is polluting the water of your destiny by using strange powers. God has demonstrated the use of such a weapon in the scriptures. **Ezekiel 29:4**

> ***"But I will put hooks in thy jaws, and I will cause the fish of thy rivers to stick unto thy scales, and I will bring thee up out of the midst of thy rivers, and all the fish of thy rivers shall stick unto thy scales."***

AN AWESOME WEAPON

This is one weapon that will disgrace the enemy and sack all the agents of the power of your father's house. God is an awesome warrior. He can use one weapon of spiritual warfare and deliverance to destabilize a whole army. How does He do this? He will put hooks in a dangerous place in the body of the enemy and the whole satanic force will be routed, paralyzed and captured. I want you to examine the scenario described in **Ezekiel 38:4.**

> ***"And I will turn thee back, and put hooks into thy jaws, and I will bring thee forth, and all thine army, horses and horsemen, all of them clothed with all sorts of armour, even a great company with bucklers and shields, all of them handling swords:"***

ENOUGH IS ENOUGH

God has decreed that a great company of soldiers with all their weapons of war will be arrested through the use of hooks. You need this weapon when you want to declare enough is enough battle. The mystery of this weapon is that when you invoke the hooks of the Lord, you will put an end to silly attacks emanating from the camps of the enemy. The moment you use this weapon, unchallengeable victory and incontestable deliverance will be yours.

This is a weapon which students in the school of deliverance and spiritual warfare must learn how to use. You need prayer points that will act as hooks which will hold captivity captive and grant you victory.

Strange prayer points that will put the hook in the enemy's mouth is your surest weapon of deliverance. This weapon is not a weapon for weak soldiers on the field of battle. You will need to get to a point when your hands are taught to do serious battle. The time is now.

PRAYER POINTS

1. Father, let Your hook go into the waters and disgrace every marine banker that has stolen from me, in the name of Jesus.
2. Father, release Your hooks into the water and disgrace every dragon power that has swallowed my destiny, in the name of Jesus.
3. Hook of the Lord, be released by the thunder of his power to fish out every power from the water troubling in my life, in the name of Jesus.
4. Let the hook of the Lord disgrace the Pharaoh in the waters that has been boasting against my breakthroughs, in the name of Jesus.
5. Let the hook of the Lord destroy every power of the Leviathan assigned against me from the water, in the name of Jesus.
6. O hook of the Lord, arise put to shame every agent of darkness hanging around my environment, in the name of Jesus.
7. Let the angels of the living God begin to use the hook of the Lord to fish out every hidden serpent and scorpion troubling my life.

WEAPON 20

HORRIBLE TEMPEST

- ***IT CAN BE USED WHEN YOU ARE BOMBARDED BY REPEATED ATTACKS.***
- ***WHEN YOU WANT POWER TO CHANGE HANDS.***
- ***WHEN YOU WANT TO EXPERIENCE QUICK AND UNCHALLENGEABLE VICTORY.***
- ***WHEN YOU DECIDE TO FIGHT THE ENEMY TO A STAND STILL.***
- ***WHEN YOU WANT TO DEAL A HEAVY BLOW UPON THE HEAD OF STUBBORN PURSUERS.***
- ***WHEN YOU WANT TO EXPERIENCE TOTAL DELIVERANCE.***

There are weapons, and there are weapons. When God uses the weapon of horrible tempest demonic agents are in trouble. Horrible tempests can be described as a destructive wind or an evil blast. It is a type of wind that will suffocate and destroy the enemy of your freedom.
Evil powers are able to carry out their activities when there is no threat. But, when the tempest of the Almighty threatens them they would release their victims. When the Bible describes a weapon as horrible, it will surely spread tragedy across the camp of the enemy. There is a time in spiritual warfare when the only way the enemies can be forced to turn back is when we issue a cry that will be transformed into a terrible tempest. **Psalm 56:9**

> ***"When I cry unto thee, then shall mine enemies turn back: this I know; for God is for me."***

FRIGHTEN THE ENEMY

When you understand the deep meaning of spiritual warfare you will discover that the devil deserves no pity or mercy. The enemies who raise satanic storms against you deserve being stomped and horrified by the tempest of the Almighty. **Psalm 11:6**

> ***"Upon the wicked he shall rain snares, fire and brimstone, and an horrible tempest: this shall be the portion of their cup."***

When the rain of divine judgment falls from heaven and the terrifying wind from heaven blows against your foundational bondage, the enemy shall be petrified. God can use any method to disgrace the enemy and set his children free. To

confuse the powers that are holding you in bondage, God can introduce a storm in a cup and make the enemy to stagger like a drunkard.
There is no method God cannot use when your victory or deliverance is at stake. This is a season of vengeance. God is set to unleash terror upon the enemy. The tempest is so violent that it will blow off every power behind your problem. Beloved, a million winds may be un-noticed, but a horrible tempest will bring devastating consequences that will remain indelible.

TACKLE THE ENEMY

A lot of God's children are busy going about with the victim mentality. The moment you begin to invoke horrible tempest from heaven, the spirit of terror will grip household witchcraft, foundational powers, and powers behind terrible curses and covenants. We live in a terrible local environment where evil is perpetrated with reckless abandon. We, therefore, need uncommon weapons of spiritual warfare and deliverance.
God has not created special weapons for them to lie fallow and unused. The environment in which we live is dangerous. I am sure you know that the enemy has his own evil wind. This wind has made many blind, crippled multitudes, and paralyzed promising destinies.
The only way out is to tackle the enemy fire for fire. When the enemy comes like a flood, you must raise prayer points that will act like horrible tempest that will steer away the evil tide. When stubborn enemies vow to make your life miserable, stand up and confront them with your weapon of horrible tempest.

PRAYER POINTS

1. Oh horrible tempest, arise and trouble every warfare waged against my life, in the name of Jesus.
2. Horrible tempest from the Lord, march in your fury to pursue my pursuers, in the name of Jesus.
3. Father, let the horrible tempest be released upon every evil gathering summoned to trouble me, in the name of Jesus.
4. Father let the horrible tempest be released to secure my portion in the land of the living, in the name of Jesus.
5. Every cleverly concealed warfare, assigned against me be scattered by the horrible tempest from the Lord, in the name of

Jesus.

6. Every storm of darkness assigned against me, let the horrible tempest from the Lord scatter the tempest, in the name of Jesus.
7. Oh God, arise with Your horrible tempest and scatter every wicked association designed against my life, in the name of Jesus.

WEAPON 21

ENGINE OF WAR

▶ *WHEN YOU WANT TO FIGHT AGAINST THE HOSTS OF DARKNESS.*
▶ *THIS IS A WEAPON YOU CAN USE WHEN YOU WANT TO CONFRONT THE ENEMY FIRE FOR FIRE.*
▶ *IT IS A WEAPON YOU CAN USE WHEN YOU WANT TO SET THE CAPTIVES FREE AND HELP THE OPPRESSED TO OBTAIN FREEDOM.*

The Bible says: **Exodus 15:13**

> ***"Thou in thy mercy hast led forth the people which thou hast redeemed: thou hast guided them in thy strength unto thy holy habitation."***

Here, we discover that God is the General of all generals. He is the greatest fighter in the whole universe. He fights with terrible weapons. When God comes into the field of battle, He appears with weapons that are far more sophisticated than atomic bombs and machine guns. If human beings can invent military weapons of destruction, how much more the Almighty God whom the Bible calls the man of war.

THE LORD OF HOSTS

God is referred to as the God of host. He is the generalissimo of the armies of heaven. The term the Lord of hosts depicts God in warfare. Beloved, there is good news for every child of God. In our battles the Lord of host is with us.

Psalm 46:7

> ***"The LORD of hosts is with us; the God of Jacob is our refuge. Selah."***

The powerful truth which you need to discover, at this point, is that the Lord of hosts has engines of war. These engines of war are diverse. There is a time when God sets engine of war against the enemy. For example if you have been struggling with deep bondage you simply need to ask God to set his engines of war against the foundation of your bondage.

Ezekiel 26:9

> ***"And he shall set engines of war against thy walls, and with his axes he***

shall break down thy towers."

FEARFUL ENGINES

Divine engines of war are terrible. If God should open your eyes to the nature of such engines you will know that they are more fearful and deadly than any engine ever invented by man. Engines of war are used when God wants to finish the enemy. They are brought to the field of battle when ordinary weapons that we are familiar with are inadequate. Engines of war have been invented by God to make you victorious. Engines of war are massive weapons of deliverance.

Ezekiel 26:9

> ***"And he shall set engines of war against thy walls, and with his axes he shall break down thy towers."***

When God decides to set engines of war against the walls of the enemy, you will experience unchallengeable victory. When we take some terrible prayer points we are actually setting engines of war against the enemy. Engines of war will scatter the enemy. Engines of war have bulldozing power. Engines of war will pull down satanic strongholds. Engines of war will uproot every bondage militating against you from the root. You need engine of war prayer points to dislodge the enemy and enforce your deliverance.

WEAPON OF VIOLENCE

In the Mountain of Fire and Miracles Ministries, God has taught our hands to war and fingers to fight. We fight with all kinds of weapons. Our prayer point may appear strange. But we know that there are some battles that will not be fought victoriously without strange prayers. Soft prayers cannot function like engines of war. That is why I have stated, time and again, that the only language the devil understands is the language of holy violence. The truth is that the enemy will not leave you alone until you set engines of war from the armory of the Almighty against unrepentant Pharaohs, wicked Herod, and stubborn pursuers. This is the weapon you must use without pity. You need to invoke engines of war against the powers of your father's house and other satanic agents assigned to rubbish your destiny.

PRAYER POINTS

1. You power of darkness, the engine of war of the Almighty is against you today, in the name of Jesus.
2. You engine of war, gather yourself together and attack every stronghold mounted against my life, in the name of Jesus.
3. You engine of war of the Lord, arise in the thunder of your power and defend my interest, in the name of Jesus.
4. Every land of my life troubled by the enemy, I send the engine of war of the Almighty against you, in Jesus name.
5. You engine of war of the Almighty, set yourself in array and begin to fight all my battles, in the name of Jesus.
6. Any area where the enemy has gathered, against me, let the engine of war of the Lord, be set up against the camp of the enemy, in the name of Jesus.

WEAPON 22

EVIL ANGEL

▶ TO BE USED WHEN YOU WANT TO SEND EVIL ARROWS BACK TO SENDER.
▶ WHEN YOU WANT TO DISGRACE BOASTING POWERS.
▶ WHEN YOU WANT TO TROUBLE YOUR TROUBLES.
▶ IT IS USEFUL FOR VICTIMS OF HOUSEHOLD WICKEDNESS.
▶ IT IS A USEFUL WEAPON FOR TOUGH BATTLES.
▶ IT IS A WEAPON YOU CAN USE FOR PERSISTENT DREAM BATTLES.

Divine methods are often strange. When it comes to deliverance and spiritual warfare God chooses his weapons in strange manners. The weapon we are going to look at here is so strange that God uses it when he wants to demonstrate the fierceness of His anger. **Psalm78:49**

> ***"He cast upon them the fierceness of his anger, wrath, and indignation, and trouble, by sending evil angels among them."***

A STRANGE ACTION

When God wants to finish the stubborn enemies that are on a hot chase with an eye on rubbishing your destiny and making you a permanent resident in a terrible cage, He will take an uncommon action. When God decides to dispatch evil angels into the gathering of your enemy casualties will be innumerable.
If God can open your eyes to the wicked activities of the enemy you will discover that he deserves terrible judgment from the court of the Almighty. Immediately God sends evil angels to the gathering of witches and wizards it will be confusions galore. When eaters of flesh and drinkers of blood have concluded their agenda, evil angels will be dispatched to them and they will begin to eat their own flesh and drink their own blood.

THE AGENDA OF SELF DESTRUCTION

The appearance of evil angels from God will sentence satanic agents to a mission of self-destruction; evil angels will bring terrible calamities upon the enemy. An invasion of evil angels will spell disaster in the enemy's camp.
Evil angels have no mercy. When God decides to use them He generally gives agents of darkness a taste of the wickedness which they perpetrate against

God's children. When enemies continue to harass you and it appears as if evil powers have placed you in a cage and thrown the key away, you only need to pray for evil angels to visit them and make life uncomfortable for them until they become so troubled that they will open the cage and let you go.

When evil angels spread calamity in the camp of the enemy the devil and his agents will discover that you are untouchable. Powers of darkness will continue to mess up with you unless you pray evil angels into their camp. Beloved it takes the wrath, the anger and the indignation of the Almighty to make Him send evil angels to trouble your enemies.

TROUBLE YOUR TROUBLE

When you want to trouble your trouble, you need to pray and draw evil angels into the arena where powers that are troubling your destiny can be found. God has reserved evil angels for the day of trouble. It might appear strange but it is true that evil angels are kept for the day of God's wrath. They can be invoked during seasons of violent battles.

The enemy may continue to carry out his wicked activities, but the moment evil angels appear on the scene, they will run helter-skelter and be subjected to several somersaults until they receive the sentence of death. Evil angels are part of God's weapons. You can send them to attack agents of darkness. This is the type of weapon to use when the battle gets hot and you want to get out of the prison of bondage at all costs.

PRAYER POINTS

1. Father, let evil angels trouble the troublers of my Israel, in the name of Jesus
2. Oh evil angels, arise in anger, attack any satanic bird assigned against me, in the name of Jesus.
3. Father, let evil angels pick up every vulture of darkness assigned against my destiny, in the name of Jesus.
4. Father, let evil angels move into every complex situation terrorizing my destiny, in the name of Jesus.
5. O evil angels, move in an uncommon way and attack every enemy of my progress, in the name of Jesus.

6. Let heavens command evil angels to fight my battles for me, in the name of Jesus.
7. Every satanic bird assigned against my destiny be destroyed by evil angels, in the name of Jesus.
8. Oh evil angels, from heaven, destroy all eaters of flesh, in Jesus name.

WEAPON 23

LOCUST

- ***TO BE USED WHEN GOING THROUGH COMPLEX PROBLEMS.***
- ***THIS WEAPON WILL INVADE AND DESTABILIZE HOUSEHOLD WICKEDNESS.***
- ***THIS IS A POWERFUL WEAPON FOR USE IN CASES OF INCOMPLETE DELIVERANCE.***
- ***THIS WEAPON CAN BE USED TO WIPE OFF MASQUERADING ENEMIES.***
- ***IT CAN BE USED TO COMBAT AN EVIL NETWORK.***
- ***IT WILL PUT AN END TO PERSISTENT BATTLES.***

Exodus 10:4

"Else, if thou refuse to let my people go, behold, tomorrow will I bring the locusts into thy coast:"

Exodus 10:12

"And the LORD said unto Moses, Stretch out thine hand over the land of Egypt for the locusts, that they may come up upon the land of Egypt, and eat every herb of the land, even all that the hail hath left."

ANALYSIS OF LOCUSTS

Locusts invade. You can invade the camp of the enemy. Locusts have consuming ability. You can command the consuming fire of God to swallow the enemies of your deliverance. Locusts have terrible capacity. The Bible says that they are very grievous. **Exodus 10:14**

"And the locusts went up over all the land of Egypt, and rested in all the coasts of Egypt: very grievous were they; before them there were no such locusts as they, neither after them shall be such"

Locusts have devouring power. **II Chronicles 7:13**

"If I shut up heaven that there be no rain, or if I command the locusts to devour the land, or if I send pestilence among my people.."

You can either command the enemies to devour themselves, or to be devoured by the divine locust. Locust comes in large numbers. **Nahum 3:15**

"There shall the fire devour thee; the sword shall cut thee off, it shall

eat thee up like the cankerworm: make thyself many as the cankerworm, make thyself many as the locusts"

You can command an army of locusts to visit everywhere your name is mentioned with the intention of swallowing your destiny. Locusts can be endowed with awesome power. **Rev. 9:3**

"And there came out of the smoke locusts upon the earth: and unto them was given power, as the scorpions of the earth have power"

You can invoke divine locusts that are endowed with destructive power to disperse every gathering put in place in order to bury your destiny and make you a prisoner in wicked satanic cages.

COMMON FEATURES

Two things are common about the locust

1. They come in large numbers and multiply fast.
2. They are often referred to as an army of locusts.

They become intimidating as a result of their large number. Often times, it is difficult to count them. **Psalm 105:34**

"He spake, and the locusts came, and caterpillars, and that without number,"

Jer. 46:23

"They shall cut down her forest, saith the LORD, though it cannot be searched; because they are more than the grasshoppers, and are innumerable."

THE METHOD

When you use the weapon of divine locusts the host that are fighting for you outnumber the company of your enemies. Locusts are often blown to specified locations by the wind. **Exodus 10:13**

"And Moses stretched forth his rod over the land of Egypt, and the LORD brought an east wind upon the land all that day, and all that

night; and when it was morning, the east wind brought the locusts."

You can therefore command the wind of the Almighty to blow divine locusts into places where agents of darkness gather together in preparation for an attack against your life. When an army of divine locusts land in a midst of household enemies, local witch crafts, and groups of people who have been put together to inflict arrows of setbacks upon you, they will scatter. Their hands shall not perform their enterprise.

AN ARMY OF LOCUSTS

One other thing we should take note of concerning the locust is that it has four incisive teeth which transverse each other like scissors. Their function is to grip or cut. When you make use of the weapon of divine locusts you can command their teeth to act like scissors and cut into shreds every demonic agenda factored against you by wicked powers. **Joel 1:6**

> ***"For a nation is come up upon my land, strong, and without number, whose teeth are the teeth of a lion, and he hath the cheek teeth of a great lion."***

Locusts constitute special squads in God's army. Their mission is to consume. **Deut. 28:38**

> ***"Thou shalt carry much seed out into the field, and shalt gather but little in; for the locust shall consume it."***

METHODS OF USING THE WEAPON

You need to pray and ask God's locust to unleash judgment upon the powers that will not cooperate with your freedom. Locusts are instruments of divine judgment. You need to send locusts to the enemy's camp. Since enemies are bent on wasting your destiny, you must waste them before they waste you. Their labour must be consumed by devouring locusts. **Psalm 78:46**

> ***"He gave also their increase unto the caterpillar, and their labour unto the locust."***

As long as the enemy is determined on keeping you in the land of bondage, you must also be determined to command a terrible invasion upon them by God's locusts. This weapon is useful when an array of enemies confront you. This weapon comes handy when your battles are passed from hand to hand by a network of dark powers. You need this weapon when it is your desire to scatter binding powers in such a way as to make it impossible for them to ever come together again.

When you want to devour the enemy without leaving remnant, the locust of the Almighty will do the job perfectly. Instances of re-current battles, incomplete deliverance, and persistent attacks can only be brought to an end when you bombard them with terrible divine locusts.

We need fresh revival of spiritual warfare. We need to go into aggressive warfare invoking locusts that eat without remnant.

With such divine invasion every enemy of your goodness will be routed and consumed.

PRAYER POINTS

1. Locusts from heaven, locate every plantation of darkness in my life and uproot them, in the name of Jesus.
2. Locusts from heaven, eat up every satanic seed planted in the garden of my life, in the name of Jesus.
3. Let the commandment of the Lord go forth and deliver me from every plantation of the enemy using the weapon of the locust, in the name of Jesus.
4. Locusts of the Most High God invade every house of the strongman and pursue them out of their hiding places, in the name of Jesus.
5. I invoke the power of the locust of God to repossess and to reposition everything the enemy has stolen, in the name of Jesus.
6. Let the locust from heaven go forth in the thunder of thy power to send confusion into the camp of my enemies, in the name of Jesus.
7. I use the weapon of the locust to clear every blockage in my way, in the name of Jesus.

WEAPON 24

THE COCKATRICE

▶ *THIS WEAPON WILL ENABLE YOU TO DEAL WITH HOUSEHOLD WICKEDNESS TOYING WITH YOUR JOY.*

▶ *WITH THIS WEAPON YOU BRING TO PUBLIC DISGRACE EVERY POWER OF FAILURE.*

▶ *MAKE USE OF THIS WEAPON WHEN YOU WANT TO UNLEASH THE RAW POWER OF GOD UPON THE POWERS THAT ARE TRYING TO BURY YOUR DESTINY.*

A lot of people wonder why our prayer points are unique. There are people who have tried to decipher our use of language during hot prayer sessions. What happens during warfare prayer sessions differs from what happens in everyday life experiences. Hence, prayer commands may appear strange and the weapon we use on the field of battle may appear somewhat uncommon.
When God begins to reveal startling details of what happens in the spiritual realm, you will understand why strange weapons are needed when fighting strange battles. In the arena of spiritual warfare and deep areas of deliverance, we must learn how to pick up new prayer terminologies and explore the depths of deliverance. The good news is that God has shared His deep secrets with His servants. Some of these uncommon secrets have been shared in this ground breaking book.

DEEP SECRETS

When you get to the realm of spiritual warfare and make use of deep secrets you will experience victory, come up with awesome testimonies and consequently become signs and wonders to those who are around you. Beloved, let me share a secret with you at this point. The giant strides which the Mountain of Fire and Miracles Ministries has taken so far can be attributed to our emphasis on prayer, deliverance, and spiritual warfare.
For quite a very long time, Christianity has not been applied appropriately to the environment of the black race. As God has given us deep insights into the goings on in the spiritual realm, a lot of people have discovered the practical realities of the spiritual realm. Deep truths have been discovered. We have learnt how to come out of our grandparent's spiritual huts. Rather than allow things to remain the way they are, we have decided to take the battle to the gates of the enemy,

fight satanic agents to a standstill and possess our possessions.

A STRANGE WEAPON

A lot of people have wondered whether spiritual warfare principles are for real. Beloved, do not wait until wicked powers deal with you before you begin to fight. Even if you are not going through any battle at the moment, one principle you can learn from or embrace is; in the time of peace, prepare for war.
The weapon of cockatrice is a strange weapon. It is one weapon that God has reserved for seasons of tough battles. The cockatrice is a fiery serpent. It is a viper's offspring. It is a venomous snake. It is believed that the cockatrice can poison with its ordinary breath.

Proverb 23:32

> ***At the last it biteth like a serpent, and stingeth like an adder.***

Isaiah 59:5

> ***They hatch cockatrice' eggs, and weave the spider's web: he that eateth of their eggs dieth, and that which is crushed breaketh out into a viper.***

The word cockatrice is an old English word that describes a serpent of highly venomous character.

Jeremiah 8:17.

> ***For, behold, I will send serpents, cockatrices, among you, which will not be charmed, and they shall bite you, saith the LORD.***

Amos 9:3

> ***And though they hide themselves in the top of Carmel, I will search and take them out thence; and though they be hid from my sight in the bottom of the sea, thence will I command the serpent, and he shall bite them:***

It is a dangerous viper that is about a foot long. In fact, the cockatrice is one of the most dangerous serpents. It is extremely hostile and fearsome because of its poison. One of the characteristics of the cockatrice is that its bite will automatically result in death. The cockatrice is, therefore, a member of God's elite army. It is a tough weapon.

DEADLY WEAPONS

Whenever agents of darkness toy with God's children, they must embrace the poison of the cockatrice. Beloved, there is no mercy for the enemy on the field of battle.

Deadly weapons are allowed when demonic agents are sent to assassinate you and consequently swallow your destiny. You must take tough prayer points against them. You need to be aggressive and command the cockatrice to bite and poison any power that has vowed that your marriage will fail, your business will collapse, your calling will be buried or your virtues will be swallowed by the power of your father's house.

The cockatrice is the weapon to use when certain powers are saying that you will end the journey of your life in the valley of shame and failure. Invoke this weapon against powers that bite without any remnant and you will begin to sing your song and dance your dance.

PRAYER POINTS

1. Let the power of the cockatrice be invoked to trouble every enemy of my life, in the name of Jesus.
2. Let the power of the cockatrice begin to torment my tormenters, in the name of Jesus.
3. Let the battle of the Almighty be waged against my enemies using the weapon of the cockatrice, in the name of Jesus.
4. Thou poison of the cockatrice be injected into every arena of satanic warfare waged against me and let the warfare be destroyed, in the name of Jesus.
5. Thou power of the cockatrice arise and fight my oppressors, in the name of Jesus.
6. I command the cockatrice to bite and poison any power that has vowed that my destiny will fail, in the name of Jesus.
7. Let the power of the cockatrice torment every unrepentant witchcraft and bite them to submission, in the name of Jesus.

WEAPON 25

LIGHTENING OF GOD

- *THIS WEAPON WILL GIVE THE ENEMY PUBLIC DISGRACE.*
- *IT IS A POWERFUL WEAPON THAT CAN BE USED TO ARREST AND DEFLECT SATANIC ARROWS.*
- *IT IS A SUITABLE WEAPON FOR FIGHTING FOUNDATIONAL BATTLES.*
- *YOU NEED IT WHEN YOU WANT ANTI BREAKTHROUGH POWERS TO SOMERSAULT AND DIE.*
- *YOU CAN USE THIS WEAPON WHEN YOU WANT TO TOTALLY CONFUSE EVIL SPIES.*

Lightening is a formidable weapon created by God to destroy the enemies of your destiny and enhance your deliverance. In the physical realm, lighting comes out in a frightening form. It can be visible from one end to another end of the earth. It is so palpable that it cannot be un-noticed. When God casts forth his lightening, enemies are scattered. When the enemies of your deliverance gather together to ensure that you remain perpetually under bondage, the instrument God will use to scatter them unto desolation is the weapon of explosive divine lightening. The enemies of your destiny and breakthroughs cannot escape the fierce lightening of the Almighty. **Psalm 144:6**

> ***"Cast forth lightning, and scatter them: shoot out thine arrows, and destroy them."***

When demons gather themselves together in order to fulfill their agenda of keeping you in the valley of bondage, God, the man of war, will shoot out terrific lightening in order to send disaster into their camp. With one arrow of lightening the enemies of your breakthroughs and deliverance will be dispersed.

ARROW OF LIGHTENING

The Bible makes it clear that lightening are the arrows of the Lord. **Psalm 18:14**

> ***"Yea, he sent out his arrows, and scattered them; and he shot out lightnings, and discomfited them."***

The zigzag appearance of the lightening and the pounding noise of thunder that accompanies it symbolize the fact that God is at war.
When God releases lightening, tough signals are sent to the camp of the enemy. The arrow head of the thunder, being the lightening, will surely land in witchcraft covens where enemies are busy trying to tie you down and subject you to gruesome bondage. God does not bring out this weapon all the time. However, when lightening is released from the armoury of the Almighty the battle becomes terrible. This is one weapon of deliverance we need to learn to utilize in this end time battle.

UNCHALLENGEABLE WEAPON

As no one can ignore lightening in the physical realm, no demonic gathering or perpetrators of bondage can joke with the weapon of lightening. The purpose of this weapon is to scatter, confuse, and make battalions of demonic agents to flee. When they flee an end is brought to their activities. They will abandon their mission, ignore their agenda and the totality of their activities will be aborted. All God needs to do to sentence the power that put your bondage in place to total confusion and instant burial is one powerful lightening.
The lightening of God will make the powers that hold you in bondage to do repeated summersaults until they die. When the lightening of God is shot out as an arrow the powers of your father's house will release you and let you go.

LET THE LIGHTENING STRIKE

This generation is yet to witness the full blast of God's lightening. The powers that will not let you go will be dispersed and wiped away at the onslaught of the lightening of God. You need to invoke the lightening of God against every power standing between you and your complete deliverance.
The lightening of God is needed to send hot signals to the camp of the enemy. You can, therefore, pray and ask the lightening of God to issue instant judgment upon stubborn pursuers and unrepentant enemies.

PRAYER POINTS

1. Lightening of God, arise, strike terror and fear into the camp of my enemies, in the name of Jesus.
2. O God arise by the weapon of Your lightening and scatter every

conspiracy against my life, in the name of Jesus.

3. O God arise and let the weapon of your lightening move into the camp of my pursuers, in the name of Jesus.
4. Lightening of God arise, go into the waters, go into the forest and go into the mountains and destroy every stronghold mounted against me, in the name of Jesus.
5. Lightening of God, move in an uncommon way and empower me to possess my possessions, in the name of Jesus.
6. Lightening of God, move in Your fire and in Your rage and pursue my pursuers, in the name of Jesus.
7. Let the lightening of the Lord begin to strike fear and terror to the camp of my stubborn pursuers and into the camp of my unrepentant enemy, in the name of Jesus.

WEAPON

26

HAIL STONES

► IT IS A WEAPON OF VENGEANCE.
► IT IS MEANT FOR HOT BATTLES.
► IT CAN BE USED TO WIPE OFF AN ASSEMBLY OF THOSE WHO HAVE GANGED UP AGAINST YOU.
► IT WILL SACK WITCHCRAFT BARBERS AND NIGHT CATERERS.
► IT WILL DISGRACE UNFRIENDLY FRIENDS.
► THIS WEAPON WILL MOVE YOU FROM THE VALLEY TO THE MOUNTAIN TOP.

Hail stones are terrible weapons of deliverance and spiritual warfare. The Bible says in **Psalm 18:12-13.**

> ***"At the brightness that was before him his thick clouds passed, hail stones and coals of fire. The LORD also thundered in the heavens, and the Highest gave his voice; hail stones and coals of fire."***

The use of hail stones reminds us of violent exhibition of divine power. It is a symbol of divine vengeance. God can go any length to fight our battles. The prince of the power of the air may not respect ordinary weapons but when God dispatches terrible hail stones even the legions of hell will be scattered.

GOD OF VENGEANCE

There is no extent the Almighty will not go to protect us. Any power that wants to keep you under bondage is inviting destruction. Hail stones from God are the answer. The wicked acts of the enemy often attract terrible divine wrath. God responds and vengeance is unleashed upon the enemy.

There is a moment when God throws hail stones whose mission is to locate the head of every Goliath behind your bondage and attacks. Hail stones can be described as divine balls of fire. Once these hail stones are triggered off, they hit the powers behind bondage like killer gunshots.

The truth is that the enemy has been having a field day because God's children have not learnt how to make use of these weapons as destructive divine missiles.

Hail stones are tough weapons. They come into play whenever God declares. **Isaiah 63:4**

"For the day of vengeance is in mine heart, and the year of my redeemed is come".

Romans 12:19

"Dearly beloved, avenge not yourselves, but rather give place unto wrath: for it is written, Vengeance is mine; I will repay, saith the Lord."

WHEN GOD IS PROVOKED

The powers that put you under bondage are inviting divine vengeance. When God's wrath is provoked, angels that have no mercy are dispatched bringing acidic hail stones into the camps of the enemy.
According to *(Psalm 18:12-13 - At the brightness that was before him his thick clouds passed, hail stones and coals of fire. The LORD also thundered in the heavens, and the Highest gave his voice; hail stones and coals of fire.)* Hail stones are accompanied by coals of fire, in fact, they can be rightly described as stones of fire. God's hands are filled with such destructive weapons.
These weapons are needed when you are faced with an unending cycle of battles, repeated attacks and deep bondage. If you are tied down in the spirit, you need to ask God to release hail stones and coals of fire upon those who have subjected you to such gruesome captivity.

Divine hail stones are not just kept in God's armoury, they are meant for tough battles. If you have used several weapons and there are no visible results, you need to pray hail stone prayers upon the powers behind the problems. The only way you can command your bondage to die is to ask God to locate the heads of the powers behind instances of captivity, to knock their heads into unconsciousness and subsequently subject them to total annihilation.
Hail stones are terrible weapons that God has earmarked for wounding the head of your oppressors. No power can survive when confronted by powerful hail stones from heaven.

IMPORTANT EXAMPLES

In the scriptures, God demonstrated the use of hail stones as formidable weapons for dealing squarely with the enemy in the following instances.

1. **God uses hailstones to slay the enemies of His people. Josh. 10:11**

"And it came to pass, as they fled from before Israel, and were in the going down to Bethhoron, that the LORD cast down great stones from heaven upon them unto Azekah, and they died: they were more which died with hailstones than they whom the children of Israel slew with the sword."

2. **Hail stones were used to attack farms. Psalm 78:47**

"He destroyed their vines with hail, and their sycomore trees with frost."

3. **God uses hail stones as weapons of war. Isaiah 30:30**

"And the LORD shall cause his glorious voice to be heard, and shall shew the lighting down of his arm, with the indignation of his anger, and with the flame of a devouring fire, with scattering, and tempest, and hailstones."

4. **God uses hail stones to consume. Ezekiel 13:13**

"Therefore thus saith the Lord GOD; I will even rend it with a stormy wind in my fury; and there shall be an overflowing shower in mine anger, and great hailstones in my fury to consume it."

5. **God uses hail stones to deal with people. Ezekiel 38:22**

"And I will plead against him with pestilence and with blood; and I will rain upon him, and upon his bands, and upon the many people that are with him, an overflowing rain, and great hailstones, fire, and brimstone."

THE VIOLENT HOUR

There is a time when you need to become violent and pray saying oh, great hail stones fall upon the head of my enemy. **Ezekiel 13:11**

> ***"Say unto them which daub it with untempered morter, that it shall fall: there shall be an overflowing shower; and ye, O great hailstones, shall fall; and a stormy wind shall rend it."***

GREAT HAIL STONES

I want you to take cognizance of the fact that there are ordinary hail stones and there are great hail stones. **Ezekiel 38:22**

> ***"And I will plead against him with pestilence and with blood; and I will rain upon him, and upon his bands, and upon the many people that are with him, an overflowing rain, and great hailstones, fire, and brimstone."***

When your goal is great deliverance you must invoke the weapon of great hail stones. The greater the level of victory you desire, the greater the capacity of hail stones you must use. Great hail stones will wreck great havoc in the camp of powers that are responsible for your deliverance.
These are weapons you need to make use of when the enemy will not let you go. When you are tired of dwelling in the valley and when you are fighting critical battles you need this weapon.

WEAPON OF UNCHALLENGEABLE VICTORY

These weapons have been possibly hidden from believers for ages. The same God who used hail stones to inflict judgment upon the enemies of His people has not stopped using the weapon. Beloved, the truth is that some enemies will not stop harassing you unless you command hail stones to destroy them.
The powers of your father's house will not stop disturbing you until you declare enough is enough by asking God to send rains of hail stones from heaven. The power behind the foundational bondage that has rubbished your destiny can only be disgraced and destroyed when there is a repeat of the use of hail stones in Bible days, in your life today.

OFFENSIVE WARFARE

You must take the battles to the realm of the heavenlies through the use of hail stones as weapons of mass destruction. This weapon is needed by men and women who have suffered in the hands of satanic dribblers, eaters of flesh and drinkers of blood, witchcraft barbers, destructive unfriendly friends, die-hard satanic agents and hidden wicked enemies. Use this weapon today and your victory will be awesome.

PRAYER POINTS

1. Father, let Your hail stones rain into the camp of my enemies, in the name of Jesus.
2. Father, give my enemies hail stones that will make them regret ever coming to fight me, in the name of Jesus.
3. Lord, let hail stones be rained from heaven upon every witchcraft gathering assigned against my life, in the name of Jesus.
4. Hail stones from heaven, arise, pester every enchanter unto submission, in the name of Jesus
5. Hail stones form heaven, move in your rage and disgrace every activities of serpent and scorpion fashioned against me, in the name of Jesus.
6. O God arise with the power of your hail stones and possess my possessions, in the name of Jesus.
7. Father, let the hail stones from heaven move into my place of birth and recover every good thing that has been stolen from my life, in the name of Jesus.

WEAPON 27

FINGER OF GOD

- ***YOU CAN USE THIS WEAPON WHEN YOU WANT TO INVOKE THE RAW POWER OF THE ALMIGHTY.***
- ***IT IS SUITABLE FOR CANCELLING THE HANDWRITING OF DARKNESS.***
- ***IT IS AN UNCHALLENGEABLE YOKE BREAKER***
- ***IT IS AN UNCOMMON WEAPON FOR TOUGH BATTLES***
- ***IT IS A WEAPON YOU CAN USE WHEN YOU WANT TO CONFRONT FAKE PROPHETS AND FETISH PRIEST.***
- ***IT IS USEFUL FOR THOSE WHO ARE INVOLVED IN PUBLIC POWER ENCOUNTERS.***

One of the most violent weapons which God has given to us for decisive victory and total deliverance is the weapon of the finger of God. The finger of God reveals God as the man of war. Whenever God comes into the scene of the battle He appears with His finger as a weapon of dealing decisively with the enemy. When God's finger becomes visible at the place of battle, the enemy will be defeated woefully. If you know how to make use of this uncommon weapon the enemy will submit themselves and bow. They will be forced to declare. "This is the finger of God." Exodus 8:19

> ***"Then the magicians said unto Pharaoh, This is the finger of God: and Pharaoh's heart was hardened, and he hearkened not unto them; as the LORD had said."***

A UNIQUE WEAPON

The finger of God is needed when you are confronted by problems that are related to foundational bondage. To destroy any form of evil foundation, you need to use the weapon of the finger of God. To inflict fatal wounds upon the head of the enemy you need the weapon. Beloved, the powers of your father's house cannot withstand the finger of God.

When the finger of God confronts the evil cobwebs in your life, they will be roasted and converted to ashes. The finger of God was a formidable weapon in the court of Pharaoh. You need this weapon in order to obtain victory in Pharaoh's court today. The finger of God is a weapon that will remove every handwriting of darkness keeping you in the realm of bondage.

AN UNBEATABLE WEAPON

The weapon of the finger of God came to the fore when Jesus declared **Luke 11:20**

> ***"But if I with the finger of God cast out devils, no doubt the kingdom of God is come upon you"***

Here, Jesus made it categorically clear that to cast out devils, the finger of God is an unbeatable weapon. Every habitation of darkness in your life would be exposed when the finger of God sets your life on fire.

The enemy cannot joke with the finger of God. It is a fearful weapon. The finger of God is the finger of fire. The finger of God is the instrument that will set you free from any form of bondage. The finger of God will make every hidden stranger to be frightened out of their places of hiding.

THE YOKE BREAKER

Jesus reminded those who listened to Him that the instrument of casting out devils is the finger of God. When the finger of God is fully stretched, demons will be cast out, bondage will break, yokes will scatter and captives of the terrible will be delivered. If stubborn powers have kept you in bondage for a long time you must pray the finger of God into fearful operation, and you will be set free instantaneously.

No matter how deep your bondage is, when the finger of God touches your life, fire will fall from heaven and every tree which your heavenly father has not planted shall be uprooted. When the finger of God comes into manifestation in your life, satanic attacks you have suffered from for a very long time will become a thing of the past. The finger of God will cancel the hand writing of the devil. The finger of God will frustrate the token of liars and make diviners mad.

A WEAPON FOR TOUGH BATTLES

When the battle becomes tough the finger of God is the weapon to use. The finger of God comes with the totality of the power of God. It is loaded with the fury and wrath of the Almighty against every power that has vowed that your deliverance will not be complete.

The finger of God will close every case that are opened in the courts of the enemy. The finger of God will give you uncommon deliverance and dumb-founding miracles. Try the weapon of God's fingers today, and the Almighty will respond in a terrible manner. **Psalm 65:5**

> ***"By terrible things in righteousness wilt thou answer us, O God of our salvation; who art the confidence of all the ends of the earth, and of them that are afar off upon the sea:"***

PRAYER POINTS

1. By the finger that destabilized Nebuchadnezzar, arise and fight for me O Lord, in the name of Jesus.
2. O finger of God, arise in your anger and confuse my confusion, in the name of Jesus.
3. My Father, let Your finger of fire be pointed out against every opposition to my advancement, in the name of Jesus.
4. O finger of God, arise recover my stolen virtues, in the name of Jesus.
5. O finger of God, arise, write the judgment against my oppressors, in the name of Jesus.
6. Father, let the weapon of your finger overcome every opposition to my promotion, in the name of Jesus.
7. Thou finger of God, disappoint all the devices of the crafty working against my life, in the name of Jesus.
8. O finger of God, arise ravage the camp of my enemies, in the name of Jesus.

WEAPON 28

FEAR OF THE DAY

▶ YOU NEED IT WHEN YOU WANT TO UNLEASH AN ATMOSPHERE OF PANIC INTO THE SATANIC BARRACKS OF YOUR FATHER'S HOUSE.

▶ YOU CAN USE THIS WEAPON TO FRUSTRATE THE SATANIC VULTURES IN YOUR TERRITORY.

▶ USED TO RENDER THE POWERS OF YOUR FATHER'S HOUSE AND OTHER WICKED AGENTS LAME, BLIND DEAF AND DUMB.

God is a strategist. He is a great fighter. There are dangerous weapons in the divine armoury. As long as the enemy continues to invent destructive weapons, God will continue to come up with deadlier weapons. No wonder the Bible says when the enemy comes like a flood the Spirit of the Lord shall raise up a standard against him. The weapon we are considering now is one of such raised standards.

Beloved when the enemy is busy rejoicing that he has just manufactured a wicked weapon, God will simply raise a higher standard and come up with a weapon that will make the enemy's invented weapon look like a toy. God has a great sense of humour. He takes delight in laughing at the enemy. No wonder the Bible says He that sitteth in heaven shall laugh.

POWER TO DETHRONE EVIL KINGS

Beloved, there is no weapon that God cannot invent and make use of, just to make sure that the enemy is disgraced and destroyed. Here, we are looking at a very strange weapon. The fear of the day is a terrific weapon. When God has finished making the night an uncomfortable atmosphere for wicked powers to carry out their evil activities, heaven will switch the gear to the realm of the day.

When the fear of the day overshadows the hearts of agents of darkness, they will be prevented from carrying out their activities. The fear of the day is a weapon of terror. When this weapon grips the heart of unfriendly friends, the powers of your father's house and other wicked agents they will be rendered lame, blind deaf and dumb.

CYCLICAL WARFARE

One of the strategies of God is to embark on cyclical warfare. When the enemies are routed, arrested and imprisoned in the night they will also be made to meet their waterloo during the day. They face terror in the night, and terror in the day, leaving them with no moment for their nefarious and wicked activities.
The Bible says that wicked powers that will not let you fulfil your destiny shall receive the arrow of the astonishment of heart. **Deut. 28:28**

> ***"The LORD shall smite thee with madness, and blindness, and astonishment of heart:"***

POWER TO HARASS THE ENEMY

With astonishment of heart during the day and fear in the night the enemy will be thrown out of business. The fear of the day is a deadly weapon given to us by God to use to harass the enemy instead of being harassed by wicked powers. The fear of the day is a weapon you can use to paralyze the enemy and make it impossible for wicked powers to attack you during the day. If evil powers decide that you will not rest during the day and night, you can come up with a higher decree and decide to withdraw the arrests by programming fear into their lives.
Deut. 28:66

> ***"And thy life shall hang in doubt before thee; and thou shalt fear day and night, and shalt have none assurance of thy life:"***

HOW TO CAPTURE THE ENEMY

The principle here is to stop them before they stop you. This weapon will enable you to capture the enemy before you are captured. Rather than allow the devil to fill your heart with terror and fear in the day, you can make the enemy to be at the receiving end by making use of these back to sender weapons.
A lot of believers are suffering today because of the ignorance of the use of spiritual warfare weapons. As God's children, we are not supposed to be harassed by fear in the day and in the night, we are the ones to paralyze wicked forces and plant such fear that will make them to become barking dogs that cannot bite. This is our day of victory. This is the weapon that we need to torment all the tormentors and celebrate the victory that God has given us.

PRAYER POINTS

1. Let all my stubborn enemies receive the arrow of the fear of the day, in the name of Jesus.
2. Let all my enemies receive the arrow of the fear of the day, in the name of Jesus.
3. Let the fear of the day come upon my stubborn pursuer, in the name of Jesus
4. Let the fear of the day envelope my midnight enemies, in the name of Jesus.
5. Let every divination, let every spell issued against me in the day be nullified by the fear of the day, in the name of Jesus.
6. Holy Ghost arise in your power and overshadow my enemies with the fear of the day, in the name of Jesus.
7. Blood of Jesus arise in your power over shadow my enemies with fear of the day, in the name of Jesus
8. Father, let great fear of the day be upon every enemy of righteousness, in the name of Jesus.
9. Oh Lord, arise, and let the fear of the day pursue my pursuers, in the name of Jesus.

WEAPON

29

FEAR OF THE NIGHT

- ***THIS WEAPON WILL SPREAD TERROR IN THE ENEMY'S CAMP.***
- ***IT WILL ENABLE YOU TO TAKE CHARGE OF THE NIGHT.***
- ***YOU CAN USE THIS WEAPON WHEN YOU WANT TO DISGRACE THE POWERS OF THE NIGHT.***
- ***YOU CAN USE THIS WEAPON WHEN YOU WANT TO SUSPEND EVIL ACTIVITIES THAT GO ON IN THE NIGHT.***
- ***IT CAN BE USED TO ARREST WICKED NIGHT CATERERS.***

Students of spiritual warfare are aware of the fact that wicked satanic activities are carried out in the night. Evil powers often make use of the cover of darkness to perpetrate uncommon wickedness. But the good news is that our heavenly Father is greater than the greatest, stronger than the strongest and is able to come up with divine warfare strategies that will swallow dark strategies.

The weapon we are considering here is the weapon of the fear of the night. God has given us this weapon to arm us sufficiently to deal squarely with the evil forces. When the weapon of the fear of the night comes upon night caterers and birds that fly in the night, they will be paralyzed and they will not be able to carry out their activities.

The fear of the night is a very powerful weapon. **Deut. 28:66**

> ***"And thy life shall hang in doubt before thee; and thou shalt fear day and night, and shalt have none assurance of thy life:"***

THE PARALYSING FORCE

When fear invades the camp of the enemy, they will abandon their evil plans, and their agenda shall be frustrated. As a believer you can invoke the fear of God upon your environment. This fear will become the fear of the night. It will get to a point when agents of darkness will be confronted by powers that are greater than them and for fear will not be able to perform their wicked plans.

Evil powers have carried out their activities because no one has challenged them. In the days of Apostle Joseph Ayo Babalola, whenever he invaded any locality with the awesome power of God, it was said that no witch could stay around thirty kilometers radius near where the great apostle ministered. That kind of power that invoked palpable fear is the weapon we need to make use of today. Since evil powers have vowed that they will continue to carry out their activities in the night, we must also learn how to spread the fear of God in the night.

POWER TO SPREAD FEAR

The fear of the night will be so strong that it will sack and destroy powers of darkness. If you live in an environment where evil birds fly in the night, you can attack them with strange prayer points. These prayer points will spread the fear of the night. The moment the fear of the night becomes strong, the glory of God will spread fear and the atmosphere of the night will be so charged with positive power that evil powers will not be able to operate or attack you.

Beloved, you can actually command the fear of the night to grip the hearts of all wicked spirits released and dispersed into the atmosphere to either harm you or put you under bondage. These are the end times. This is an era where God's children must take control of the night. Evil powers have done enough in the night. Now is the time when the situation must change. Power must change hands. We must arise and take captivity captive.

The same fear that the enemy uses to trouble our hearts must be sent back to them in form of the weapon of the fear of the night.

PRAYER POINTS

1. Let all my stubborn enemies receive the arrow of the fear of the night, in the name of Jesus.
2. Let all my enemies receive the arrow of the fear of the night, in the name of Jesus.
3. Let the fear of the night come upon my stubborn pursuer, in the name of Jesus.
4. Let the fear of the night envelope my midnight enemies, in the name of Jesus.
5. Let every divination, let every spell issued against me in the night be nullified by the fear of the night, in the name of Jesus.

6. Holy Ghost, arise in Your power and overshadow my enemies with the fear of the night, in the name of Jesus.
7. Blood of Jesus, arise in Your power and overshadow my enemies with fear of the night, in the name of Jesus.
8. Father, let great fear of the night be upon every enemy of righteousness, in the name of Jesus.
9. O Lord, arise, and let the fear of the night pursue my pursuers, in the name of Jesus.

WEAPON 30

GREAT HEAT

- ***THIS IS AN OUTSTANDING FIRE WEAPON.***
- ***IT IS A WEAPON FOR UNLEASHING DIVINE JUDGMENT UPON THE ENEMIES OF YOUR DESTINY.***
- ***IT CAN BE USED TO SEND THE JUDGMENT OF DEATH UPON WITCHCRAFT.***
- ***THIS WEAPON WILL FRIGHTEN EVERY STRANGER OUT OF THEIR HIDDEN PLACES.***
- ***IT WILL OVER THROW THE POWER OF DARKNESS.***
- ***IT IS A POWERFUL WEAPON FOR SERIOUS BATTLES.***
- ***YOU CAN USE THIS WEAPON WHEN YOU WANT TO SING YOUR SONG AND DANCE YOUR DANCE.***

There are diverse weapons which we are yet to discover and make use of in this era of intense warfare. It is unfortunate that many believers are not tutored on the importance of spiritual warfare. The devil has dribbled many believers. Hence, they are casualties in the field of battle. Many believers who are supposed to be riders of horses are busy trekking as if they have no connection to divine royalty. Many are miles away from the realities of the victory of Calvary. Unfortunately, a lot of modern day Christians are victims of oppression. Victory appears elusive. The overcoming lifestyle has become difficult to come by. The reasons are not farfetched.

THE CHARGED ATMOSPHERE

We have not learnt how to make use of spiritual warfare weapons. The more we make use of the weapons of spiritual warfare, the more we will experience and celebrate victory. The weapon of great heat is an awesome spiritual warfare weapon. God can use heat to fight the enemy to a standstill. When God decides to "command deliverances unto Zion" he makes use of strange weapons like great heat. The heat charges the atmosphere and makes things unbearable for the enemy.

When household wickedness, unrepentant witchcraft, stubborn marine powers, and other types of satanic agents are subjected to great heat, they will let you go. The story of Pharaoh comes to mind here. Initially, Pharaoh was stubborn. When he was told "let my people go" he would not budge, God intensified the heat of the various strange attacks until it rose to a boiling point that made him to say "please go and set me free. Let me be free from this horrible heat."

SUFFOCATING HEAT

If the powers of your father's house have held you captive all through these years, you need to pray and invoke great heat from above to suffocate and kill the powers in charge of your case.
The weapon of great heat is used when God is provoked and He decides to give vent to His anger. Deut. 29:24-25

> ***"Even all nations shall say, Wherefore hath the LORD done thus unto this land? what meaneth the heat of this great anger? Then men shall say, Because they have forsaken the covenant of the LORD God of their fathers, which he made with them when he brought them forth out of the land of Egypt:"***

Here, the Bible tells us that the heat of God's anger will become great heat that will set the enemy on edge. When God begins to increase the intensity of the heat of his anger there shall be burning sensations in witchcraft covens and other places where your enemies are gathered together. The Bible makes it clear that the invasion that is carried out through the use of great heat will make the territory of the enemy to be turned to a desert.

THE OVERTHROWING HEAT

Deut. 29:23

> ***"And that the whole land thereof is brimstone, and salt, and burning, that it is not sown, nor beareth, nor any grass groweth therein, like the overthrow of Sodom, and Gomorrah, Admah, and Zeboim, which the LORD overthrew in his anger, and in his wrath:"***

Psalm 107:34

> ***"A fruitful land into barrenness, for the wickedness of them that dwell therein."***

Jer. 17:6

> ***"For he shall be like the heath in the desert, and shall not see when good cometh; but shall inhabit the parched places in the wilderness, in a salt land and not inhabited."***

DIVINE DESOLATION

God can make use of the weapon of great heat to turn the enemy's territory to a habitation of perpetual desolation. Great heat is a weapon you must learn to use. We have had enough of ice cream prayers. There are certain powers that one minute prayers said by those who mumble in the name of the father, son and Holy Ghost cannot move. Mechanical prayers cannot generate enough heat that will drive out demonic invaders.

Your prayers must generate enough heat. This type of prayer was prayed by Jesus in the garden of Gethsemane. The prayer of Jesus was so intensive that blood mixed with water and emerged as sweat.

THE HEAT GENERATOR

How do you want to make use of the weapon of great heat, when you cannot even sweat at the place of prayer? If you pray and you dose off, how can your prayers gather heat? What we need today is the weapon of great heat. This is the prayer that will make water to boil. **Isaiah 9:5**

> ***"For every battle of the warrior is with confused noise, and garments rolled in blood; but this shall be with burning and fuel of fire."***

Isaiah 64:2

> ***"As when the melting fire burneth, the fire causeth the waters to boil, to make thy name known to thine adversaries, that the nations may tremble at thy presence!"***

Beloved, you must make the enemies to tremble according to the Scriptures.

PRAYER POINTS

1. Father, by the power of the blood of Jesus, I invoke the power of great heat to melt away the coven of darkness, in the name of Jesus.
2. Father, let great heat from heaven melt away every conspiracy working against me, in the name of Jesus.
3. Father, let great heat from heaven remove from their stronghold every plantation of darkness, in the name of Jesus.

4. Great heat from heaven, arise in your power and pursue my pursuers, in the name of Jesus.
5. Great heat from heaven, move into the stronghold established against me and melt the stronghold to pieces, in the name of Jesus.
6. Great heat from heaven chase away every stranger assigned to my body, assigned to my soul, assigned to my spirit, in the name of Jesus.
7. Great heat from heaven, locate and evacuate every plantation of sorrow, in the name of Jesus.

WEAPON

31

OVERFLOWING SCOURGE

► ***IT IS A WEAPON THAT CAN BE USED AGAINST STUBBORN PURSUERS.***
► ***THIS WEAPON WILL DESTABILIZE WICKED DEMONS ON ASSIGNMENT.***
► ***IT WILL PUT AN END TO THE SEASON OF AFFLICTION.***
► ***IT WILL END SATANIC STORMS.***
► ***IT WILL DISGRACE YOUR GOLIATH.***
► ***IT WILL DROWN PHARAOH AND HIS DEMONIC SOLDIERS.***

This is one of the most powerful weapons in God's armoury. There are times when the enemy will not give up unless God uses a weapon that is highly destructive. The battles of life cannot be fought and won by lily-livered believers. It is indeed true that a drastic situation needs a drastic cure. Stubborn enemies can only be dealt with through the use of tough spiritual warfare weapons.

When God wants to visit the abode of powers of the occult and high-class satanic agents, He will dispatch the overflowing scourge. The weapon in question is described below. **Isaiah 28:18**

> "And your covenant with death shall be disannulled, and your agreement with hell shall not stand; when the overflowing scourge shall pass through, then ye shall be trodden down by it."

FORTIFIED AGENTS

We need to take note of the background from which this weapon is introduced. The entities to be dealt with had made covenant with death and hell. This shows that this weapon must be used when we want to deal with fortified demonic agents. Beloved, I do not generally quote secular authors and great men but I am going to quote this particular one.

General Dwight Eisenhower a former president of the United States of America said; "Your enemy is well trained, well equipped and battle hardened. He will fight savagely. Thus the need to beseech the blessing of the Almighty God on this great and noble undertaking, but I also feel that as warriors on whom the survival of democratic institutions rest, you cannot afford to faint. You need to pray hard." If an American Army General could describe an enemy as well equipped and battle hardened, as end time Christians, we cannot afford to be buried by the sand of ignorance.

HARDENED ENEMIES

Hardened enemies need hardened weapons. All unrepentant enemies must be confronted with equal aggression. Hence, one of the weapons that suits hardened enemies is the weapon of overflowing scourge. A scourge can be described as a plague, an epidemic, a terrible affliction. But when the Bible describes it as overflowing scourge we are given a picture of a storm that is capable of washing away communities of wicked enemies. Boasting powers cannot withstand the weapon of overflowing scourge. Hardened demonic warriors need just one single flood or storm of calamity and their covenant with death, wicked charms and occult powers shall be buried by the power of God.

The overflowing scourge cannot visit the domain of dark powers and it will be business as usual. Hardened spiritual criminals can only be dealt with by using the weapon of overflowing scourge. The weapon of overflowing scourge surpasses any form of tsunami or hurricane. Beloved, God has His own overflowing scourge for dealing with deaf and dumb powers.

You need this weapon when you are attacked by mesmerizing powers, satanic dribblers, and unrepentant enemies. Any Pharaoh that will not let you go will receive the judgment of overflowing scourge. This weapon will leave devastating casualties in the habitation of wicked powers.

PRAYER POINTS

1. Overflowing scourge from heaven, be released against every force of Senacherub assigned against me, in the name of Jesus.
2. Let the overflowing scourge from heaven put an end to every organized warfare fashioned against me, in the name of Jesus.
3. Let the overflowing scourge from heaven move and destroy every serpent, in the name of Jesus.
4. Let the overflowing scourge from heaven move and put to shame every force of Pharaoh and Herod, in the name of Jesus.
5. Let the overflowing scourge from heaven move and deliver me from environmental oppressions, in the name of Jesus.
6. Let the overflowing scourge from heaven move and deliver me from the power of oppression, in the name of Jesus.

WEAPON 32

STONE OF OFFENCE

- ***YOU CAN USE THIS WEAPON WHEN YOU WANT TO CRUSH THE ENEMY.***
- ***YOU CAN USE IT WHEN YOU WANT TO BOMB DARK FORCES.***
- ***THIS WEAPON CAN BE USED TO SILENCE BOASTING POWERS.***
- ***STUBBORN PURSUER CAN BE DEMOLISHED WITH THE USE OF THIS WEAPON.***
- ***IT IS THE WEAPON THAT CAN BE USED TO ARREST SPIRITUAL TERRORISTS.***
- ***IT CAN BE USED TO ARREST POWERS THAT ARE SENT TO ARREST YOU.***

God is a man of war. He knows how to deal with the enemy. There are classes of weapons for classes of enemies. There are bad and good news. The bad news is that the enemy is busy doing a lot of havoc in this generation. The good news is that God has specific weapons for nullifying every arrow coming from the camp of dark powers.

Satanic terrorism is on the increase in our days. However, the good news is that there is a counter terrorism squad established by the Almighty to locate and destroy the efforts of spiritual terrorist.

A TRAGIC WEAPON

The weapon we are considering in this section is a unique weapon for deflecting satanic arrows and commanding them to go back to sender. The weapon of the stone of offense is a weapon that the enemy cannot run away from. The Bible calls it the stone of offence. **Isaiah 8:14**

> ***"And he shall be for a sanctuary; but for a stone of stumbling and for a rock of offence to both the houses of Israel, for a gin and for a snare to the inhabitants of Jerusalem."***

It functions as a double edged sword. **Matt. 21:44**

> ***"And whosoever shall fall on this stone shall be broken: but on whomsoever it shall fall, it will grind him to powder"***

A SPIRITUAL TIME BOMB

If the enemy falls on the stone, the enemy will be shattered and broken into pieces. When the stone of offense lands on the enemy it will grind him to powder. In other words, head or tail; the enemy loses. **Luke 20:18**

> ***"Whosoever shall fall upon that stone shall be broken; but on whomsoever it shall fall, it will grind him to powder."***

The weapon called the stone of offense is a spiritual time-bomb; when it lands on the enemy, there is disaster. It is a very mysterious weapon. It is also called a burdensome stone. Wherever this stone lands in the territory of the enemy calamity or disaster will spread. Any enemy who toys with this weapon, toys with disaster. **Zach. 12:3**

> ***"And in that day will I make Jerusalem a burdensome stone for all people: all that burden themselves with it shall be cut in pieces, though all the people of the earth be gathered together against it."***

Toying with this weapon can be described as toying with God's sword. Beloved, any enemy that decides to run his fingers across the sharp sword of the Almighty will have such fingers cut to pieces. When this weapon is in operation, the enemy has two options; the enemy either gets broken or is grinded to powder.

A DEADLY WEAPON

The stone of offense is a very heavy stone. It is a deadly weapon. When the stone of offense lands upon the enemy it will reduce him to dust so that he may be scattered by the winds. When a burdensome stone falls on the enemy the results are fatal. Such an experience will be terminal. It will result in irreparable destruction.

You need this weapon when you are dealing with wicked enemies. This weapon is needed when you are in the throes of a conflict that is sponsored by territorial powers and drawers of power from the heavenlies. You need to make use of this weapon when you want to unseat demonic kings and queens. You need this weapon when you want to deal with ancestral powers. Stubborn pursuers will be sent to their graves when you make use of this weapon. Just one stone of offense and boasting powers will become silent.

PRAYER POINTS

1. Let the stone of offense grind to powder every hand writing of darkness, in the name of Jesus.
2. Let the stone of offense be released to destabilize every wicked plantation, in the name of Jesus.
3. Let the stone of offense be released to bring down the head of my Goliath, in the name of Jesus.
4. Let the stone of offense break every satanic serpent assigned against me, in the name of Jesus.
5. Let the stone of offense move into my situation and capture every unfriendly friend, in the name of Jesus.

WEAPON 33

STORMING DELUSION OF OFFENCE

- ***THIS WEAPON WILL SCATTER THE FORCES OF DARKNESS.***
- ***IT CAN BE USED WHEN YOU WANT TO DRIBBLE AND CONFUSE THE ENEMY.***
- ***YOU CAN ALSO USED IT TO LURE THE ENEMY INTO THE CAGE THAT WAS MEANT FOR YOU.***
- ***THIS WEAPON WILL ENABLE YOU TO HOLD DEMONIC SOLDIERS CAPTIVE.***
- ***YOU CAN USE THIS WEAPON WHEN YOU WANT TO DISGRACE ANTI-BREAKTHROUGH POWERS.***
- ***IT WILL ALSO PUT AN END TO THE ACTIVITIES OF THE POWER OF YOUR FATHER'S HOUSE.***
- ***IT WILL BREAK EVERY YOKE AND CANCEL EVIL COVENANTS AND CURSES.***

There are two branches of military warfare; the weapon and the tactics or strategy. The combination of these two forces gives victory in warfare. While some weapons are outright instruments of fighting battles, a class of weapons bother on war strategy. A good number of battles are best won through the use of appropriate strategy. The methods of warfare must be strategic for some battles to be won.

When God wants to disgrace the enemy, He lays an ambush by using some uncommon tactics. This is the kind of weapon we are considering here. It is a weapon that confuses the enemy. This weapon is used when God wants to showcase His superior power and disgrace the enemy without lifting a finger. Here, there is no loud noise of war, weapons may not be visible and the enemy will not notice any impending onslaught. God comes in with divine subtlety. There is a divine camouflage.

THE DRIBBLING WEAPON

While the enemy expects an attack from the north an invasion is unleashed through an unnoticeable opening in the south. In one moment, there is apparent calm, in the next moment there is a sudden cloud and before the enemy would know anything, confusing noise is raised and in a split second the enemy is demolished. God specializes in making use of confusing noise. **Isaiah 9:5**

> ***"For every battle of the warrior is with confused noise, and garments rolled in blood; but this shall be with burning and fuel of fire."***

CONFUSED NOISE

From this passage we discover that the battle of seasoned warriors is identified with the use of confused noise. Confused noise is a weapon. It is a manifestation of stormy delusion from the Lord. It is a method that God uses in advanced warfare.

God raises a confusing noise against enemies that fortify themselves. God raises confusing noise when evil forces come against God's children. The noise becomes so loud that it orchestrates a stormy delusion. What the Bible terms as a strong delusion is a divine strategy that centres on diverting the enemy's attention. God can decide to send stormy delusion in form of a lying spirit.
1Kings 22:22

> ***"And the LORD said unto him, Wherewith? And he said, I will go forth, and I will be a lying spirit in the mouth of all his prophets. And he said, Thou shalt persuade him, and prevail also: go forth, and do so."***

God can also bring a stormy delusion to the heart of the enemy by deceiving the enemy. **Ezekiel 14:9**

> ***"And if the prophet be deceived when he hath spoken a thing, I the LORD have deceived that prophet, and I will stretch out my hand upon him, and will destroy him from the midst of my people Israel."***

God can also raise this weapon by giving the enemy over to his desire until he ends up with destruction. **Romans 1:24**

> ***"Wherefore God also gave them up to uncleanness through the lusts of their own hearts, to dishonour their own bodies between themselves:"***

SEDUCING SPIRITS

God may decide to seduce the enemy and lure him into a pit by dispatching seducing spirits. **1Timothy 4:1**

> ***"Now the Spirit speaketh expressly, that in the latter times some shall depart from the faith, giving heed to seducing spirits, and doctrines of devils;"***

This is the kind of a weapon that God used when he lured Pharaoh and hardened his heart to pursue the children of Israel until God buried him, his weapon and his entire military force in the red sea. Use this weapon today and stormy delusion will destroy every power assigned to keep you in captivity.

PRAYER POINTS

1. Father, I invoke the weapon of stormy delusion from the Lord against every power monitoring my destiny, in the name of Jesus.
2. Let stormy delusion from the Lord pursue my pursuer, in the name of Jesus.
3. Let stormy delusion from the Lord arrest my arresters, in the name of Jesus.
4. Let stormy delusion from the Lord destroy my Goliath, in the name of Jesus.
5. Let stormy delusion from the Lord scatter my oppressors, in the name of Jesus.
6. Let stormy delusion from the Lord render blind, deaf and dumb every diviner divining against me, in the name of Jesus.
7. Let stormy delusion from the Lord put to shame every operation of darkness, in the name of Jesus.

WEAPON 34

TERROR OF DEATH

- ***THIS WEAPON IS USEFUL WHEN YOU WANT TO DISPATCH ANGELS THAT HAVE NO MERCY INTO THE TERRITORY OF THE ENEMIES.***
- ***THIS WEAPON IS USEFUL FOR HIGH LEVEL SPIRITUAL BATTLES.***
- ***IT CAN BE USED WHEN YOU WANT TO UNLEASH THE SENTENCE OF DEATH UPON WITCHES AND WICKED POWERS.***
- ***YOU CAN USE IT TO FORCE POWERS THAT HAVE SWALLOWED YOUR VIRTUES TO VOMIT THEM.***
- ***IT WILL DEAL DECISIVELY WITH THE SPIRIT OF DEATH AND HELL.***

God uses the terror of death as a weapon of combating the enemy. In the field of warfare there is no mercy. God has two sides, there is the side of compassion and mercy and there is the side of judgment and wrath. It depends on the side that God decides to turn to; either his children or his enemy.
God can either hide his face in wrath, or show kindness in the demonstration of His mercy. **Isaiah 54:8**

> ***"Then shall thy light break forth as the morning, and thine health shall spring forth speedily: and thy righteousness shall go before thee; the glory of the LORD shall be thy rearward.***

Romans 9:15

> ***"For he saith to Moses, I will have mercy on whom I will have mercy, and I will have compassion on whom I will have compassion."***

THE TERROR MACHINE

God can be a terror to the enemy and show favour to His children. God can decide to plant terror in the heart of your enemies. **Psalm 55:4**

> ***"My heart is sore pained within me: and the terrors of death are fallen upon me."***

The terrors of death can fall upon the enemies like a mighty stone. The full force of the terror is described below. **Psalm 116:3**

> ***"The sorrows of death compassed me, and the pains of hell gat hold upon me: I found trouble and sorrow."***

DEADLY TERROR

Terror, fear and anguish can so destabilize the hearts of your enemies, that will lead them to death. This weapon is best described as deadly terror. When this weapon is used, God pushes the enemy to the valley of the shadow of death. Terror can become so tangible that stubborn pursuers will be gripped by it and they will suddenly find themselves in the grave. When we pray that some powers should fall down and die, we are actually using the weapon of terror of death.

One quick way of invoking death on the powers that do not let you rest is to command the terror of death to fall upon them. **Psalm 88:3**

> ***"For my soul is full of troubles: and my life draweth nigh unto the grave."***

You can sentence the enemy to installmental death by using the weapon of the terror of death. **Psalm 18:4**

> ***"The sorrows of death compassed me, and the floods of ungodly men made me afraid."***

THE TARGET

This weapon is suitable for use when you are dealing with:

1. *Fortified powers*
2. *Wicked satanic agents*
3. *The power of the emptiers*
4. *The powers that kill good things at infancy*
5. *Powers that abort dreams*
6. *Attacks from witchdoctors*
7. *Anti-breakthrough powers*
8. *Powers that carry battles from one generation to another*
9. *Bondage expanders*
10. *Powers that bury virtues*
11. *Powers that swallow destinies*
12. *The spirit of death and hell*

You must deal with these powers today.

PRAYER POINTS

1. Thou terror of death, be mobilized into the camp of demonic witchcraft, in the name of Jesus.
2. Thou terror of death, arise, and invade the houses of those who are harassing my life, in the name of Jesus.
3. Thou terror of death, be mobilized to fight all the battles of my life, in the name of Jesus.
4. Thou terror of death, envelope all my enemies and put them into shame, in the name of Jesus.
5. Thou terror of death, disgrace every plantation of the enemy, in the name of Jesus.
6. Thou terror of death, move with great speed into the heavenlies and possess my possessions, in the name of Jesus.
7. Thou terror of death move among the enemies that are saying let us scheme and see what will become of him, in the name of Jesus.

WEAPON 35

HAIL AND FIRE MINGLED WITH THE BLOOD OF THE LAMB

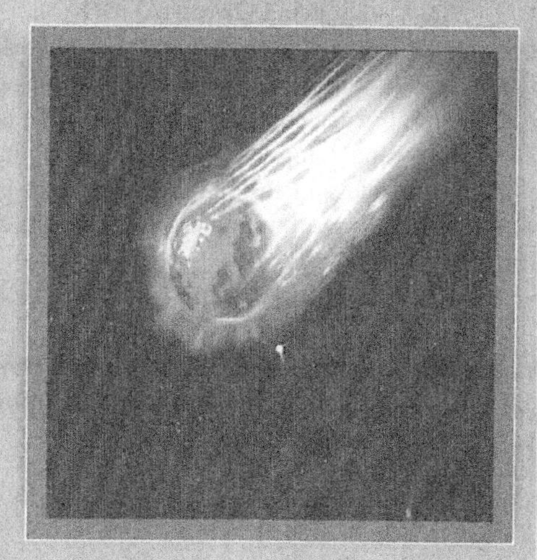

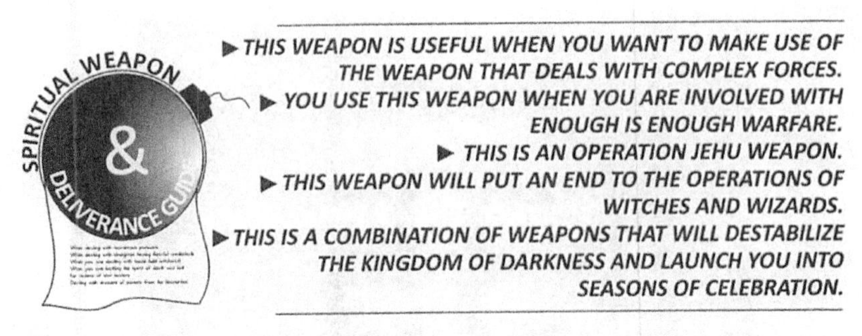

- ***THIS WEAPON IS USEFUL WHEN YOU WANT TO MAKE USE OF THE WEAPON THAT DEALS WITH COMPLEX FORCES.***
- ***YOU USE THIS WEAPON WHEN YOU ARE INVOLVED WITH ENOUGH IS ENOUGH WARFARE.***
- ***THIS IS AN OPERATION JEHU WEAPON.***
- ***THIS WEAPON WILL PUT AN END TO THE OPERATIONS OF WITCHES AND WIZARDS.***
- ***THIS IS A COMBINATION OF WEAPONS THAT WILL DESTABILIZE THE KINGDOM OF DARKNESS AND LAUNCH YOU INTO SEASONS OF CELEBRATION.***

In the physical realm, there are terrible weapons which armies of nations only bring out and make use of once in a while. Such weapons are so deadly that they dare not bring them out at the instance of any little battle.
God has created some terrible weapons that we can safely say *"woe betide that enemy upon whom it is used"*. For example, if a country like the United States of America decides to use their latest atomic bomb on a poor African nation whose population is less than a million, what do you think will happen if such a nation faces jet bombers holding cutlasses and arrows? The superior army will surely level such a nation and make it look like a new construction site or a newly bulldozed ground in readiness for agriculture.

AN AWESOME COMBINATION

The weapon we are considering, here, is perhaps the most deadly weapon available in the spiritual realm. It is a combination of the forces of hailstones, fire, and the blood of the lamb. Each of these weapons, when used singularly, will put the enemy in trouble. What happens when they are combined together? Hail is destructive. Fire is terrible and the blood of the lamb is an awesome weapon. Mix the three weapons together and you have a weapon that will put the nails of finality on the enemy's coffin.
Is such a weapon available? The answer is a resounding 'Yes'. **Rev. 8:7**

> ***"The first angel sounded, and there followed hail and fire mingled with blood, and they were cast upon the earth: and the third part of trees was burnt up, and all green grass was burnt up."***

Let me tell you the truth. Beloved, many deep weapons are hidden from the mind of man. But, they can be found in God's armoury. **Ezekiel 38:22**

> ***"And I will plead against him with pestilence and with blood; and I will rain upon him, and upon his bands, and upon the many people that are with him, an overflowing rain, and great hailstones, fire, and brimstone."***

WEAPONS OF MASS DESTRUCTION

God has weapons of mass destruction. Heaven has weapons that can destroy the enemy in a split second. This kind of multi-purpose weapon will ensure that every department of the kingdom of darkness is reduced to ashes. Fire will consume one part; hailstones will consume another part while the destructive power that resides in the blood of the lamb will consume another part of the gathering of the enemy. This is operation Jehu in action.

Undoubtedly, no power can withstand such destructive divine artillery. You can make use of this weapon when witches and wizards are in charge of your case. You can also make use of this weapon when evil powers have passed your case from one hand to another. You can also make use of this combined weapon when you are confronted by wicked powers from the heavenlies.

FATAL CONSEQUENCE

This weapon will subject your enemies to shameful summersaults. It will change your story and re-write your history. This weapon is needed when you need nothing but victory. It will move you from the valley to the mountain top. It will also grant you spiritual immunity. This is the weapon you need for total deliverance. You need to make use of these prayer points when you want to put an end to repeated failure and defeat on the field of battle.

PRAYER POINTS

1. Let the hail and fire mingled with the blood of the lamb arise and destroy the powers hindering me from possessing my possessions, in the name of Jesus.
2. Let hail and fire mingled with the blood of the lamb pursue my sisera, in the name of Jesus.
3. Let hail and fire mingled with the blood of the lamb move into

every coven assigned against me and scatter them, in the name of Jesus.

4. Let hail and fire mingled with the blood of the lamb move in a new way to give me my possessions, in the name of Jesus.
5. Let hail and fire mingled with the blood of the lamb fall upon every satanic soldier assigned against me, in the name of Jesus.
6. Let the hail and fire mingled with the blood of the lamb fall upon every oppression assigned against me, in the name of Jesus.
7. Let the hail and fire mingled with the blood of the lamb fight all my battles, in the name of Jesus.

WEAPON 36

GREAT EARTHQUAKE

- ***THIS WEAPON CAN BE USED WHEN YOU WANT TO CAUSE AN UPROAR IN THE ENEMY'S KINGDOM.***
- ***YOU CAN USE THE WEAPON WHEN YOU WANT TO DEAL WITH STUBBORN ENEMIES.***
- ***IT IS A WEAPON THAT WILL GRANT YOU UNCHALLENGEABLE VICTORY.***
- ***THIS WEAPON WILL SILENCE EVERY ENEMY OF YOUR PROGRESS.***
- ***WITH THIS WEAPON IN YOUR HANDS, YOUR DESTINY WILL BE FULFILLED.***

God can raise great earthquakes and use them as a weapon to deal with the kingdom of darkness. Some enemies deserve devastating blows. Such blows can be received in form of a great earthquake. An earthquake creates a landmark. It is a violent eruption that shakes everywhere. When God wants to silence the enemy completely he commands an earthquake to destabilize them.
Matt 27:51

> ***"And, behold, the veil of the temple was rent in twain from the top to the bottom; and the earth did quake, and the rocks rent;"***

A POWERFUL SIGNAL

The earthquake being referred to here is not a common earthquake. God uses great earthquakes to deal, in an unforgettable manner with the enemy. One event that shook heaven and earth was the crucifixion of Jesus. To show the world that something great was taking place there was a great earthquake. When God wants to send powerful signals to the camp of your enemy, He would use the weapon of the great earthquake. It is my prayer for you that God will silence your enemies through a great earthquake.

God is ever ready to bring out and use the weapon of great earthquake. He has promised. **Isaiah 13:13**

> ***"Therefore I will shake the heavens, and the earth shall remove out of her place, in the wrath of the LORD of hosts, and in the day of his fierce anger."***

Joel 3:16

> ***"The LORD also shall roar out of Zion, and utter his voice from Jerusalem; and the heavens and the earth shall shake: but the LORD***

will be the hope of his people, and the strength of the children of Israel."

Haggai 2:6

"For thus saith the LORD of hosts; Yet once, it is a little while, and I will shake the heavens, and the earth, and the sea, and the dry land;"

Haggai 2:21

"Speak to Zerubbabel, governor of Judah, saying, I will shake the heavens and the earth;"

THIS IS WAR

With these powerful prophetic promises God is set for war. The Almighty is battle ready. He is ready to cause a great earthquake that will shake both the heavens and the earth. Invoke these weapons today and terrible catastrophes will hit the camp of the enemy.

PRAYER POINTS

1. Father, release great earthquakes of deliverance and set me free from bondage, in the name of Jesus.
2. Father, let great earthquakes be released and let every bondage be shaken into pieces, in the name of Jesus.
3. Father let great earthquakes be released, let the power of God move me from strength to strength and from glory to glory, in the name of Jesus.
4. Let the great earthquake of the Lord be released and let whatever belongs to me being held in any satanic warehouse be released, in the name of Jesus.
5. Let the great earthquake of the Lord begin to shake every environment and let me possess my possession, in the name of Jesus.
6. Let the great earthquake of the Lord move into every situation concerning me and give me uncommon blessings, in the name of Jesus.
7. Let the great earthquake of the Lord tear to pieces any form of internal or external bondage, in the name of Jesus.

WEAPON 37

SEA QUAKE

- ***THIS WEAPON WILL PULL DOWN SATANIC STRONG HOLDS.***
- ***IT IS A POWERFUL WEAPON FOR DEALING WITH MARINE POWERS.***
- ***MEN AND WOMEN FROM RIVERINE AREAS WILL EXPERIENCE TOTAL VICTORY.***
- ***IT IS A POWERFUL WEAPON OF DELIVERANCE.***
- ***THIS WEAPON WILL FORCE AGENTS OF DARKNESS TO VOMIT WHAT THEY SWALLOWED.***
- ***THIS WEAPON WILL BRING OUT YOUR VIRTUES THAT ARE BURIED IN THE SEA.***

The Bible says in **2Cor 10:4**

> ***"For the weapons of our warfare are not carnal, but mighty through God to the pulling down of strong holds;"***

Satanic strongholds can only be pulled down through mighty weapons. God has surveyed the entire gamut of areas of bondage and spiritual warfare and he has given us weapons with which we can combat dark forces. The Bible makes it very clear that the weapons that God has given to us are tough weapons. We shall consider one of such weapons in this section.
Let the devil take the battle to any realm, there are mighty weapons for such realms. All manners of battles can be won through the use of mighty weapons. The weapon of the seaquake can locate hidden enemies even when they draw their powers from the marine world.

MARINE SPIRITS

Stubborn areas of bondage can be traced to the activities of marine spirits. For some people, what has kept them under bondage can be found under bodies of water in several parts of the world. The weapon of the sea quake can make water turbulent and heat up any river until marine warders have no options than to let their prisoners go free. God can move rivers or cause violent sea quakes in order to grant you total deliverance or give you victory over marine battles. **Jer.46:8**

> ***"Egypt riseth up like a flood, and his waters are moved like the rivers; and he saith, I will go up, and will cover the earth; I will destroy the city and the inhabitants thereof."***

MARINE BOMBS

Just like we have the earthquake there is also what can be called the sea quake. When God uses the sea quake as a weapon there will be no hiding place for demons that hide in the rivers. You can make use of this weapon if you happen to come from riverine areas. This weapon will also prove invaluable when you make use of it to deal with any bondage that is rooted in the river. It is tailor-made for anyone who has suffered marital turbulence because evil powers have locked the padlock and thrown the key of their marriage into the river. Again, men and women who are named after rivers or their names have anything to do with water will need to make use of this weapon in order to obtain your deliverance and experience unchallengeable victory.

When there is a sea quake marine oppression will cease, destinies that are buried in the sea will be recovered. The virtues that have gone down into the deep shall be fetched out. You can use the weapon of divine sea quake to overcome marine powers, today.

PRAYER POINTS

1. Father, let the seaquake be released to secure my portion captured by marine powers, in the name of Jesus.
2. Let there be a seaquake in the belly of the sea to shake down the citadel of darkness, in the name of Jesus.
3. Let the seaquake of the Lord shake out any good thing that belongs to me buried in the waters, in the name of Jesus.
4. Let there be a release of the seaquake that will trouble all powers from the waters troubling my destiny, in the name of Jesus.
5. Thou seaquake, arise in your anger and shake out every enchantment assigned against me inside the waters, in the name of Jesus.
6. Thou seaquake, move with your fire and with your power and disgrace every Pharaoh in the waters, in the name of Jesus.
7. Thou seaquake, move with lightning speed to destabilize every conspiracy from the waters, in the name of Jesus.

WEAPON

38

AIR QUAKE

- *THIS WEAPON WILL ENABLE YOU TO SUMMON ANGELIC ASSISTANCE.*
- *IT WILL GIVE YOU VICTORY OVER TERRITORIAL POWERS.*
- *YOU WILL EXPERIENCE VICTORY OVER WICKED SPIRITS IN HIGH PLACES.*
- *YOU WILL SCORE VICTORY OVER ANCESTRAL POWERS.*
- *THIS WEAPON WILL MAKE EVIL ARROWS TO GO BACK TO THE SENDER.*
- *THIS WEAPON WILL MAKE YOU TOO HOT FOR THE ENEMY TO HANDLE.*

An air quake is superior to an earthquake. It is a violent eruption that emanates from heaven and lands on the earth. One instance of an air quake happened at the instance of the resurrection of the Lord Jesus Christ. **Mat. 28:2**

> ***"And, behold, there was a great earthquake: for the angel of the Lord descended from heaven, and came and rolled back the stone from the door, and sat upon it."***

God wanted to showcase His military might. So He dispatched an air quake from heaven.

A TOUGH WEAPON

An air quake is God's weapon of enabling us to fight from heaven. **Judges 5:20**

> ***"They fought from heaven; the stars in their courses fought against Sisera."***

When you fight from heaven you are fighting from the platform of victory. An air quake makes power to change hands from the hands of your enemy to the hand of the Holy Spirit. This weapon takes you to a realm where you are empowered to fight with ease with the anointing of ease upon you.

AN IRRESISTIBLE WEAPON

The weapon of divine air quake disorganises the enemy and gives you an upper hand. When an air quake falls from heaven and drops upon the camp of the enemy, satanic agents will flee and hide themselves after the order of Daniel's vision. **Daniel 10:7**

> ***"And I Daniel alone saw the vision: for the men that were with me saw not the vision; but a great quaking fell upon them, so that they fled to hide themselves."***

If you want to destabilize, the enemies of your destiny, you must command air quakes to fall upon them.

THE ONSLAUGHT

The weapon of the air quake is irresistible. It emanates from the raw power of the Almighty. To deal with stubborn enemies you need this weapon. It is a weapon you can use to deflect evil arrows and consequently send them back to the power behind those arrows. The weapon of divine air quake will always hit the target with mathematical precision. No power can withstand this uncommon weapon.

PARALYSING EVIL POWERS

When the full force of the air quake shakes the heavenlies, the first thing that would happen is that drawers of power from the heavenlies shall be destabilized, wicked Spirits in high places shall be arrested and their counterparts on earth shall receive stones of fire. The weapon will enable you to paralyse and overcome the powers of the air. This weapon will also enable you to deal with territorial powers. This is a weapon that will completely blind evil spies and clip the feathers of evil birds.

No power can escape an air quake. Once a divine air quake creates holy confusion in the air, demonic powers will remain powerless. You need to know how to make use of prayer points that cause airquakes. This will place you on a new pedestal of advanced spiritual warfare.

PRAYER POINTS

1. Let the air quake be released to trouble every power working against me from the heavenlies, in the name of Jesus.
2. Let the air quake of the Lord shake down every spiritual wickedness in high places, in the name of Jesus.

3. Let the air quake of the Lord release the wind of fire upon the camp of the oppressors in the sky, in the name of Jesus.
4. Let the air quake of the Lord tear away every evil handwriting fastened to the heavenlies against me by the power of the Holy Spirit to recover any good things that belong to me that they have stolen, in the name of Jesus.
5. Let the air quake of the Lord, cry against of every Ahitophel and Absalom spirit targeted against me, in the name of Jesus.
6. Let the air quake of the Lord go to the North, South, East and the West and recover my stolen possessions, in the name of Jesus.

WEAPON 39

THE BLOOD OF JESUS

► *THIS IS A POWERFUL WEAPON OF SPIRITUAL IMMUNITY.*
► *IT IS ALSO A WEAPON THAT WILL GRANT YOU TOTAL DELIVERANCE.*
► *IT IS A POWERFUL SANITIZING WEAPON.*
► *YOU USE THIS WEAPON WHEN YOU ARE FACING TOUGH BATTLES.*
► *YOU USE THIS WEAPON WHEN YOU WANT TO ESTABLISH YOUR VICTORY.*
► *IT IS THE WEAPON YOU CAN USE TO COMBAT EVIL FORCES.*
► *YOU CAN USE THIS WEAPON WHEN YOU WANT TO BARRICADE YOUR LIFE.*

The blood of Jesus is a weapon that will forever confuse the enemy. Years of spiritual warfare has kept satanic agents in the valley of defeat as a result of the instrumentality of the blood of Jesus. The blood of Jesus is a destructive weapon. It destroys the habitations of darkness. The blood of Jesus is a speaking weapon. It speaks against the kingdom of darkness. The blood of Jesus is our weapon of victory. The blood of Jesus is a powerful deliverance weapon. The blood of Jesus is a weapon that cancels curses and erases evil covenants.

When you apply the blood of Jesus to the foundation of your live the Holy Spirit will carry out and consolidate the work of repair and restoration. The blood of Jesus is one weapon that can wipe off the hand writing of darkness against your destiny. It is one weapon that will cancel the agenda of darkness.

The blood of Jesus has zero tolerance for ugly spiritual attacks. The blood of Jesus sanitizes and disinfects. The blood of Jesus is one weapon that counters spiritual terrorism. It is loaded with power to capture wicked arrows and render them null and void.

SPIRITUAL IMMUNITY

The blood of Jesus is a weapon that gives you spiritual immunity, the blood of Jesus is backed up by the totality of the power of God, the blood of Jesus has immense spiritual charge to power your deliverance and sustain victory. The blood of Jesus is a weapon that will reduce all the weapons of the enemy to useless toys. When deliverance reaches a critical stage the blood of Jesus is the answer. When battle assumes a complex dimension the blood of Jesus is the solution. When you are dealing with multiple enemies, the blood of Jesus will give you an edge over them. When you fight face to face with ancient powers,

the blood of Jesus is your winning formula.
There is no power the blood of Jesus cannot arrest. There is no spiritual case the blood of Jesus cannot settle. The blood of Jesus places you on the platform of victory.

POWERFUL RESOURCES

It enables you to draw upon the powerful resources that reside in the greatest force in the universe.
The blood of Jesus converts your battles to the Lord's battles. You cannot understand the awesome power that resides in the blood of Jesus until you decide to make use of it as your weapon of deliverance. **Rev 12:11**

> ***"And they overcame him by the blood of the Lamb, and by the word of their testimony; and they loved not their lives unto the death."***

Romans 16:20

> ***"And the God of peace shall bruise Satan under your feet shortly. The grace of our Lord Jesus Christ be with you. Amen"***

PRAYER POINTS

1. I stand on the ground of the blood of Jesus to proclaim victory over sin, in the name of Jesus.
2. I apply the blood of Jesus to every stubborn problem in my life, in the name of Jesus.
3. I plead the blood of Jesus upon my body from the top of my head to the sole of my feet, in the name of Jesus.
4. I soak my life in the blood of Jesus.
5. I paralyse all satanic oppressors delegated against me with the blood of Jesus.
6. I hold the blood of Jesus as a shield against any power that is already poised to resist me, in the name of Jesus.
7. Let the power of the blood of Jesus be released on my behalf and let it speak against every dead bone in my life, in the name of Jesus.

WEAPON 40

WEST WIND OF DELIVERANCE

- ***THIS IS PRIMARILY A DELIVERANCE WEAPON.***
- ***YOU USE THIS WEAPON WHEN YOU WANT GOD TO ARISE AND FIGHT YOUR BATTLES.***
- ***THIS WEAPON CAN BE USED WHEN YOU WANT TO BRING YOURSELF OUT OF ANY FORM OF EVIL UMBRELLA.***
- ***THIS WEAPON WILL MAGNETISE DIVINE BLESSINGS INTO YOUR LIFE.***
- ***IT IS A WEAPON YOU CAN USE WHEN YOU WANT TO CELEBRATE THE DEFEAT OF OPPOSING POWERS.***
- ***IT WILL ENABLE YOU TO PUT AN END TO SATANIC SLAVERY.***
- ***THIS WEAPON WILL LEAD YOU TO YOUR SEASON OF DIVINE RESTORATION.***

This is a powerful deliverance weapon. It is a weapon that will deliver the gains of deliverance when other weapons fail when it matters most. When you command the west wind of deliverance to blow upon your life, your deliverance will be activated in the spiritual realm.

The west wind is a conveyor of divine blessings, freedom, refreshment, renewal and revival. The spiritual connotation of the west wind is a force that brings blessings, just as the east wind brings rain and refreshing. It is crystal clear that bondage makes life uncomfortable. But, when the west wind of deliverance blows, bondage is broken. The sign of the west wind is highlighted below.

Luke 12:54

> ***"And he said also to the people, When ye see a cloud rise out of the west, straightway ye say, There cometh a shower; and so it is."***

SHOWERS OF DELIVERANCE

The west wind and the cloud bring the good news of imminent showers of blessing. When you receive showers of blessing it shows that you are out of the cage of bondage.

The west wind of deliverance is a very strong weapon of spiritual warfare. It is a weapon that shows the strength of the Almighty. **Ex 10:19**

> ***"And the LORD turned a mighty strong west wind, which took away the locusts, and cast them into the Red sea; there remained not one locust in all the coasts of Egypt."***

DIVINE JUDGEMENT

Just as a mighty strong west wind cast an army of locusts into the Red sea and there was no longer any locust in the coast of Egypt, God will also wipe away all the enemies of your deliverance and bury them in a sea of judgement.

The west wind of deliverance is a weapon you can use to terminate the reign of wickedness.

When the west wind of deliverance blows, your bondage will go. The west wind of deliverance will give total deliverance. The wind of deliverance will blow away every residue of bondage from your life. The west wind of deliverance will separate you from the powers of your father's house. When you make use of prayer points that activate the west wind of deliverance, you will take the battle to a level where demons are scattered and the weapons of the enemy are destroyed.

The weapon of the west wind of deliverance will empower you to vomit fire into the territory of the enemy. The west wind of deliverance will make you an overcomer, and set you free from the shackles of spiritual slavery. Beloved, this is your moment of unchallengeable victory and complete deliverance.

PRAYER POINTS

1. Thou West wind of deliverance, arise from your abode and scatter the camp of my enemies, in the name of Jesus.
2. West wind of deliverance, blow and cause confusion in the camp of my oppressors, in the name of Jesus.
3. West wind of deliverance, cause deliverance to happen in every situation concerning me, in the name of Jesus.
4. West wind of deliverance, attack every plantation of darkness assigned against me, in the name of Jesus.
5. Oh West wind of deliverance, go to the North, South, East and shake down every wickedness positioned against me, in the name of Jesus.
6. Thou West wind of deliverance, move in the amazing name of Jesus and cause great deliverance to happen in my body, soul and spirit, in the name of Jesus.
7. West wind of deliverance, move and contend with those that contend with me, in Jesus name.

WEAPON 41

BATTERING RAM

- ***IT IS A WEAPON YOU CAN USE AGAINST THE POWER BEHIND WITCHCRAFT.***
- ***YOU CAN USE THIS WEAPON WHEN YOU WANT TO PULL DOWN JERICHO WALLS.***
- ***YOU USE THIS WEAPON WHEN YOU ARE FACING STRANGE BATTLES.***
- ***YOU USE THIS WEAPON WHEN YOUR SITUATION REQUIRES SPIRITUAL MACHINE GUNS.***
- ***IT IS A WEAPON YOU CAN USE WHEN YOU WANT TO EXPERIENCE UNCOMMON VICTORY.***

Battering rams constitute an integral part of violent weapons of spiritual warfare. In Bible days what was called Battering rams was a military engine. It was a long beam with a head of brass like the head and horns of a ram. Hence, it was named battering rams. The instrument was pushed back and forth by hefty men. Then, suddenly they will let it hit the wall with great force to batter it and bring it down. This beloved, is a very terrible weapon. The purpose of the weapon of the battering rams is to bring down the kingdom of darkness with military force. The weapon is described below. **Ezek. 4:2**

> ***"And lay siege against it, and build a fort against it, and cast a mount against it; set the camp also against it, and set battering rams against it round about."***

A BULLDOZING WEAPON

The battering rams are a bulldozing weapon. It is a weapon that empowers you to carry the battle to the gates of the enemy. When this weapon collides with the walls of the kingdom of darkness the tottering walls will collapse like a pack of cards. **Ezek. 21:22**

> ***"At his right hand was the divination for Jerusalem, to appoint captains, to open the mouth in the slaughter, to lift up the voice with shouting, to appoint battering rams against the gates, to cast a mount, and to build a fort."***

The moment you demolish the gates of darkness your offensive strategy will give you unchallengeable victory.

AN OFFENSIVE WEAPON

The weapon of battering rams can be used to bore holes in the walls of witchcraft covens. It will pull down demonic Jericho walls and make you more than a conqueror. When you set battering rams round about the territory of the enemy you are on the offensive rather than on the defensive.

Beloved, battening rams are strange weapons. Some prayer points can be termed battering rams prayers points. We often teach believers how to convert prayer points to spiritual machine gun weapons. This weapon will grant you quick deliverance and swift victory.

A FORCEFUL WEAPON

It is a forceful weapon. The strength of battering rams cannot be resisted by the enemy. The moment their Jericho walls fall down flat their evil deeds will be exposed and they shall be arrested by the fire of the Holy Ghost. When you are instructed to take some prayer points seven or twenty one times you are being taught how to utilize the weapon of battering rams.

Some powers cannot yield when you issue a single command. Most stubborn powers will require repeated bombardments and aggressive persistence. Use this weapon today and you will experience wonderful results.

PRAYER POINTS

1. Father, use Your battering ram to dispossess every strongman and every power holding tight to the instruments of my breakthroughs, in the name of Jesus.
2. Father, use Your battering ram to shake down the power of the strongman that has stolen from me, in the name of Jesus.
3. By the battering ram of the Holy Spirit, let every stronghold of the oppressor be dashed to pieces, in the name of Jesus.
4. By the battering ram of the Lord, let every evil structure constructed against me be demolished, in the name of Jesus.
5. By the battering ram of the Lord, I pull down the devices of the enemy, in the name of Jesus.
6. By the battering ram of the Lord, I move to my place of destiny
7. By the battering ram of the Lord, I disgrace every opposition, in the name of Jesus.
8. By the battering ram of the Lord, I possess all my possessions, in

the name of Jesus.

9. By the battering ram of the Lord, I enter into my place of rest and remove every power blocking my way, in the name of Jesus.
10. By the battering ram of the Lord, I enter into my place of celebration, in the name of Jesus.

WEAPON

42

BLAST OF HIS NOSTRILS

- ***THE WEAPON WILL DEMOLISH THE WEAPON OF DARKNESS.***
- ***IT WILL QUASH SATANIC REBELLION.***
- ***IT IS A POWERFUL DELIVERANCE WEAPON.***
- ***YOU NEED THIS WEAPON WHEN YOU ARE AT THE VERGE OF GIVING UP.***
- ***IT WILL CONSUME HOUSEHOLD WITCHCRAFT.***
- ***IT IS A POWERFUL WEAPON FOR DEFEATING ENEMIES OF YOUR DESTINY.***

The breath of God has been described as a blast in the scripture. The blast of God's nostril is a serious weapon. **Psalm 18:15**

> ***"Then the channels of waters were seen, and the foundations of the world were discovered at thy rebuke, O LORD, at the blast of the breath of thy nostrils."***

POWER TO DEMOLISH

The breath of God comes out as a blast to demolish the enemy. No power can withstand the blast of the Almighty. When the Almighty breathes, devouring fire will fall into the camp of the enemy. The blast of God's breath can become a flood that will drown the enemy. It can also dry up the evil waters that the enemy has brought into the boat of your life. **Exodus 15:8**

> ***"And with the blast of thy nostrils the waters were gathered together, the floods stood upright as an heap, and the depths were congealed in the heart of the sea."***

God can send a blast upon the enemy to destroy him. **Isaiah 37: 7**

> ***"Behold, I will send a blast upon him, and he shall hear a rumour, and return to his own land; and I will cause him to fall by the sword in his own land."***

CONSUMING WEAPONS

Stubborn pursuers will be consumed by the blast of God, you can command God's judgment to come out through the weapon to the blast of God's nostril and locate the head of all the powers that have come together to fight against you.

Use this weapon when you are confronted by multiple enemies. The blast of God's nostril is the weapon you need when terrible demons are coming so close to you to the point of bringing fear into your heart. You need this weapon when you want your battle to become God's battles. The blast of God will blow away every evil wind limiting your destiny. This is an important weapon for end time battles.

PRAYER POINTS

1. Father, by the blast of Your nostril, shake away every stubborn aggressor, in the name of Jesus.
2. By the blast of Your nostril, O God, shake away every plan of the oppressor, in the name of Jesus.
3. Let the heat from the blast of God's nostril melt away every coven agenda and its dwelling place, in the name of Jesus.
4. Let the glory of the living God arise with the blast of God's nostril to torment every tormentor, in the name of Jesus.
5. O God, arise by the weapon of the blast of Your nostril and let me possess my possessions, in the name of Jesus.

WEAPON 43

GREAT FURNACE

► ***THIS WEAPON IS HANDY WHEN YOU WANT TO HARASS THE POWERS THAT HARASS YOU.***
► ***THIS IS A WEAPON THAT WILL ENABLE YOU ACHIEVE UNCOMMON VICTORY.***
► ***IT IS A WEAPON YOU CAN USE WHEN THE ENEMY IS CHALLENGING YOUR GOD.***
► ***WHEN DELIVERANCE BECOMES HARD TO OBTAIN, MAKE USE OF THIS WEAPON.***
► ***YOU CAN USE THIS WEAPON WHEN YOU WANT GOD TO PROVE HIMSELF IN YOUR LIFE.***
► ***IT IS A WEAPON FOR OPPRESSING YOUR OPPRESSORS.***

God has a great array of weapons that have things to do with fire. An easy explanation for this is that fire will be the final weapon of dealing with Satan and all enemies of God. Fire is a great weapon of judgment; a strong weapon for defeating the enemy. It is a weapon for silencing evil voices. It is used to disgrace satanic soldiers. It is the divine weapon for chasing hidden enemies out of their place of hiding. It is a weapon for show-casing the supremacy of the power of God over the power of the enemy.
Weapons that are rooted in fire constitute the most formidable weapons made available for us in the realm of spiritual warfare. When a particular weapon is cased in the envelope of fire, such a weapon has superlative powers for granting us speedy, final and decisive victory.

THE PREPARED FURNACE

The weapon we are looking at in this section is the weapon of great furnace. There is a department in heaven where God prepares a great furnace in readiness for use in dealing with his enemies. No matter the military power of a particular army, if the opposing army can make use of a great furnace to destabilize the enemy, the army that uses furnace will obtain quick and cheap victory.
I learnt one of the greatest lessons of my life when I was very young. A bully of a boy kept harassing me on daily basis. My stature was so small in those days. The boy kept cheating and obtaining from me whatever I went to school with. He would come and say; give me what you brought to school today and I would hand over everything with timidity

BLIND THE ENEMY

He kept on taking advantage of me until one day I decided to tackle him boldly but intelligently. The bully challenged me as usual. But, on that particular day I told him that he shouldn't mess up with me. As he tried to beat me up I located his two eyes and dipped my fingers filled with hot balm into his eyes. That was how I overpowered him. Before he could scamper for safety he found himself on the floor with his eyes filled with forced tears. Since my weapon was superior that was the last time he ever challenged me.

The correlation here is that if you make use of a weapon that blinds the enemy your victory will be unchallengeable or uncontestable. Beloved, heaven has a great furnace. This weapon has been reserved for seasons of great battles. The power and the devastating effects of a great furnace cannot be quantified. Beloved, God does not need to create this weapon. He has already created it, waiting for us to make use of it. The Bible describes the immense power of a great furnace below. **Rev. 9:2**

> ***"And he opened the bottomless pit; and there arose a smoke out of the pit, as the smoke of a great furnace; and the sun and the air were darkened by reason of the smoke of the pit."***

If the smoke of a great furnace has blinding power, can you imagine the effect of its raw fire? This is the weapon to use when the enemy is challenging your God and evil powers are boasting saying "who is that God." This is a weapon to use when you are tired of being tossed to and fro by powers that keep people under bondage. This weapon will surely put an end to your bondage.

PRAYER POINTS

1. Every power that wants me to die, die in my place in the great furnace, in the name of Jesus.
2. Father utilize the power of Your great furnace and burn to ashes every plantation of the enemy, in the name of Jesus.
3. Father, utilize the weapon of Your great furnace to swallow every power that has swallowed my destiny, in the name of Jesus.

4. Father, utilize the power of Your great furnace to burn to ashes every serpent and scorpion assigned against me, in the name of Jesus.
5. Father, let the power of the great furnace be released to burn to ashes every plantation of darkness, in the name of Jesus.

WEAPON 44

HOT THUNDERBOLT

▶IT IS A WEAPON FOR AGGRESSIVE WARFARE.
▶ IT IS A WEAPON YOU CAN USE TO ATTACK WITCHCRAFT COVENS.
▶THIS WEAPON WILL SET CAPTIVES OF THE TERRIBLE FREE.
▶ WITH THIS WEAPON YOU CAN PURSUE YOUR PURSUER.
▶ FOR THOSE WHO ARE STRUGGLING WITH THE FEAR OF UNTIMELY DEATH.
▶ A WEAPON THAT PUTS AN END TO EVIL OCCURRENCES AND TRAGEDIES.

Beloved, God is mighty in battle. **Psalm 24:8**

> ***"Who is this King of glory? The LORD strong and mighty, the LORD mighty in battle."***

Our Father is the king of Glory who displays the totality of His energy when it comes to the destruction of the enemy. He is the Almighty who is strong and mighty in battle. When God fights he disgraces the enemy.
When the Almighty goes into battle He does the uncommon by leading captivity captive. With the weapon of the Almighty, the enemy is caught in the trap set by him.

A DIVINE TWIST

Hence, when we talk about tough spiritual warfare weapons, we refer to weapons that are indeed terrible. God sets captives of the terrible free and subjects the terrible to ignominious captivity.
The weapon of hot thunderbolt is no doubt a fearful weapon that will hit the enemy and he will be left with no option than to let you go. This is the type of weapon that was used in the days of Pharaoh. There was hot thunderbolt and Pharaoh was forced to release the people of God. **Exod. 9:28**

> ***"Intreat the LORD (for it is enough) that there be no more mighty thunderings and hail; and I will let you go, and ye shall stay no longer."***

THE THREAT

This weapon is a weapon that threatens. It is a weapon that paralyzes captains of the kingdom of darkness. It is a weapon that roasts satanic emissaries alive. It is

a weapon that declares that the time is up. It is a weapon for the declaration of victory. It is a weapon of sudden death.
This weapon will go to your place of birth and strike the powers that are holding you captive, dead. The weapon of hot thunderbolt is what is needed to enforce your victory and validate your deliverance. When this weapon is in use, elemental powers will bow. Evil spirits will be struck down, strong ancestral bondage will break and persistent attacks will stop, while evil arrows will go back to sender. When you are conscious of the fact that hot thunderbolts are in God's armory, you will make use of them and the powers that have resisted prayers will be forced to flee.

THE ANSWER

If the enemy has been harassing you day and night, hot thunderbolt from heaven is the answer. If wicked forces have placed evil marks on you, you must counter them with hot thunderbolt. When hot thunderbolt from above hits the enemy, it will land with liquid fire upon the head of the enemy. Hot thunderbolt is not a small weapon at all, it is a weapon of total defeat. No enemy can withstand hot thunderbolt when it is launched as a terrific missile.
You can command hot thunderbolt from heaven to land on the spot where demons are gathered. Immediately this happens, hot fire from divine thunderbolt will force the enemy to withdraw in shame. What you need in order to obtain your final release and deliverance is hot thunderbolt that will descend from heaven and leave terrible casualties in the enemy's camp.

PRAYER POINTS

1. Hot thunderbolt from the Lord, move in an uncommon anger and make me to possess my possessions, in the name of Jesus.
2. My Father, order the hot thunderbolt from Your throne to pass through the camp of my enemy, in the name of Jesus.
3. My Father, arise by Your hot thunderbolt and pursue my pursuers, in the name of Jesus.
4. I decree, the hot thunderbolt of the Lord, to move against every evil conspiracy targeted against my destiny, in the name of Jesus.

WEAPON 45

DIVINE FANNERS

SPIRITUAL WEAPON & DELIVERANCE GUIDE

▶ POWER MUST CHANGE HANDS PRAYERS. BACK TO SENDER WEAPONS.
▶ IT IS A WEAPON THAT WOULD DEMOLISH THE STRONGHOLD OF DARKNESS.
▶ YOU CAN USE THIS WEAPON TO CANCEL SATANIC EMBARGOES.
▶ TO OBTAIN VICTORY OVER LOCAL SATANIC TECHNOLOGY.
▶ IT IS A POWERFUL WEAPON FOR OBTAINING VICTORY OVER THE STRONG ENEMY.

The army of heaven has some dangerous departments. The activities of some of these departments are frightening. You cannot understand some of the divine weapons until God opens your eyes and you begin to see the havoc that the enemy is doing among men. We live in the end times. There are terrible dangers in this era. Some powers have swallowed whole members of families in one day. Some demonic agents have occasioned the death of hundreds of innocent people in one day. In some families, witchcraft powers have placed embargoes on everyone. In some communities people are being eaten alive by wicked powers.

CRUEL DOMAINS

There are graveyards of darkness in several places. Promising destinies have been swallowed. Virtues have been thrown into the dustbin. The spirits of death and hell have swallowed entire occupants of busses or vehicles. It is, indeed, true that many places are habitations of cruelty. **Psalm 74:20**

> ***"Have respect unto the covenant: for the dark places of the earth are full of the habitations of cruelty."***

If God gives you insight to the height of cruelty that is being perpetrated globally you will understand why God has created terrible weapons to combat the forces of darkness.

BACK TO SENDER

Beloved, until we begin to make use of strange weapons, strange battles may never be won. We cannot overcome wicked powers without going to the armory

of the Almighty and bring out deadly weapons that will send evil arrows to their sender with speed and terrible aggression.
When you are faced with tough battles all you need is invoke divine fanners and dispatch them into the camp of the enemy. The weapon of divine fanners is needed when you are faced with an unending cycle of wicked attacks. You need this weapon when you are fighting tough battles. **Jeremiah 51:2**

> ***"And will send unto Babylon fanners, that shall fan her, and shall empty her land: for in the day of trouble they shall be against her round about."***

You need this strong weapon when you are dealing with strong enemies. You need this weapon when you want eaters of flesh and drinkers of blood to eat their own flesh and drink their own blood. You need this strange weapon when you are dealing with ancestral powers. You need this weapon when you are confronting fortified Babylonian-warriors.

YOUR SEASON OF VICTORY

You need this weapon when you want to disgrace your Goliath. You need this weapon when you are fighting enough is enough battles. You need this weapon when you want to put an end to satanic harassment. You need this weapon when it is time to face Pharaoh and declare let my people go.
You need this weapon when you want power to change hands. You need this weapon when you want the horse and it's rider to be buried in the sea. This weapon will make you to be more than conquerors. It will also frustrate the token of liars and make diviners mad.
This is a weapon that will turn the kingdom of darkness upside down.

PRAYER POINTS

1. Let divine fanners fan away every negative power hanging around me, in the name of Jesus.
2. Let the fanners of God fan away every dark power hiding in my environment, in the name of Jesus.
3. Let the fanners of the Lord begin to blow away every hand of the oppressor and the enemy, in the name of Jesus.

4. Let the fanners of the Lord begin to destroy every stronghold of wickedness, in the name of Jesus.
5. Let the fanners of the Lord begin to put to shame every agenda of darkness, in the name of Jesus.

WEAPON

46

RUMOUR

▶ *IT IS A STRATEGIC WEAPON FOR STRATEGIC WARFARE.*
▶ *THIS WEAPON CAN BE USED TO CAPTURE STUBBORN SATANIC WEAPONS.*
▶ *USE THIS WEAPON WHEN YOU WANT TO OBTAIN VICTORY OVER FAMILIAR SPIRITS AND HOUSEHOLD WITCHCRAFT.*
▶ *THIS WEAPON WILL CAPTURE AND DISGRACE BOASTING ENEMIES.*
▶ *IT IS A WEAPON FOR PUTTING AN END TO LONG TERM PROBLEMS.*
▶ *IT IS A WEAPON FOR CAPTURING SATANIC SPIES.*

The Almighty is a strategist. No man can predict the angle from which He will fight the enemy. Sometimes, God can decide to use a weapon that appears insignificant. But, when He is through with the use of the weapon, great personalities in the demonic kingdom will appear like ants and their weapons will become toys.

With the array of weapons that God has created as weapons of victory and deliverance, no child of God has anything to do with defeat or bondage. The greatest problem in this modern generation can be traced to acute ignorance. Many have failed to enrol in the school of spiritual warfare.

The truth many have failed to understand is that there is no power on earth that God cannot tame. There is no demonic agenda God cannot destroy. There is no fetish power or spiritual household entity that God cannot command to somersault and die. The greatest witch doctor in the world needs just one little but unique weapon in Gods armory to knock him into unconsciousness.

AN UNUSUAL WEAPON

The weapon we are going to examine in this section is one of God's strategic weapons of warfare. Beloved, God is the best and greatest military tactician. The weapon of divine rumour works in a very strange manner. **Isaiah 37:7**

> ***"Behold, I will send a blast upon him, and he shall hear a rumour, and return to his own land; and I will cause him to fall by the sword in his own land."***

God can lure the enemy into destruction. He can also ordain terrifying noises to deceive the enemy. God can decide to capture the entire company of your pursuers by using a little rumour. This weapon is very suitable for dealing with household wickedness.

A DIVINE RUMOUR

It is also a weapon that can be used to deal with powers that have been threatening and harassing you. It is also one weapon you can use with the enemy that is monitoring your destiny. Witches, wizards and familiar spirits that are monitoring your life will swallow disaster through this weapon. God can lure His enemies to their death through a rumour and it is my prayer that a divine rumour will be spread that will magnetize your enemies to their destruction.
Isaiah 37:37-38

> ***"So Sennacherib king of Assyria departed, and went and returned, and dwelt at Nineveh. And it came to pass, as he was worshipping in the house of Nisroch his god, that Adrammelech and Sharezer his sons smote him with the sword; and they escaped into the land of Armenia: and Esarhaddon his son reigned in his stead."***

If your enemies are waiting for you in a particular spot, God will cause them to hear a rumour that will make them to abandon the spot, a few minutes before you get there.

DIVINE MISCHIEF

This is a weapon for dealing with household witchcraft, unfriendly friends, evil monitoring spirits and other satanic agents that have vowed that your destiny would never be fulfilled. God can multiply this weapon in several folds until the enemy is destroyed. **Ezekiel 7:26**

> ***"Mischief shall come upon mischief, and rumour shall be upon rumour; then shall they seek a vision of the prophet; but the law shall perish from the priest, and counsel from the ancients."***

Just as it was predicted in the Bible, a rumour destroyed a king. A rumour shall also destroy every power assigned to destroy your destiny. **2Kings 19:7**

> ***"Behold, I will send a blast upon him, and he shall hear a rumour, and shall return to his own land; and I will cause him to fall by the sword in***

his own land.

Isaiah 37:37-38

> ***"So Sennacherib king of Assyria departed, and went and returned, and dwelt at Nineveh. And it came to pass, as he was worshipping in the house of Nisroch his god, that Adrammelech and Sharezer his sons smote him with the sword; and they escaped into the land of Armenia: and Esarhaddon his son reigned in his stead."***

The weapon of divine rumour is such a complex weapon that the enemy cannot fathom its depth. Use this weapon today and you shall destroy your destroyers.

PRAYER POINTS

1. Let my enemy hear rumours and let them make mistakes, in the name of Jesus.
2. Let my enemies that are gathered in the coven hear a rumour that will make them run perpetually without stopping, in the name of Jesus.
3. O rumour of God, arise by Your power, evacuate every negative power from my life, in the name of Jesus.
4. Let the rumour of the Lord move round the North, South, East and West and cause the enemies to make mistakes that will advance my cause, in the name of Jesus.
5. Let the rumour of the Lord be stretched out to make every satanic conspiracy against me scatter, in the name of Jesus.

WEAPON 47

SERPENT OF THE LORD

► ***IT IS A WEAPON FOR CONFRONTING THE HOST OF DARKNESS.***
► ***USE THIS WEAPON WHEN YOU NEED TO EXPERIENCE REMARKABLE VICTORY OVER THE DEVIL.***
► ***IT WILL SWALLOW THE WEAPONS OF DARK AGENTS.***
► ***THIS WEAPON WILL DISGRACE AND SWALLOW THE SERPENT OF THE MAGICIANS.***
► ***USE IT WHEN YOU SENSE ANY FROM OF SATANIC INVASION.***

Serpents constitute an important part of God's weapon. **Job 26:13**

"By his spirit he hath garnished the heavens; his hand hath formed the crooked serpent."

Please note the following facts:

1. Serpents are endowed with biting power. **Prov. 23:32**

"At the last it biteth like a serpent, and stingeth like an adder."

2. Serpents have poison or venom. Psalm 58:4

"Their poison is like the poison of a serpent: they are like the deaf adder that stoppeth her ear;"

3. There are flying serpents. **Isaiah 14:29**

"Rejoice not thou, whole Palestina, because the rod of him that smote thee is broken: for out of the serpent's root shall come forth a cockatrice, and his fruit shall be a fiery flying serpent."

Isaiah 30:6

"The burden of the beasts of the south: into the land of trouble and anguish, from whence come the young and old lion, the viper and fiery flying serpent, they will carry their riches upon the shoulders of young asses, and their treasures upon the bunches of camels, to a people that shall not profit them."

4. There is what is known as the piercing serpent.
5. God can command serpents to bite and devour your enemies.

Amos 9:3

"And though they hide themselves in the top of Carmel, I will search and take them out thence; and though they be hid from my sight in the bottom of the sea, thence will I command the serpent, and he shall bite them:"

6. Serpents inflict injury.

Luke 10:19

"Behold, I give unto you power to tread on serpents and scorpions, and over all the power of the enemy: and nothing shall by any means hurt you."

THE LORD'S ARMY

God deals with stubborn enemies without mercy. The serpent of the Lord can be dispatched into the camp of the wicked when they are trying to execute their wicked agenda. Flying witches who go on a mission of destruction can be attacked and cast down in their flight, when flying serpents of the Lord locate them in the air.

Beloved, enough is enough. Children of God have stayed long enough on the victim's side. If you happen to be a deliverance minister who has listened to terrible stories that bother on oppression, suppression, the attack of night caterers, the wicked attacks of eaters of flesh and drinkers of blood, the activities of star hunters, the evil acts of tragedy activators and all kinds of powers that have subjected humanity to cruel bondage, you will agree with me that we need to discover and make use of hidden spiritual warfare weapons.

A DEVASTATING WEAPON

The serpent of the Lord is a devastating weapon. God has created weapons that can inflict one blow upon the enemy and every noise made by dark powers would be turned to pin drop silence. Evil powers can only continue their wicked operations when we allow them to have their ways or when we are making use of inferior weapons.

My heart yearns for a time when enemies will flee when they discover that the weapon we are making use of are both terrible and frightening. It is unfortunate that the devil has invested wicked weapons long ago when many believers were snoring and sleeping. When the devil came out with terrible weapons many were busy singing and dancing in churches where little or nothing is known about the fire of God. For a very long time strange spiritual warfare weapons have not been discovered not to talk of being used.

TERRIBLE AGGRESSION

Beloved, these are the end times. There is no time in Christian history when the rage of warfare has been hotter than now. In this era of tough warfare the only weapon that will save the day is the weapon of terrible aggression.

You need strange weapons that will make the enemy to surrender. You need weapons that will feed the enemy with their own flesh and cause them to drink their own blood. This is the only type of weapon that will make your deliverance fast, decisive and complete.

PRAYER POINTS

1. Let the serpent of the Lord arise swallow every serpent of darkness, in the name of Jesus.
2. Thou serpent of the Lord, go into the belly of the waters and destroy every serpent working against me, in the name of Jesus.
3. Thou serpent of the Lord arise and strike to death every plantation of darkness, in the name of Jesus.
4. Thou serpent of the Lord arise and fish out every cleverly concealed enemy, in the name of Jesus.
5. Thou serpent of the Lord arise and let the name of the Lord alone be glorified in my life, in the name of Jesus.
6. Thou serpent of the Lord arise and destroy every plantation contrary to my life, in the name of Jesus.
7. Thou serpent of the Lord, move into impossible situations and make them possible, in the name of Jesus.
8. Thou serpent of the Lord, bite every serpent hiding anywhere against me, in the name of Jesus.

WEAPON 48

STUMBLING BLOCK

▸ THIS WEAPON WILL MAKE YOU TOO HOT TO HANDLE.
▸ IT WILL GIVE YOU POWER TO TROUBLE YOUR TROUBLE.
▸ THIS WEAPON MUST BE USED WHEN YOU WANT TO ANNOUNCE THE OBITUARY OF THE POWERS OF YOUR FATHER'S HOUSE.
▸ IT IS NEEDED WHEN YOU WANT TO KEEP THE ENEMY AWAY FROM YOUR FAMILY AND IMPORTANT PROJECTS.
▸ IT IS A WEAPON YOU CAN USE WHEN YOU WANT TO EXPERIENCE ACCELERATED PROMOTION.

With the array of weapons that God has manufactured and kept ready for our use, no child of God has any business with defeat and bondage. Instances of defeat and bondage cannot be attributed to God. He has already given unto us all things that pertain to our victory and total wellbeing. No power can defeat God. No enemy can challenge him. No demonic entity can dribble the Almighty.
The truth is that God has not created any power he cannot tame. The Almighty has a solution to every problem, ready victory for every battle, deliverance for every bondage and suitable weapons to counter any form of satanic invasion. The weapon we are considering in this section is the weapon of divine stumbling block.

AN UNCOMMON WEAPON

Enemies prevail when God's children lack knowledge. Enemies prevail when believers are naïve. Enemies overcome when Christians are lazy. Enemies record victory when children of God live in the dark as far as weapons of outstanding victory are concerned. You can score cheap victory against the enemy when you make use of this uncommon weapon.
Here, you may not confront the enemy with arms and ammunition. You simply lay stumbling blocks on the pathway of the enemy. We can learn a few lessons from physical warfare. When some battles are fought,. a particular army may decide to use land mines. These are buried in the ground. They are programmed to explode at will, and at that moment, multiple explosions are triggered off and an advancing opposing army will be left with no option than to either surrender or flee.

A LANDMINE

The spiritual stumbling block is comparable to a land mine. **Isaiah 8:14**

> ***"And he shall be for a sanctuary; but for a stone of stumbling and for a rock of offence to both the houses of Israel, for a gin and for a snare to the inhabitants of Jerusalem."***

I want you to picture an enemy that charges at you, poised for battle. Such an enemy will keep running just to frighten you. But, when the Almighty places an unseen stumbling block, the enemy will stumble. To defeat the enemy you can command the stumbling block of the Almighty to be scattered upon the enemy. Each stone will earn the enemy resounding defeat. **1Peter 2:8**

> ***"And a stone of stumbling, and a rock of offence, even to them which stumble at the word, being disobedient: whereunto also they were appointed."***

A GREAT STONE

There is a mystery in the above verse. Beloved, the size of the enemy will determine the size of the stumbling block to be used. By the spirit of prophesy the Apostle Peter describes two types of stumbling blocks. One is a stone while the other is a rock. The stone causes the enemy to stumble while the rock puts the enemy to trouble. Of course, you know that any enemy that goes into a head-on collision with the rock of ages will have that head shattered into pieces that cannot be gathered together.

PRAYER POINTS

1. Father, put stumbling blocks on the way of my oppressors, in the name of Jesus.
2. Father, put a stumbling block to barricade the enemies from gaining access to the garden of my life, in the name of Jesus.
3. Father, put a stumbling block in the way of those that despise my Zion, to be put to shame, in the name of Jesus.
4. Thou weapon of stumbling block arise, fight my enemies and let them make mistakes that will advance my cause, in the name of Jesus.
5. Thou power of stumbling block, hinder my oppressors from moving into my territory, in the name of Jesus.

WEAPON 49

ANGEL OF DEATH

- ***THIS WEAPON WILL ARREST THE SPIRIT OF DEATH AND HELL.***
- ***YOU NEED THIS WEAPON IN ORDER TO ACTIVATE THE LAW OF DIVINE SUBSTITUTION.***
- ***IT WILL GIVE YOU VICTORY OVER THE ARROW OF UNTIMELY DEATH.***
- ***IT IS A POWERFUL WEAPON OF DELIVERANCE.***
- ***IT IS AN OFFENSIVE WEAPON THAT WILL TURN THE TIDE AND MAKE YOU A THREAT TO THE KINGDOM OF DARKNESS.***

It is crystal clear that there are diverse weapons in the armory of the Ancient of Days. Beloved, some of these weapons are fearful and intimidating. There are seasons when God reveals His veracious power. God has the capacity to deal with the enemy mercilessly, decisively, and in a tragic manner. The Bible declares that the Lord killeth, in other words; God is a killer. Deut. 32:39

> ***"See now that I, even I, am he, and there is no god with me: I kill, and I make alive; I wound, and I heal: neither is there any that can deliver out of my hand."***

THE POWER OF LIFE AND DEATH

The power of life and death resides in the hands of the Almighty. No matter what we think about the mercy of God there are seasons when God issues death sentence against the enemy. On such occasions, God will simply dispatch angels of death to the camp of agents of darkness. God can command angels of death to invade the camp of your enemies after the order of his unforgettable dealings with Pharaoh. Heb. 11:28
Through faith he kept the Passover, and the sprinkling of blood, lest he that destroyed the firstborn should touch them.

GOD'S MESSENGERS

God can also command angels of death to invade the camp of your enemies after the order of the onslaught of the Assyrians. **2 king 19:35**

> ***"And it came to pass that night, that the angel of the LORD went out, and smote in the camp of the Assyrians an hundred fourscore and five thousand: and when they arose early in the morning, behold, they***

were all dead corpses."

The angel of death is God's messenger or weapon for terminating powers that have vowed to terminate your life. This weapon will enable you to enforce the sentence of death that God has issued against witchcraft.

THE MYSTERY OF SUBSTITUTION

This weapon will turn the table against your enemies and make them die in your place. This particular weapon cannot be understood or used by amateur students in the field of spiritual warfare. It can also be used by those who are ready to move in the spirit and power of Elijah. It is a weapon that God has reserved for those who merit the severity of His judgment. You can command this weapon to locate the powers of your fathers' house and the powers that swallow good virtues.

PRAYER POINTS

1. Thou angel that visited the Egyptians to let the children of Israel go, visit my enemies, in the name of Jesus.
2. Thou agent of death that destroyed Senacherib, arise and destroy my multiple enemies, in the name of Jesus.
3. Thou angel of God that fought Joshua's battles, arise and fight my battles, in the name of Jesus.
4. Thou angel of death that arose to fight Sisera, let the same angel arise and fight for me, in the name of Jesus.
5. Oh angel of death, hear the word of the Lord and stop those who want to stop me and destroy those who want to destroy me, in the name of Jesus.

WEAPON 50

THE WHIRLWIND

► *YOU NEED THIS WEAPON WHEN YOU NEED COMPLETE DELIVERANCE.*
► *IT IS A WEAPON THAT BULLDOZES EVIL STRUCTURES MOUNTED BY THE ENEMY.*
► *IT WILL DEMOLISH THE POWERS OF THE EMPTIERS.*
► *IT IS A WEAPON FOR EFFECTING THE BURIAL OF HOUSEHOLD WITCHCRAFT.*
► *IT WILL CUT EVIL ROPES TYING YOU TO THE SAME SPOT.*
► *IT GIVES VICTORY OVER WICKED SATANIC AGENTS.*

One of the toughest weapons that God has established for winning the battles of life, obtaining deliverance by fire, and overcoming the enemy is the weapon of the whirl wind. This is a weapon that is quite strange. This weapon is actually used when the enemy deserves it. It is the best weapon to use against the powers that court the anger and displeasure of the Almighty. **Hosea 8:7**

> ***"For they have sown the wind, and they shall reap the whirlwind: it hath no stalk: the bud shall yield no meal: if so be it yield, the strangers shall swallow it up."***

A SPIRITUAL LAW

This weapon is used in accordance to the law of sowing and reaping. Those who have sown into the wind shall reap the whirl wind. Satanic agents who fuel the anger of God shall reap severe judgment. Beloved, evil powers actually get what they deserve. When this weapon is used against them they will end up with the fruit of what they have sown.

The weapon of the whirl wind is a symbol of the anger of the Almighty. When a whirl wind is in motion, it announces the fierce wrath of the Ancient of Days. A whirl wind is a tempest or a strong wind that destroys whatever is on its way. Some people wonder why we pray hard prayers against agents of darkness. Our answer is that nobody can be more righteous than God. It is the decree of heaven that those who sow into the wind shall reap the whirl wild.

NO PITY

When the weapon of whirl wind begins to devour the enemy there is no need for pity, since it is what the enemy has sown that has metamorphosised into the whirl wind. It is better not to provoke the Almighty as no force can stop the motion of the whirl wind. Another word for the whirl wind is the destroying storm. The Bible declares that God has a mighty and strong weapon otherwise known as the whirl wind. Job 40:6

> ***"Then answered the LORD unto Job out of the whirlwind, and said,***

Is 40:24

> ***"Yea, they shall not be planted; yea, they shall not be sown: yea, their stock shall not take root in the earth: and he shall also blow upon them, and they shall wither, and the whirlwind shall take them away as stubble."***

Is 41:16

> ***"Thou shalt fan them, and the wind shall carry them away, and the whirlwind shall scatter them: and thou shalt rejoice in the LORD, and shalt glory in the Holy One of Israel"***

er 30:23

> ***"Behold, the whirlwind of the LORD goeth forth with fury, a continuing whirlwind: it shall fall with pain upon the head of the wicked.'***

Is 66:15

> ***"For, behold, the LORD will come with fire, and with his chariots like a whirlwind, to render his anger with fury, and his rebuke with flames of fire."***

Jer 23:19

> ***"Behold, a whirlwind of the LORD is gone forth in fury, even a grievous whirlwind: it shall fall grievously upon the head of the wicked.***

WHEN TO USE THE WEAPON

This is a weapon that you can use against.

1. Enemies that will not let you rest
2. Powers that have vowed that you will not eat the fruit of your labour
3. Anti-breakthrough powers
4. The power of the emptiers
5. Ancestral spirits

6. Powers that keep people under prolonged bondage
7. Eaters of flesh and drinkers of blood
8. Household witchcraft
9. The powers behind shame and ridicule
10. Powers that promote re-current diseases and untimely death
11. Forest powers
12. The powers of your father house

When you have tried elementary weapons and nothing has happened, command the whirl wind of the Almighty to blow away every power constituting stumbling blocks on the pathway of your destiny.

PRAYER POINTS

1. I invoke the weapon of the whirlwind to scatter every camp of darkness, in the name of Jesus.
2. I invoke the weapon of the whirlwind to arise and cause confusion in the camp of my enemies, in the name of Jesus.
3. O whirlwind of the Lord, arise in your power and mightiness and fight for me, in the name of Jesus.
4. Oh whirlwind of the Lord, go into the North, go into the South, go into the East, go into the West and cause my portion to be released, in the name of Jesus.
5. Thou whirlwind of the Lord, blow away every bad luck, jinx, spell and every enchantment, in the name of Jesus.
6. Thou whirlwind of the Lord, put your fear into the hearts of people and make me untouchable, in the name of Jesus.

WEAPON 51

POISON

► ***THE IS A SUITABLE WEAPON FOR WICKED ENEMIES.***
► ***IT IS A BACK TO SENDER WEAPON.***
► ***IT IS A UNIQUE WEAPON FOR TOUGH BATTLES.***
► ***IT IS YOUR WEAPON OF TOTAL DELIVERANCE.***
► ***IT IS A WEAPON FOR KILLING THE AGENDA OF DARKNESS.***
► ***IT WILL WREST YOUR DESTINY OUT OF THE HANDS OF STAR HUNTERS.***

The enemy cannot afford to toy with weapons of spiritual warfare. When the battle becomes hot, God introduces strange and uncommon weapons. As far as God is concerned, he that must die must die. God can apply the law of divine substitution when it comes to dealing with the enemy. The entire army of Pharaoh can be buried in the sea in order to let the children of Israel go.

THE POISONOUS WEAPON

God can wipe away the army of the dark kingdom if that is the only thing that will grant you freedom or liberty. The weapon we are considering in this section is not common at all. When God uses uncommon weapons His intention is to deal with a group of enemies that can only be stopped by such weird weapons. The Bible highlights the weapon of poison below. **Deut. 32:24**

> ***"They shall be burnt with hunger, and devoured with burning heat, and with bitter destruction: I will also send the teeth of beasts upon them, with the poison of serpents of the dust.***

One of the arrows of the Almighty that has been soaked in a strange poison is the weapon that we are going to need in this end times. Some enemies need the poison of the serpent and other warfare weapons that function like poison.

POISONOUS ARROWS

Beloved, agents of the devil will not think twice before they poison their victims. You must poison them before they poison you. There are some prayer points that function as poison in the body of the enemy. It should not be strange to us when God kills those who are bent on killing stars that God wants to raise up.
You need to pray that God should send poisonous arrows into every witchcraft

coven where your issues have been tabled and your destiny is targeted for destruction. The weapon of poison has been created to enable us inject poison into agents of darkness set to poison us.
Beloved, you are allowed to poison the enemy and put him out of circulation. This weapon has been specifically earmarked for the end time battle.

PRAYER POINTS

1. Father, release heavenly poison against eaters of flesh and drinkers of blood who have vowed to attack me, in the name of Jesus.
2. Father, release Your poison against those who are against my breakthroughs, in the name of Jesus.
3. Father, release Your poison from heaven to kill all serpents of darkness hiding to attack me, in the name of Jesus.
4. Father, release Your poison to kill every spiritual pest around me, in the name of Jesus.
5. Father, release Your poison to put to shame, every power swallowing my blessing, in the name of Jesus.
6. Let the poison of the Lord swallow every satanic poison, in Jesus name.

WEAPON 52

FIRE OF THE HOLY GHOST

► ***THIS WEAPON WILL TACKLE MOST PROBLEMS.***
► ***IT IS A POWERFUL DELIVERANCE WEAPON.***
► ***YOU CAN USE THIS WEAPON TO ATTACK ALL MANNER OF FOUNDATION PROBLEMS.***
► ***YOU CAN USE THIS WEAPON WHEN YOU ARE IN THE MIDST OF INTENSIVE WARFARE.***
► ***WHEN YOU USE THIS WEAPON, HIDDEN ENEMIES WILL BE FRIGHTENED OUT OF THEIR CLOSED OR HIDDEN PLACES.***
► ***IT WILL PUT AN END TO ANCESTRAL BATTLES.***

Fire is a strange weapon. It's consuming power is awesome. When Fire confronts the kingdom of darkness, there will be relics of ashes. Fire is a fearful weapon. Of all spiritual warfare weapons, the fire of the Holy Ghost is one of the toughest. No power can come against the fire of the Holy Ghost and not get roasted or burnt to ashes. Fire does not tolerate any nonsense. Fire can kill instantly. It can roast alive. It can demolish the entire territory of the enemy.

The power that resides in fire is huge and indescribable. Of all weapons, the most fearful one is the fire of the Holy Ghost. When fire begins to burn snakes and serpents will be frightened out of their hiding places. When you challenge the foundation of your life with Holy Ghost Fire you will experience strange manifestations. The activities of the enemy will be put on hold when you use the weapon of the fire of Holy Ghost.

AN UNCOMMON COMBINATION

The combination of the force of Holy Ghost and fire has remained the weapon that will quickly pluck you out of the valley of oppression. ***Matt 3:11-12***

> ***"I indeed baptize you with water unto repentance: but he that cometh after me is mightier than I, whose shoes I am not worthy to bear: he shall baptize you with the Holy Ghost, and with fire: Whose fan is in his hand, and he will throughly purge his floor, and gather his wheat into the garner; but he will burn up the chaff with unquenchable fire "***

Malachi 3:2

> ***"But who may abide the day of his coming? and who shall stand when he appeareth? for he is like a refiner's fire, and like fullers' soap:"***

Mark 1:8

"I indeed have baptized you with water: but he shall baptize you with the Holy Ghost."

Acts 2:3

"And there appeared unto them cloven tongues like as of fire, and it sat upon each of them."

AWESOME POWER

This generation is yet to witness the awesome power of the weapon of the fire of the Holy Ghost. Holy Ghost fire is a bondage breaker. The fire of the Holy Ghost can go into the territory of the enemy and bring out your confiscated blessings. The fire of the Holy Ghost is able to disgrace your stubborn oppressors. When the fire of the Holy Ghost is used to confront dark powers, you will enjoy swift victory.

The fire of the Holy Ghost will not allow the enemy to invade the territory of your life. The fire of the Holy Ghost will always keep you on the side of victory. To deal with hardened enemies, the fire of the Holy Ghost is to the right weapon to use.

THE BONDAGE BREAKER

Ancient powers will bow when they come face to face with the fire of the Holy Ghost. The fire of the Holy Ghost will put and end to the evil cry of your family idol. The fire of the Holy Ghost will knock out every evil label attached to your forehead.

The fire of the Holy Ghost is one cure for all satanic bondage, evil attacks, and dark manifestations. When the fire of the Holy Ghost falls, your bondage will break and you will escape the fowler's snare. When you invoke the fire of the Holy Ghost in your prayer, there will be Holy pandemonium and your victory will be pronounced in heaven and on earth.

PRAYER POINTS

1. O fire of the Holy Ghost, arise and burn to ashes every plantation of the wicked, in the name of Jesus.
2. Thou fire of the Holy Ghost, arise and put every enemy of my destiny to shame, in the name of Jesus.
3. Thou power of the Holy Ghost arise put to shame every agent of

darkness, in the name of Jesus.

4. Thou power of the Holy Ghost arise and let every prophet of Baal be disgraced, in the name of Jesus.
5. Thou power of the Holy Ghost arise and let every power chasing my blessings away be put to shame, in the name of Jesus.

WEAPON

53

THRESHING INSTRUMENT

► *USE THIS WEAPON WHEN YOU ARE CONFRONTED BY COMPLEX SATANIC ATTACKS.*

► *THIS WEAPON WILL MAKE STUBBORN PURSUERS TO TURN BACK.*

► *THIS IS THE WEAPON TO USE WHEN YOU ARE FACING SEVERE HINDRANCES.*

► *USE THIS WEAPON WHEN YOU WANT YOUR STORY TO CHANGE IN A DRASTIC MANNER.*

► *IT IS A SUITABLE WEAPON FOR COMBATTING ANTI MARRIAGE FORCES.*

► *IT WILL BULLDOZE SATANIC STUMBLING BLOCKS.*

There are lots of strange weapons that God has given us to enable us overcome dark powers with ease. The type of weapon you make use of in warfare goes a long way to determine the level of victory as well as the time it will take you to obtain victory. As far as God is concerned, victory is not hard as long as you use the right weapon.

God has settled your victory and your deliverance. You only need to obtain your freedom by complying with the divine instruction. People make mistakes when they put a square peg in a round hole. But, when you use the right instrument you will experience the mystery of sweat victory.

THE KEY

No matter, how hard or deep the bondage of the enemy is there is a key that opens the door of deliverance. With the right key, the door will be thrown open and you will be free. The Bible has declared in ***Isaiah 49:25***

> ***"But thus saith the LORD, Even the captives of the mighty shall be taken away, and the prey of the terrible shall be delivered: for I will contend with him that contendeth with thee, and I will save thy children."***

From the foregoing, it is clear that even for those who are victims of layers of bondage the right weapon will change the situation. There is freedom for captives of the mighty. Beloved there is liberty for the prey of the terrible. When you invoke the right weapon against stubborn enemies your victory will be awesome.

A DEVASTATING WEAPON

The weapon of threshing instruments is a devastating weapon. It can break through fortified gates of iron, leap over high walls and locate stubborn pursuers

and deal squarely with them.
Threshing instruments are sharp. They have teeth for devouring. They can thresh mountains and reduce them to powder. ***Isaiah 41:15***

> ***"Behold, I will make thee a new sharp threshing instrument having teeth: thou shalt thresh the mountains, and beat them small, and shalt make the hills as chaff."***

POWER TO CONQUER

In other words, with this weapon you will be able to destroy all your enemies even if they tower high like a lofty mountain. Beloved, when God gives you a new sharp threshing instrument, no power will be able to hinder you. The weapon that has teeth for threshing is a weapon that will enable you to deal with the strong enemy. You can confront your Goliath and destroy your Pharaoh through the use of new sharp threshing instruments.
When God places this instrument into your hands, you will move from the valley to the mountain top and your status will change from that of a victim to a victor. This is a fearful weapon to invoke upon enemies that are bent on destroying your destiny.

PRAYER POINTS

1. Father, employ Your threshing instruments to grind to powder every serpent and scorpion assigned against me, in the name of Jesus.
2. I call upon the weapon of the threshing instruments to go into the habitations of my oppressors and force them to release my possessions, in the name of Jesus.
3. I command the threshing instruments of the Almighty God to arise and destabilize every power of darkness, in the name of Jesus.
4. Let the weapon of the threshing instruments release my breakthroughs, in the name of Jesus.
5. Let the weapon of the threshing instruments recover my breakthroughs, in the name of Jesus.
6. Let the threshing instruments of the Holy Spirit arise in an amazing way and do great wonders in my situation, in the name of Jesus.
7. Let the weapon of the threshing instruments of the Lord, do great and mighty wonders by fighting my enemies for me, in the name of Jesus.
8. Oh Lord, arise with Your threshing instrument and fight for me in the morning, in the noon, and in the night, in the name of Jesus.

WEAPON

54

THE BATTLE AXE OF GOD

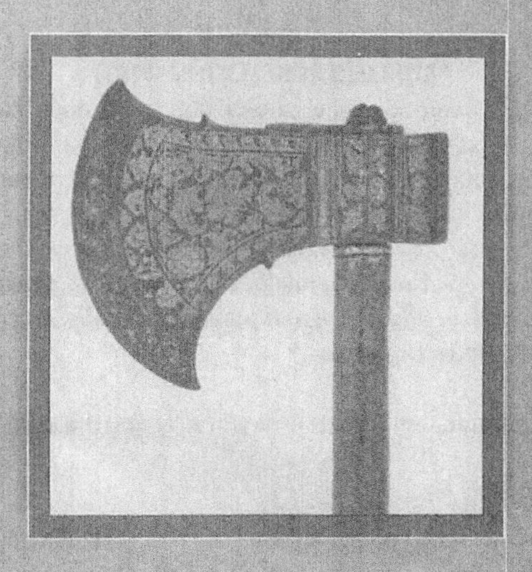

- ***THIS WEAPON WILL ENABLE YOU TO ARREST SATANIC IMMIGRATION OFFICERS AT THE EDGE OF YOUR BREAKTHROUGHS.***
- ***THIS WEAPON WILL OVERCOME SATANIC BOASTING POWERS.***
- ***IT IS A POWERFUL WEAPON FOR FIGHTING THE BATTLES OF LIFE.***
- ***THIS IS YOUR WEAPON OF BOMBARDMENT WHEN SATANIC LOFTY MOUNTAINS ARE THREATENING YOUR PROGRESS.***
- ***USE THIS WEAPON WHEN YOU WANT TO COME OUT OF THE CAGE OF DARKNESS.***
- ***IT IS ONE OF THE MOST POWERFUL END-TIME WEAPONS.***

The battle axe is a weapon of warfare and deliverance. When the axe of God falls on the root of your bondage you will experience instantaneous deliverance. God has designed the battle axe for cutting off demonic trees that have been used to keep you under bondage. The battle axe is a fierce weapon. When you make use of the battle axe, enemies flee, evil powers bow. No wonder the Bible says in ***Jer 51:20***

> ***"Thou art my battle axe and weapons of war: for with thee will I break in pieces the nations, and with thee will I destroy kingdoms;***
> ***God wants to use the battle axe to destroy the kingdom of darkness, scatter evil associations and break in pieces the weapons of the enemy. "***

TACKLING REBELLIOUS SPIRIT

The battle axe has been specially carved out for serious battles. God has designed the battle axe for scattering rebellious spirits and hacking demonic agents who are bent on destroying your destiny. To deal with eaters of flesh and drinkers of blood, you need God's battle axe.

When enemies threaten you, you must go for the battle axe. The axe of God is a weapon of Judgment reserved for rebellious satanic agents. ***Ezekiel 26:9***

> ***"And he shall set engines of war against thy walls, and with his axes he shall break down thy towers."***

To break down the stronghold of darkness you will need the axe of God.

DIVINE ENGINES

The axe of God will enable you to break down demonic towers. It is part of divine engines of war. There is no satanic gathering that the axe of God cannot scatter. Even fortified cages will be broken by the axe of God. Jesus declared that the axe has been laid at the root of every evil tree.

Luke 3:9

> ***"And now also the axe is laid unto the root of the trees: every tree therefore which bringeth not forth good fruit is hewn down, and cast into the fire."***

In the end time battle, we will be required to make use of the battle axe. When evil powers appear resistant, command the battle axe of God to cut them to pieces and destroy them.

Use this weapon today and you will overcome the host of darkness. As long as the battle axe of God is in place, no power will be able to contend with your deliverance.

THE ENEMIES

The battle axe of the Lord can be used in the following instances:

1. When you want to cut down stubborn evil trees
2. When you want to address evil foundations
3. When you want to demolish the proud towers of the enemy
4. When you want to silence boasting powers
5. When you want to put an end to satanic oppression
6. When you want to fight the battles of life
7. When you want to destabilize the kingdom of darkness
8. When you want to enforce the decree of God

The battle axe of God will enable you to celebrate the defeat of the enemy.

PRAYER POINTS

1. Battle axe of God, uproot every evil tree planted against my destiny, in the name of Jesus.
2. O battle axe of God, arise and cut down every evil tree planted in the

garden of my destiny, in the name of Jesus.

3. O battle axe of God, arise and cut down every tree of stagnation in my life, in the name of Jesus.
4. O battle axe of God cut down every tree of frustration in my life, in the name of Jesus.
5. O battle axe of God cut down the tree of hopelessness in my life, in the name of Jesus.
6. I receive the battle axe of God to fight and war a good warfare, in the name of Jesus.
7. Let the power of the battle axe of God put to shame every enemy of my life, in the name of Jesus.
8. Thou battle axe of God, move in an amazing way and do great and mighty things in my life, in the name of Jesus.
9. Let the battle axe of God, arise and scatter to the North, South, East and West, every agenda of darkness against my life, in the name of Jesus.
10. Let the battle axe of God remove every bad thing planted by the enemy in my life, in the name of Jesus.
11. Thou battle axe of God, begin to fight my battles now, in the name of Jesus.

WEAPON

55

CUP OF FURY AND TREMBLING

▶ ***IT IS A WEAPON OF DIVINE VENGEANCE.***

▶ ***USE IT WHEN YOU WANT TO MAKE THE ENEMY TREMBLE.***

▶ ***THIS WEAPON WILL MAKE EATERS OF FLESH AND DRINKERS OF BLOOD TO EAT THEIR OWN FLESH AND DRINK THEIR OWN BLOOD.***

▶ ***YOU NEED THIS WEAPON WHEN YOU WANT TO COMMAND EVIL ARROWS BACK TO THE SENDER.***

▶ ***IT IS THE RIGHT WEAPON TO USE WHEN YOU WANT THE ENEMY TO SUBMIT.***

▶ ***IT IS A POWERFUL WEAPON TO USE WHEN YOU ARE FACED WITH WITCHCRAFT ATTACKS.***

There are weapons that are reserved for stubborn enemies. These weapons must be used without mercy. The weapons in question have been created to demonstrate the deep wrath of the Almighty. The weapons are released and used when God has brought out His full wrath. It is used when the cups of iniquity and wickedness of agents of darkness have reached a capacity that is full and overflowing.

The tragedy of this weapon, beloved, is that the moment God brings it out there is no going back. It is referred to as the cup of fury and trembling.

Isaiah 51:17

> ***"Awake, awake, stand up, O Jerusalem, which hast drunk at the hand of the LORD the cup of his fury; thou hast drunken the dregs of the cup of trembling, and wrung them out."***

WHEN THE ENEMY TREMBLES

The cup of fury will make the enemy to tremble. ***Isaiah 51:22***

> ***"Thus saith thy Lord the LORD, and thy God that pleadeth the cause of his people, Behold, I have taken out of thine hand the cup of trembling, even the dregs of the cup of my fury; thou shalt no more drink it again:"***

God is set to put the weapon of the cup of fury in your hands. ***Jer. 25:15***

> ***"For thus saith the LORD God of Israel unto me; Take the wine cup of this fury at my hand, and cause all the nations, to whom I send thee, to drink it.***

FIERCE WRATH

This weapon is also called the cup of fierce wrath. ***Rev. 16:19***

> ***"And the great city was divided into three parts, and the cities of the nations fell: and great Babylon came in remembrance before God, to give unto her the cup of the wine of the fierceness of his wrath."***

This is the time when you must make the enemies of your destiny to drink the cup of the fierce wrath of the Almighty. Beloved, the cup of the fierce wrath of the Almighty contains spiritual poison.

THE RESULTS

Immediately the enemy tastes from the cup of God's wrath, the following things will happen.

1. *They will somersault and die*
2. *The content of the cup of fierce wrath destroy them*
3. *When they taste from the cup of the wrath of God they will be forced to drink their own blood and eat their own flesh.*
4. *The cup of God's wrath will send satanic agents on a mission of self destruction; your enemies will be given useless assignments that advance your cause.*
5. *When you locate and command satanic agents to drink from the cup of fierce wrath there will be violent manifestation.*
6. *Evil spirits will release their victims.*

This is one weapon that will poison the powers that are planning to poison you. The fierce wrath of the Almighty will be released. This is our finest hour of victory. Now is the time when we must posses our possessions and triumph over dark powers.

PRAYER POINTS

1. Let my enemies drink the cup of fury and trembling, in the name of Jesus.
2. Let my full time enemies begin to experience the fury and the trembling of the cup of the Almighty, in the name of Jesus.
3. My Father, arise in Your fury and let my enemies tremble and be confused, in the name of Jesus.

4. My Father, put Your cup of fury in the hand of my enemies and make me to possess my possessions, in the name of Jesus.
5. Oh Lord, let Your cup of fury and trembling be poured upon my stubborn enemies and pursuers, in the name of Jesus.
6. Let the cup of fury and trembling of the Lord be the portion of every arrester in dark clothes, in the name of Jesus.

WEAPON 56

FAMINE

▶ ***THIS IS A STRANGE WEAPON TO USE WHEN YOU FACE STRANGE BATTLES.***

▶ ***USE THIS WEAPON WHEN YOU WANT GOD TO SENTENCE POWERS THAT ARE ASSIGNED AGAINST YOU TO GET BUSY WITH ACTIVITIES THAT WILL PROMOTE YOUR DESTINY.***

▶ ***IT IS A WEAPON OF VENGEANCE***

▶ ***IT IS A WEAPON YOU CAN USE WHEN YOU WANT YOUR BURIED VIRTUES TO BE EXHUMED.***

▶ ***THIS WEAPON WILL LEAD YOU TO THE MOUNTAIN OF TESTIMONIES.***

The quiver of the Lord is filled with all manner of poisonous arrows. When these arrows are shot, the enemy will regret ever confronting you as a child of God. One of the weapons which God uses to fight is the weapon of famine. When famine hits the enemy's camp, agents of darkness will find it difficult to carry out their operations. God can attack the evil company that is working night and day to perpetuate your bondage.

If some agents of darkness are busy attacking you, the weapon of famine will scatter them unto desolation. You can ask God to send the gift of famine to the camp of your enemies. You can specifically ask for a type of famine that is deadly and tragic.

THE WEAPON

A season of famine will not only spell disaster in the camp of the enemy, it will also subject them to total burial. Boastful enemies can be silenced through the use of the weapon of famine. This weapon is described in the scriptures as the evil arrows of famine. The agenda of this famine is destruction. ***Ezekiel 5:16***

> ***"When I shall send upon them the evil arrows of famine, which shall be for their destruction, and which I will send to destroy you: and I will increase the famine upon you, and will break your staff of bread:"***

The arrow of famine is one of the tough weapons that can be found in the armory of heaven. The powers that are attacking you will certainly lose focus when they are invaded by the arrow of famine. When God dishes out prolonged famine to the camp of wicked powers they will be thrown into panic and confusion.

2Sam 21:1-3

> ***"Then there was a famine in the days of David three years, year after year; and David enquired of the LORD. And the LORD answered, It is for Saul, and for his bloody house, because he slew the Gibeonites. And the king called the Gibeonites, and said unto them; (now the Gibeonites were not of the children of Israel, but of the remnant of the Amorites; and the children of Israel had sworn unto them: and Saul sought to slay them in his zeal to the children of Israel and Judah.) Wherefore David said unto the Gibeonites, What shall I do for you? and wherewith shall I make the atonement, that ye may bless the inheritance of the LORD?***

A STRATEGIC WEAPON

Such a weapon is often used by God to put a halt to the evil activities of the enemy. It is unfortunate, however, that children of God are the victims. A lot of believers are busy grappling with famine, whereas the power of commanding famine to hit the camp of the enemy lies in our hands. There are times when children of darkness are busy molesting God's children. Whereas, if believers have prayed famine into the territory of such agents, the famine would have brought them into such a state of confusion that they will not be able to lift up a finger.

Beloved, the weapon of famine is a strategic weapon. Our inability to use this weapon accounts for the proliferation of attacks against the people of God. This secret weapon will shut the mouth of angry lions. When the lion becomes so hungry, it will no longer be able to walk or roar. The use of this weapon will give you uncommon testimonies, take you to the highest realm of victory and make you an overcomer.

These end times call for the use of the weapon of famine. Do not wait until you are attacked by the enemy. Attack your attackers and you will defeat the powers that are busy mocking your God. This is a weapon you need to use before it is too late. *I challenge you to pray like a wounded lion.*

PRAYER POINTS

1. Oh God, arise and wage war with the instrument of famine against my opposition, in the name of Jesus.
2. Let the famine of the Almighty descend on the camp of eaters of flesh

and drinkers of blood, in the name of Jesus.

3. Power of divine famine, visit the stronghold of demonic caterers, in the name of Jesus.
4. Power of divine famine, fall upon every demonic famine, in the name of Jesus.
5. Oh divine famine of the Lord, arise in the rage of your power and scatter every power devouring my finances, in the name of Jesus.
6. Holy Ghost fire, and divine famine of God visit the camp of my strong opposition, in the name of Jesus.
7. Father let the famine of heaven visit every power bent on devouring my destiny, in the name of Jesus.

WEAPON

57

DEVOURING STORM

► *TO BE USED WHEN THERE IS SATANIC GATHERING AGAINST YOU.*
► *WHEN YOU ARE AWARE THAT THERE IS A NETWORK OF WITCHCRAFT; LOCAL OR INTERNATIONAL GATHERED AGAINST YOU.*
► *WHEN YOU ARE TIRED OF SATANIC CONSPIRACY AGAINST YOUR LIFE.*
► *WHEN THERE ARE EVIL CONGREGATIONS OF THE WICKED FRUSTRATING YOUR EFFORTS.*
► *WHEN THERE IS AN ARRAY OF MOCKERS AROUND YOU.*
► *WHEN STRANGE PROBLEMS AND DISEASES ARE BOMBARDING YOUR HELPERS.*
► *WHEN GETTING ANYTHING TO WORK BECOMES VERY HARD.*

God has designed terrible weapons for dealing with all forms of satanic wickedness. One of these weapons is the weapon of devouring storm. As the name of the weapon implies, it is a weapon for devouring of destruction. Wicked satanic agents and their weapons deserve no other thing but total destruction. God has created a storm that specializes in arresting and devouring wicked enemies and their weapons of destructions. You can invoke this weapon when you want to put an end to satanic activities aimed at destroying you or your destiny.

Psalm 83:15-17

> ***So persecute them with thy tempest, and make them afraid with thy storm. Fill their faces with shame; that they may seek thy name, O LORD. Let them be confounded and troubled for ever; yea, let them be put to shame, and perish:***

A tempest is another word that describes a violent storm. This weapon has been created by God to pursue, terrify and consume every stubborn pursuer.

You must use this weapon when your purpose is to make enemies of your destiny confounded, put to shame and destroyed. We use it when you want people to know that He whose name alone is Jehovah, is the most high over all the Earth.

"If you want to witness God in action, you need this weapon".

Psalm 50:3

> ***Our God shall come, and shall not keep silence: a fire shall devour before him, and it shall be very tempestuous round about him.***

The devouring storm is a weapon that announces the fearful presence of the most high. You need to release a tempestuous storm against the camp of the enemy. To silence boastful powers, you need to unleash a fiery stream against them.

Daniel 7:10

> ***"A fiery stream issued and came forth from before him: thousand thousands ministered unto him, and ten thousand times ten thousand stood before him: the judgment was set, and the books were opened.***

Devouring storm will uproot and devour the stronghold of wickedness.

Job 27:20-23

> ***Terrors take hold on him as waters, a tempest stealeth him away in the night. The east wind carrieth him away, and he departeth: and as a storm hurleth him out of his place. For God shall cast upon him, and not spare: he would fain flee out of his hand. Men shall clap their hands at him, and shall hiss him out of his place.***

Now is the time to arrest and destabilize every wicked mechanism fashioned against you. You can invoke a divine overflow that will flush the enemy out of his hiding place.

Isaiah 28:17

> ***Judgment also will I lay to the line, and righteousness to the plummet: and the hail shall sweep away the refuge of lies, and the waters shall overflow the hiding place.***

This weapon is used for divine justice. You need it when you want to pay wicked enemies back in their own coins. This weapon will enable you to sweep away the enemy and his weapon of war after the order of Pharaoh and his army at the

Red sea.

Exodus 14:26-28

> ***"And the LORD said unto Moses, Stretch out thine hand over the sea, that the waters may come again upon the Egyptians, upon their chariots, and upon their horsemen. And Moses stretched forth his hand over the sea, and the sea returned to his strength when the morning appeared; and the Egyptians fled against it; and the LORD overthrew the Egyptians in the midst of the sea. And the waters returned, and covered the chariots, and the horsemen, and all the host of Pharaoh that came into the sea after them; there remained not so much as one of them.***

You can command every stubborn Pharaoh to be swept away by the devouring storm of the Almighty. This weapon will do its wonders in your life. It will spread disaster across the length and breadth of the camp of the enemy.

PRAYER POINTS

1. O God, arise and provoke your devouring storm against every evil gathering, summoned against my destiny, in Jesus name.
2. O devouring storm of the Almighty, pursue my pursuers unto desolation, in the name of Jesus.
3. Every agenda of wicked covens against my progress, receive the devouring storm of the Almighty, in Jesus name.
4. My Father, provoke your devouring storm to silence every power divining against me, in the mighty name of Jesus.
5. Every good thing stolen from my life, I invoke the devouring storm of the Almighty to repossess them.
6. Every company of hardened and unrepentant enemies, be scattered by the devouring storm of the Almighty, in Jesus name.
7. O, heavens arise and call into activity the power of the devouring storm of the Almighty to stop my spiritual embargoes, in Jesus name.

WEAPON 58

SCORPIONS

▶ ***THIS IS A POWERFUL DELIVERANCE WEAPON.***
▶ ***YOU NEED THIS WEAPON WHEN YOU WANT TO TORMENT YOUR TORMENTORS.***
▶ ***IT IS A POTENT WEAPON WHEN USED AGAINST HOUSEHOLD WICKEDNESS.***
▶ ***YOU NEED THIS WEAPON WHEN YOU NEED UNCOMMON VICTORY IN LIFE'S BATTLES.***
▶ ***IT IS AN APPROPRIATE WEAPON AGAINST BLOOD SUCKING DEMONS.***

In this part of the world a lot of people are under bondage to strange powers. When God wants to set you free from strange bondage he might use a strange method of deliverance. Since the bondage of mankind is in diverse areas God has also created an array of strange weapons.

Those who need deep deliverance have been provided with appropriate weapons and instruments. One of these weapons is the weapon of scorpions. There are weapons in God's armory that are capable of stinging the enemy to death. Divine scorpions are loaded with poison. I am yet to see an enemy or any power of the enemy that will be invaded by divine scorpions and remain alive. God has scorpions in abundance.**Deut. 8:15**

> ***"Who led thee through that great and terrible wilderness, wherein were fiery serpents, and scorpions, and drought, where there was no water; who brought thee forth water out of the rock of flint;"***

THE SQUAD OF SCORPIONS

The scorpions form a squad in the divine army. Scorpions have tormenting power. Immediately they inject their poison, it is death. **Rev. 9:5**

> ***And to them it was given that they should not kill them, but that they should be tormented five months: and their torment was as the torment of a scorpion, when he striketh a man.***

When enemies decide that they will not stop molesting you, you can discharge divine scorpions into their midst. You can simply order the scorpions to keep on carrying their destructive mission in the camp of the enemy for the next six months. Any wound inflicted by scorpions is fatal. There is enormous poison in the tail of the scorpion. The poisonous sting of the scorpions is suitable for the persistent enemy or the stubborn pursuer.

ENEMIES TO ATTACK

You can unleash this weapon on the following classes of powers or enemies.

1. The power of the emptiers
2. Powers that make life unbearable
3. Household wickedness
4. The spirit of Pharaoh
5. The spirit of Herod
6. Witchcraft powers
7. Evil spies
8. The spirit of death and hell
9. Destiny amputations
10. Anti-marriage forces
11. Anti-breakthrough powers

These classes of enemies must be seriously dealt with. The weapon of scorpions will sweep them away.

PRAYER POINTS

1. Oh heaven, dispatch Your scorpions against every scorpion assigned against my life, in the name of Jesus.
2. Oh Lord, let Your scorpions move into the hiding places of the oppressors and expose their weakness, in the name of Jesus.
3. Scorpions from heaven arise, fight my battles for me, in the name of Jesus.
4. Let every scorpion assigned to bite my destiny be destroyed by the scorpion of God, in the name of Jesus.
5. O scorpion of the Most High God, walk through the length and breadth of everything that concerns me and destroy every plantation of dark scorpions, in the name of Jesus.
6. My Father, arise in Your anger and send your scorpions against every wild beast moving about in the garden of my life, in the name of Jesus.

WEAPON 59

THE SWORD OF THE LORD

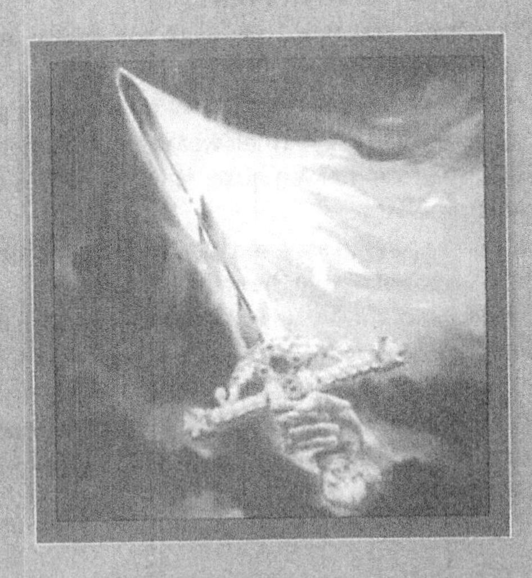

► ***THIS WEAPON WILL ENABLE YOU TO CUT DOWN EVIL PLANTATIONS.***

► ***WITH THIS WEAPON YOU WILL BRUSH AWAY EVIL COBWEB.***

► ***THIS IS THE RIGHT WEAPON TO SECURE THE KEY TO YOUR DOMINION.***

The sword of God is the sword that has slain multitudes of enemies. The sword of God is a weapon that has bathed in the blood of stubborn pursuers. A single stroke of the sword of the Almighty can slay ten thousand enemies. The sword of the Almighty can cut off evil trees that have been planted for over two hundred years. The sword of God is your weapon of fire. It is a sword of vengeance. It is a sword that has been assigned for giving the enemy an appropriate measure of the judgment he deserves.

The sword of God will brush away every evil cobweb. The sword of God can invade the territory of the enemy and grant you victory and deliverance on a platter of gold. No power can confront the sword of God and not be cut to pieces. The sword of God is your weapon of victory, it is your survival strategy. To be free from the yoke of oppression you need the sword of God. **Gen 27:40**

> ***"And by thy sword shalt thou live, and shalt serve thy brother; and it shall come to pass when thou shalt have the dominion, that thou shalt break his yoke from off thy neck."***

YOUR DOMINION KEY

The sword of God is the key of dominion. The sword of the Almighty is the express way that takes you to the realm of total deliverance. **Ephesians 6:17**

> ***"And take the helmet of salvation, and the sword of the Spirit, which is the word of God: "***

A MIGHTY SWORD

God has introduced a mighty sword to facilitate our victory and deliverance **Matt 10:34**

> ***"Think not that I am come to send peace on earth: I came not to send peace, but a sword."***

You can command the sword of God to severe every link between you and the powers of your father's house. When the sword of God is active your blood will become bitter to the enemy. The sword of God will place an embargo on satanic oppression.

THE SWORD OF DELIVERANCE

The sword of God will arrest every evil tide. The sword of God will facilitate your deliverance and get rid of every satanic yoke. The sword of God will convert your life to a-no-go area for the enemy. When you make use of the sword of God as a great weapon of deliverance, no power will be able to subject you to any form of bondage again. When you cry saying; thou weapon of the Almighty, locate every enemy of my destiny and crush them, your story will change and you will witness the disgrace of the powers that are in charge of your case.

PRAYER POINTS

1. Oh sword of God, move forth on my behalf and cut down the citadel of the wicked, in the name of Jesus.
2. Oh sword of God, arise and move into battle and defend my interest, in the name of Jesus.
3. By the sword of God, I arise and declare war against my oppressors, in the name of Jesus.
4. By the sword of God I arise and destroy every satanic manipulator working against my destiny, in the name of Jesus.
5. Oh sword of God, rise up in your anger and cut to pieces every eater of flesh and drinker of blood, in the name of Jesus.
6. O sword of the Lord, pass through the camp of my oppressors, in the name of Jesus.

7. O sword of God, pass through the camp of my oppressors, in the name of Jesus.
8. O sword of God, pass through the camp of my hardened enemies, in the name of Jesus.
9. Oh sword of God, pass through the camp of the evil companies gathered against me, in the name of Jesus.

WEAPON 60

THE NAME OF JESUS

- ***THIS IS AN ALL PURPOSE WEAPON.***
- ***IT FUNCTIONS AS A BULLDOZER.***
- ***THIS WEAPON ENABLES YOU TO SMITE THE ENEMY.***
- ***IT IS A WEAPON THAT WILL GIVE YOU TOTAL DELIVERANCE.***
- ***YOU NEED THIS WEAPON WHEN YOU ARE DEALING WITH PRINCIPALITIES AND POWERS.***
- ***YOU NEED THIS WEAPON WHEN YOU NEED PROTECTION AND SECURITY.***

The name of Jesus is one of the classified weapons of spiritual warfare and deliverance. Being an exclusive weapon, it supersedes all other weapons. It is a weapon that swallows every weapon that the enemy can boast of. When this weapon collides with the entire force of the enemy, there will be pandemonium.

The name of Jesus will swallow the name of all principalities and powers. It will make the chain of oppression to break like a weak thread. The name of Jesus cancels ancestral curses, negates the agenda of darkness and deflects evil arrows. It is one name that makes every other name in the universe to be rendered null and void. The name of Jesus is a weapon that bulldozes satanic roadblocks and demonic stumbling blocks. It is a weapon of terror, an instrument of destruction and a divine missile that will inflict fatal wounds on the head of the enemy.

AN IRRESISTABLE WEAPON

For members of the dark kingdom, it is an irresistible weapon. For God's children it is the tower of protection. The name of Jesus emits fire, breathes power and can reach the enemy that hides in the most remote part of he world. The name of Jesus is a weapon you can operate in all nations and among every tribal group.

The name of Jesus summarizes the entire weaponry of the Almighty. It is an umbrella under which other weapons assemble in readiness for exploits

(Phil 2:10)

> ***"That at the name of Jesus every knee should bow, of things in heaven,and things in earth, and things under the earth;"***

beloved this weapon transcends the heaven, the earth and under the earth.
Romans 14:11

> ***"For it is written, As I live, saith the Lord, every knee shall bow to me, and every tongue shall confess to God."***

Rev. 5:13

> ***"And every creature which is in heaven, and on the earth, and under the earth, and such as are in the sea, and all that are in them, heard I saying, Blessing, and honour, and glory, and power, be unto him that sitteth upon the throne, and unto the Lamb for ever and ever."***

Ancient powers bow at the mention of the name of Jesus. Modern occult powers will be forced to bend their knee at the mention of the name of Jesus. The name of Jesus is a weapon of perfect protection and utmost safety. **Prov 18:10**

> ***"The name of the LORD is a strong tower: the righteous runneth into it, and is safe."***

THE SEAL OF DELIVERANCE

The name of Jesus is the seal of your deliverance **(Psalm 144:2).**

> ***"My goodness, and my fortress; my high tower, and my deliverer; my shield, and he in whom I trust; who subdueth my people under me. "***

When you want to deal with ancestral curses and ancient handwriting of darkness simply use the name of Jesus. **Col 2:14**

> ***"Blotting out the handwriting of ordinances that was against us, which was contrary to us, and took it out of the way, nailing it to his cross;"***

To spoil principalities and powers, use the weapon of the *name of Jesus.*
Col 2:15

> ***"And having spoiled principalities and powers, he made a shew of them openly, triumphing over them in it."***

THE GREATEST WEAPON

The name of Jesus is the greatest name given to us as a weapon. **Acts 4:12**

> ***"Neither is there salvation in any other: for there is none other name under heaven given among men, whereby we must be saved."***

Use the weapon of the name of Jesus today and you will experience unchallengeable victory.

PRAYER POINTS

1. By the name of Jesus I destroy every camp of the oppressor, in the name of Jesus.
2. By the name of Jesus I pursue all my spiritual pursuers, in the name of Jesus
3. Every warfare in the heavenlies, on the earth and in the sea, let the name of Jesus pursue them and eliminate them.
4. Let the name of Jesus catapult me above my enemies. in the name of Jesus.
5. Let the name of Jesus defeat every frustration, disappointment and stagnation in my life, in the name of Jesus.
6. Let the name of Jesus enforce power to change hands from the hands of wickedness to my hands, in the name of Jesus.

WEAPON 61

THE WORD OF GOD

- ***THIS WEAPON WILL ENABLE YOU TO CANCEL NEGATIVE UTTERANCES.***
- ***WITH THIS WEAPON YOU WILL COUNTER DEMONIC INCANTATIONS.***
- ***THIS IS THE RIGHT WEAPON TO USE WHEN YOU ARE DEALING WITH STRONGHOLDS.***
- ***MAKE USE OF THIS WEAPON WHEN YOU WANT TO UNLEASH THE RAW POWER OF GOD UPON THE POWERS THAT ARE TRYING TO BURY YOUR DESTINY.***
- ***YOU CAN CHALLENGE THE POWERS THAT ARE CHALLENGING GOD IN YOUR LIFE.***

The word of God is a powerful weapon. It conveys the totality of the power of God. There is nowhere the word of God cannot penetrate. There is no power it cannot arrest. The word of God is loaded with unstoppable spiritual missiles. No wonder the Bible says;. **Eccl 8:4**

> ***"Where the word of a king is, there is power: and who may say unto him, What doest thou?"***

The word of God is the word of the King of kings and Lord of Lords. God's word is an eternal decree. No power can contest *"thus saith the Lord."* Seasoned deliverance ministers know that it is unnecessary to go into fruitless dialogue with demons. The moment you say; demon thus saith the Lord, the demon will have no option than to accept the divine decree.

POWER IN THE WORD

The word of God pulsates with power. Members of the dark kingdom know that there is fire in the word of God. When you handle the weapon of the word of the lord, it will work with the speed of lightening and the result will be characterized by accuracy, effectiveness and power. The Bible says; **Hebrews 4:12.**

> ***"For the word of God is quick, and powerful, and sharper than any twoedged sword, piercing even to the dividing asunder of soul and***

spirit, and of the joints and marrow, and is a discerner of the thoughts and intents of the heart"

THE DYNAMIC WORD

God's word is more dynamic than any physical weapon. It is a double sided sword, it penetrates the domain of darkness. God's word works wonders.
God's word breaks the rock in pieces. **Jer 23:29**

"Is not my word like as a fire? saith the LORD; and like a hammer that breaketh the rock in pieces?"

The weapon of God's word will discover the secret of the enemy,

CASTING DOWN IMAGINATIONS

The word of God will cast down negative imaginations and arrest every power that challenges God in your life. **2Cor 10:4-5**

"For the weapons of our warfare are not carnal, but mighty through God to the pulling down of strong holds; Casting down imaginations, and every high thing that exalteth itself against the knowledge of God, and bringing into captivity every thought to the obedience of Christ;"

The word of God holds captivity captive. The word of God is a sword that devours the enemy. **Eph 6:17**

"And take the helmet of salvation, and the sword of the Spirit, which is the word of God:"

THE DEVOURING WORD

The word of God is the sword that comes out of the mouth of the Lord **Rev 2:16.**

"Repent; or else I will come unto thee quickly, and will fight against them with the sword of my mouth"

When the powers of your father's house confront you, command the word of God to demolish them. When household witchcraft charges at you, fire the arrow of God's word toward their direction. When the scourge of the tongue is being unleashed upon you, take up the amour of God's word and fight back. God's word is at a stake in the weapon of the word of God. The power of God is unleashed at every instance of the use of this weapon. This weapon will give you victory in every battle and power to overcome every attack. Your deliverance is settled when you make use of the weapon of the word of God. Unfortunately, Bible illiterates cannot make use of this weapon. Your word power will determine the level of your victory.

PRAYER POINTS

1. Thou power of God's word, arise and fight against every negative word spoken against my destiny, in the name of Jesus.
2. I invoke the awesome power in the word of God against every enemy of my prophetic destiny, in the name of Jesus.
3. O word of God, arise and bulldoze every hindrance to my breakthroughs, in the name of Jesus.
4. Thou power of the word of God, arise and resist every dark word spoken against me in the coven of witchcraft, in the name of Jesus.
5. I release the power of the word of God, to go into the camp of my enemies and withdraw all my stolen and confiscated blessings, in the name of Jesus.
6. My father, let the power of your word be released from heaven to fight my battles and give me victory, in the name of Jesus.
7. Thou word of God, arise and swallow every evil threat made against me by the enemy, in the name of Jesus.

WEAPON 62

THE FURNACE OF AFFLICTION

▶ ***THIS IS A WEAPON THAT WILL GRANT YOU TOTAL VICTORY OVER THE ENTIRE FORCES OF DARKNESS.***

▶ ***IT IS A WEAPON YOU CAN USE TO OPPRESS YOUR OPPRESSORS.***

▶ ***MAKE USE OF THIS WEAPON WHEN YOU WANT THE POWER OF THE ENEMY TO BE ROASTED.***

▶ ***THIS WEAPON WILL ENABLE YOU TO DEAL WITH UNFRIENDLY FRIENDS AND HIDDEN TORMENTORS.***

▶ ***THIS IS THE RIGHT WEAPON TO USE WHEN YOU WANT TO***

▶ ***EXPERIENCE INSTANT MANIFESTATIONS ON THE DELIVERANCE GROUND.***

▶ ***IT IS A POWERFUL WEAPON FOR ATTACKING STUBBORN SPIRITS.***

God operates by fire. But He puts the fire in different jackets and containers. Since fire is God's toughest weapon, He has therefore created various modules of the weapon of fire. One of these modules is what I call the furnace of affliction. This is a unique weapon for dealing with all kinds of satanic agenda.
This weapon is very effective. When the furnace of affliction collides with the attacks of the enemy the attacks are put on hold. When the furnace of affliction heats up the territory of attackers, they will drop their agenda and confess that your life is too hot to be handled.

TOTAL VICTORY

The weapon of the furnace of affliction is one weapon you can use and you will cause eaters of flesh and drinkers of blood to eat their own flesh and drink their own blood. The furnace of affliction is God's weapon for winning total victory over the enemy. The furnace of affliction is the weapon for melting the weapon of darkness. This weapon will burn all evil programmes, incantations and demonic wishes against your destiny. ***Ezekiel 22:20***

> ***"As they gather silver, and brass, and iron, and lead, and tin, into the midst of the furnace, to blow the fire upon it, to melt it; so will I gather you in mine anger and in my fury, and I will leave you there, and melt you."***

HOT FURNACE

What God is set to do is to gather your stubborn pursuers, household wickedness, local witchcraft, the power of the emptiers, the power of the waster and the spirit of untimely death into the midst of the hot furnace, blow fire upon them and melt them in His anger. Beloved, the furnace of affliction is one of the hot manifestations of the anger and fury of the Almighty.
When you use the weapon of the furnace of affliction the environment of the enemy will become unbearable for them to operate in. God will demonstrate what He did in the days of Daniel. The enemies who tried to place you in a hot furnace will be roasted to ashes while God will turn the table and convert the furnace the enemy tried to put you into, to an air conditioned room for you.

TOUGH JUDGEMENT

For the enemy, the furnace of affliction is the height of divine judgment. When you sentence the enemy and command him to enter the furnace of affliction, you will witness several manifestations.
On the deliverance ground, when you command demons to enter the furnace of affliction you will begin to witness horrible manifestation in the lives of the deliverance candidate. No one can joke with the weapon of the furnace of affliction. ***Isaiah 48:10***

> ***"Behold, I have refined thee, but not with silver; I have chosen thee in the furnace of affliction."***

Ezekiel 22:22

> ***"As silver is melted in the midst of the furnace, so shall ye be melted in the midst thereof; and ye shall know that I the LORD have poured out my fury upon you."***

A TOUGH WEAPON

The furnace of affliction is one of the highest weapons in God's military warehouse. Try the weapon today and you will witness the practical implication of what it takes for strangers to be frightened out of their hidden places.

PRAYER POINTS

1. My Father, let the furnace of affliction swallow every affliction assigned against my life, in the name of Jesus.
2. O heaven arise, throw every arm of the wicked rising up against me into the furnace of affliction, in the name of Jesus.
3. Let the furnace of affliction pursue and overtake every enemy of my destiny, in the name of Jesus.
4. Oh God, push those who want to push me to death into the furnace of affliction, in the name of Jesus.
5. Let the power that delivered Shedrack, Meshach and Abednego push my attackers into the furnace of affliction, in the name of Jesus.

WEAPON 63

THE SNARE

▶ THIS IS A DIVINE DEVICE FOR CATCHING SATANIC AGENTS IN THEIR OWN TRAP.

▶ THIS IS ONE WEAPON YOU CAN USE WHEN YOU WANT TO SUBJECT CAPTIVITY TO CAPTIVITY.

▶ YOU NEED THIS WEAPON WHEN YOU WANT TO SING YOUR SONG AND DANCE YOUR DANCE.

▶ YOU CAN MAKE USE OF THIS WEAPON WHEN YOU WANT TO CAPTURE THE ENEMIES OF YOUR DESTINY AND KEEP THEM UNDER LOCK AND KEY.

▶ THIS WEAPON WILL EMPOWER YOU TO CAPTURE YOUR PURSUERS AND MOVE INTO THE REALM OF GLORIOUS DESTINY.

God specializes in setting traps to catch the enemy. There are various war strategies. To defeat some enemies you have to catch them alive. Some enemies have to be kidnapped and kept in the prison house meant for the enemies of God. When satanic agents decide that you will know no peace or that you will not be able to fulfil, your destiny, you need to simply set up a snare that will catch them.

What is a snare? Job 18:8

"For he is cast into a net by his own feet, and he walketh upon a snare."

Job 18:10

"The snare is laid for him in the ground, and a trap for him in the way."

Ps 69:22

"Let their table become a snare before them: and that which should have been for their welfare, let it become a trap."

Ps 91:3

"Surely he shall deliver thee from the snare of the fowler, and from the noisome pestilence."

A POWERFUL DEVICE

A snare is a trap. It is a net, or a device for catching animals or birds. ***Ps 11:6***

"Upon the wicked he shall rain snares, fire and brimstone, and an horrible tempest: this shall be the portion of their cup."

The weapon of snares makes the God of the suddenlies to come upon the enemy in a negative sense. The snare is a weapon that denotes sudden, furious, and mysterious utter destruction. It is a grevious divine punishment upon the enemy. The best way to capture the enemy is to capture him in the snare of the Almighty. **Ezekiel 12:13**

"My net also will I spread upon him, and he shall be taken in my snare: and I will bring him to Babylon to the land of the Chaldeans; yet shall he not see it, though he shall die there."

THE DIVINE OVERTHROW

When God's net or snare is spread upon the enemy there will be the fulfilment of the phrase: *"he who leads into captivity shall be led into captivity"*. At that point, God will overthrow your enemies and capture them with his net. **Job 19:6**

"Know now that God hath overthrown me, and hath compassed me with his net."

God will set multiple traps or snares in order to catch the enemy wherever the enemy is located; In the sea, on air, in the heavenlies, in witchcraft covens, in your father's house, in fetish shrines, God will capture them. One way you can defeat the enemies of your destiny is to command the snare of the Almighty to catch them. When they are caught you will sing the song of victory. In fact, you will sing your song and dance your dance.

PRAYER POINTS

1. Let the hosts of heaven set up a snare against every enemy monitoring my life, in the name of Jesus.
2. Let the hosts of heaven set up a snare against every enemy whispering wickedness against me in the name of Jesus.
3. Let the witches and wizards that peep and mutter be caught in the snare of heaven in the name of Jesus.

4. Every sorcerer, enchanter and diviner assigned against me be caught by the snare of the Almighty in the name Jesus.
5. The snare of God, arrest every hunter of my soul in the name of Jesus.
6. The snare of God, arrest every hunter of my destiny in the name of Jesus.

WEAPON 64

HOST OF HEAVEN

- ***THIS WEAPON HAS BEEN RESERVED FOR TOUGH BATTLES.***
- ***YOU CAN USE THIS WEAPON WHEN YOU WANT TO SUMMON DIVINE POWERS IN YOUR BATTLES.***
- ***THIS WEAPON WILL GIVE YOU THE ANSWER WHEN YOU ARE SEARCHING FOR DEEP SECRETS.***
- ***IT IS A POWERFUL WEAPON FOR MEMBERS OF GOD'S VICTORIOUS ARMY.***
- ***YOU CAN USE THIS WEAPON WHEN YOU WANT THE ALMIGHTY TO ORDAIN TERRIFYING NOISES IN THE CAMP OF THOSE WHO ARE PLANNING TO ATTACK YOU.***
- ***YOU CAN DEAL WITH TERRIBLE ENEMIES WITH THE WEAPONS.***
- ***THIS IS ONE OF THE STRONGEST DELIVERANCE WEAPONS.***

The heavenly army is referred to in the scriptures as the host of heaven. God knows that we will fight lots of battles here on earth. He has, therefore, set up battalions of soldiers in the spiritual realm. Hence, the heavenlies squad is always on standby ready to defend God's interest and integrity at all times.

The host of heaven can be referred to as God's elite army. They operate with mathematical precision and fight with the speed of lightening. God has not established the heavenly host in vain. They are stationed in the air ready to launch an offensive against the enemies of God and His children. God is the Commander in Chief of the spiritual army. Hence, He is referred to as the Lord of hosts. ***Psalm 80:4***

> ***"O LORD God of hosts, how long wilt thou be angry against the prayer of thy people?"***

Psalm 59:5

> ***"Thou therefore, O LORD God of hosts, the God of Israel, awake to visit all the heathen: be not merciful to any wicked transgressors. Selah."***

Psalm 89:8

> ***"O LORD God of hosts, who is a strong LORD like unto thee? or to thy faithfulness round about thee?"***

VICTORIOUS SOLDIERS

Since God is the God of hosts who has never lost a battle, the heavenly soldiers constitute the strongest weapons that have been made available for us. The host of heaven are soldiers who serve in the courts of God. They are fearful and terrible. The Bible declares that these heavenly soldiers stand on the right and left hand of God. **2Chro. 18:18**

> ***"Again he said, Therefore hear the word of the LORD; I saw the LORD sitting upon his throne, and all the host of heaven standing on his right hand and on his left."***

AN INNUMERABLE HOST

The Bible also tells us that the host of heaven are innumerable. **Jeremiah 33:22**

> ***"As the host of heaven cannot be numbered, neither the sand of the sea measured: so will I multiply the seed of David my servant, and the Levites that minister unto me"***

When the battle becomes tough you can make use of the weapon of the host of heaven. When you are contending with powers that expand battles, the weapon of the host of heaven is the answer. When you draw the host of heaven into battle, you have automatically drawn the God of hosts into battle. Such a battle will surely be won and crowned with victory.

REAL WARFARE

There is no true Christianity without warfare. You cannot overcome dark powers without seeking for angelic assistance. You cannot experience victory without getting the host of heaven involved in your battles. Your deliverance cannot be complete until the host of heaven invades the cage of bondage and sets you free. This is a weapon we must begin to make use of in this generation.
The hosts of heaven have not been created by God to decorate the heavenly realm. Beloved, when you command the host of heaven to ordain terrifying noises against the powers that have vowed that you will remain a permanent candidate in the school of bondage, there will be terrible uproar in the camp of the enemy. May God teach your hands to war and fingers to fight. May you be

inspired and empowered to invite and draw the host of heaven into your battles!

PRAYER POINTS

1. Let the host of heaven gather themselves in array against every warfare that I face, in the name of Jesus.
2. Father, let the hosts of heaven defend my interests in every area of my life, in the name of Jesus.
3. Every strong warfare waged against me, be destroyed by the host of heaven, in the name of Jesus.
4. Let the power of the hosts of heaven destroy the power of the hosts of the wicked, in the name of Jesus.
5. Let the host of heaven go to the north, east, south, and the west and silence every power trying to silence me, in the name of Jesus.
6. Let the host of heaven encamp around me and send back to the sender every arrow fired against me, in the name of Jesus.
7. Let the host of heaven arise and make me victorious in every battle, in Jesus name.

WEAPON

65

SOUTH WIND

▶ USE THIS WEAPON WHEN YOU WANT TO STRIKE THE ENEMY AND INFLICT FATAL WOUNDS ON YOUR OPPRESSORS.
▶ YOU CAN COMMAND THIS WEAPON TO DESTROY WITCHCRAFT COVENS PUT IN PLACE AGAINST YOUR DESTINY.
▶ USE THIS WEAPON AGAINST ANTI-FAVOUR SPIRITS.
▶ IT IS A WEAPON TO BE USED BY VICTIMS OF CONSTANT DREAM ATTACKS.
▶ USE THIS WEAPON TO SWEEP AWAY THE INVASION OF DARKNESS.

God uses the weapon of the south wind. As far as God is concerned, every wind has a function. He uses both the north wind and south wind. However, the south wind has a distinct function. **Job 37:17**

> ***"How thy garments are warm, when he quieteth the earth by the south wind?"***

A TERRIFIC WEAPON

The function of the south wind can only be understood when read against the backdrop of ***Luke 12:55.***

> ***"And when ye see the south wind blow, ye say, There will be heat; and it cometh to pass."***

The south wind brings heat. God uses the mystery of the south wind and north wind as weapons of spiritual warfare. Just as the north wind brings rain and the south wind brings heat, God has various weapons of launching attacks against the enemy. When the south wind brings a wave of heat, you have a weapon that makes the enemy uncomfortable.

When God commands the south wind to play its role and strike the enemy, there will be an up-roar in witchcraft covens, gathering of fetish priests, occult meetings and other places where people make divinations against you. This weapon may appear ordinary to the mind of man. But, the truth is that they are terrific weapons.

THE IMPACT

The south wind will convey the heat of judgment to the midst of those who are trying to attack you. Since no one can stop the wind, No power can stop this

weapon. As long as the wind blows into every part of the world the enemies of your deliverance will feel the impact of the wind and the fire and heat of the Holy Ghost will knock them down.
When a prayer command evokes the south wind it will come with an avalanche of warm air. You will begin to witness multiple summersaults by all manner of satanic agents.

ENEMIES TO OVERCOME

This weapon can be used in the following instances.

1. When evil powers gather together in readiness to launch an attack against you.
2. When demonic spies are sent against you.
3. When anti-favour forces are warring against you.
4. When iron-like horses are being invoked upon you by ancestral powers.
5. When you are a victim of multiple bondage.
6. When demonic powers have vowed that you will not cross a particular line.
7. When you are a victim of constant dream attacks.
8. When you are surrounded by terrible enemies.
9. When wicked powers from your place of birth have predicted that you will not make it in life.
10. When stubborn pursuers are almost catching up with you.
11. When the powers of the emptier are bent on draining your destiny.

PRAYER POINTS

1. O south wind, blow with violence against every evil wind targeted against my life, in the name of Jesus.
2. O south wind, blow across the rivers, across the valleys, across the mountains, and sweep away my deeply entrenched enemies, in the name of Jesus.
3. O south wind, move in a powerful way and put to shame every power of the oppressor, in the name of Jesus.
4. O south wind of the Lord, arise by your power and by your glory

and demolish the citadel and the stronghold of darkness, in the name of Jesus.

5. Every agenda of darkness in my life be scattered by the south wind, in the name of Jesus.
6. Every evil word spoken against my life be scattered by the South wind, in the name of Jesus.
7. Every power militating against my destiny be scattered by the south wind, in the name of Jesus.
8. Every incantation and evil word spoken against my life, be scattered by the south wind, in the name of Jesus.

WEAPON 66

SPIRIT OF DEEP SLEEP

- ***THIS IS A SUPER WEAPON FOR SUPER WARFARE.***
- ***IT IS TO BE USED BY CAPTIVES OF THE STRONGMAN.***
- ***IT IS A WEAPON THAT WILL SEND DEATH SENTENCE UPON WITCHCRAFT.***
- ***YOU CAN USE THIS WEAPON WHEN YOU WANT TO ORDER THE POWERS THAT HAVE VOWED THAT YOU WILL NOT REST TO EMBRACE THE SLEEP OF DEATH.***
- ***THIS IS ONE WEAPON YOU CAN USE WHEN YOU ARE CONFRONTED BY TERRIBLE NOISES FROM THE REALM OF DARKNESS.***
- ***USE THIS WEAPON WHEN YOU WANT TO DISGRACE STUBBORN PURSUERS.***

The weapons that God has provided for our victory and deliverance are strong and dynamic. The methods of divine operations are diverse. The instruments are awesome. When God wants to deal with the enemy in an unforgettable manner, he sends the spirit of deep sleep against him. The weapon of the spirit of deep sleep is a spiritual anaesthesia that lulls the enemy to sleep. By the time those who are in the camp of the enemy wake up they will behold multiple casualties. Some enemies may not even wake up at all.

When God wants to confuse the enemy he uses the weapon of deep sleep. Sleep is one of the mysteries of life. When an army general sleeps whatever happens will remain unknown to him. If you want God to disgrace your enemies just invoke the spirit of deep sleep upon them. This weapon will make them to behave like drunkards while the divine operation is being performed.

A DIVINE PLOY

Wherever demonic agents are trying to harass you and make you restless in life you must make use of prayer points that will make a deep sleep to fall upon them. When some enemies declare war against you saying "over their dead bodies" you can decide to launch them into a deep sleep and make them numb temporarily. In that state of stupor or deep sleep, God would have brought you out of the cage of bondage before they recover themselves.

If you pray enquiry prayers to know why believers go from one deliverance programme to another without any positive change, It is because those who ministered deliverance as well as the candidate are yet to make use of the weapon of deep sleep.

A STRATEGY

You need this weapon when you want the strongman to release his captives. You need this prayer when you are dealing with stubborn witchcraft. When this weapon is in place stubborn pursuers will be thrown out of business. Charmers and powers that use incantations will suddenly discover that their memory becomes blank. This weapon can deal with gaints in the kingdom of darkness. The Bible says. **Isaiah 29:10**

> ***"For the LORD hath poured out upon you the spirit of deep sleep, and hath closed your eyes: the prophets and your rulers, the seers hath he covered."***

Romans 11:8

> ***"According as it is written, God hath given them the spirit of slumber, eyes that they should not see, and ears that they should not hear; unto this day."***

Beloved, spiritual warfare is not fought with human strength. The secret of victory can be found in the use of an appropriate spiritual strategy. **Isaiah 29:10**

> ***"For the LORD hath poured out upon you the spirit of deep sleep, and hath closed your eyes: the prophets and your rulers, the seers hath he covered."***

THE RESULTS

When deep sleep falls upon witches and wizards stubborn pursuers and the powers of your father's house, they will release you and let you go.

This particular weapon is useful for dealing with boasting powers. It is an appropriate weapon for nullifying evil decrees. When you are tired of ugly incidents and embarrassing attacks you need to command deep sleep upon the enemy and upon the powers behind your problem. If they ever wake up they will discover that you have escaped from the snare of the fowler.

PRAYER POINTS

1. My Father, send the horses and the rider assigned to trouble me into deep sleep, in the name of Jesus.
2. My Father, send every full time enemy assigned against me into deep sleep, in the name of Jesus.
3. O deep sleep of the Lord, fall upon every violent warfare targeted against me, in the name of Jesus.
4. My Father, put all my enemies into deep sleep, in the name of Jesus.
5. My Father, let my stubborn enemies sleep the sleep of death, in the name of Jesus
6. O deep sleep from the Lord, arise, trouble the troublers of my Israel, in the name of Jesus.
7. My Father, arise in Your rage and send deep sleep upon every coven assigned to give me midnight troubles, in Jesus name.
8. Every rage of the dark, every rage of the day, every rage by the enemy, be silenced by the deep sleep of the Lord, in the name of Jesus.

WEAPON

67

VENGEANCE OF THE LORD

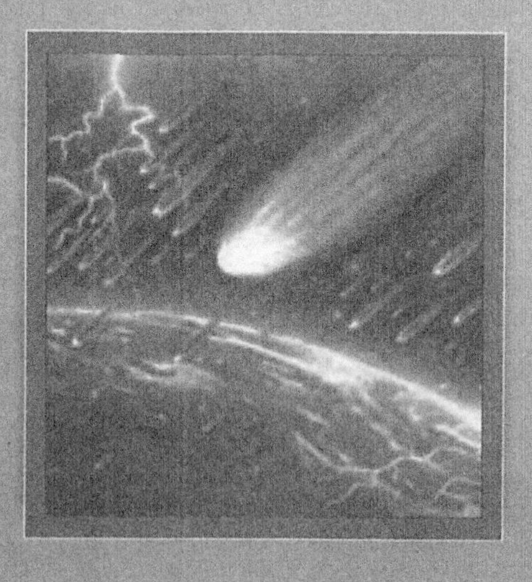

▶ *USE THIS WEAPON WHEN YOU WANT GOD TO ARISE AND LET HIS ENEMIES BE SCATTERED.*

▶ *USE THE WEAPON WHEN YOU WANT TO ACTIVATE DIVINE VENGEANCE.*

▶ *IT IS A POWERFUL WEAPON THAT WILL GRANT YOU FREEDOM FROM GENERATIONAL BONDAGE.*

▶ *USE THE WEAPON WHEN YOU WANT TO CAPTURE DESTINY ROBBERS.*

▶ *USE IT WHEN YOU WANT TO POSSESS YOUR POSSESSION.*

God is a God of vengeance. He uses instruments of vengeance. This is one instrument that God has reserved for Himself. Beloved, God knows the enemies that are supposed to be dealt with through the instruments of the weapon of the vengeance of the Lord. God watches all the activities or events that go on on earth. There are times when enemies hold the erroneous notion that bothers on getting away with their actions. Such people often loose sight of the fact that the eyes of God run to and fro throughout the whole universe.

NO ESCAPE

2Chronicles 16:9

> ***"For the eyes of the LORD run to and fro throughout the whole earth, to shew himself strong in the behalf of them whose heart is perfect toward him. Herein thou hast done foolishly: therefore from henceforth thou shalt have wars."***

Job 34:21

> ***"For his eyes are upon the ways of man, and he seeth all his goings."***

Prov 5:21

> ***"For the ways of man are before the eyes of the LORD, and he pondereth all his goings."***

Prov 15:3

> ***"The eyes of the LORD are in every place, beholding the evil and the good."***

Jer 16:17

"For mine eyes are upon all their ways: they are not hid from my face, neither is their iniquity hid from mine eyes."

GOD WATCHES

From the fore-going, God has established the fact that He watches what happens on earth meticulously. When the weapon of vengeance is used, God will inflict judgment upon wicked enemies. When the day of the Lord's vengeance begins and the weapon is unleashed upon the host of darkness casualties will be enormous. **Isaiah 34:8**

"For it is the day of the LORD'S vengeance, and the year of recompences for the controversy of Zion."

When your God comes with vengeance, no power can keep you in the cage of bondage for one split second. **Isaiah 35:4.**

"Say to them that are of a fearful heart, Be strong, fear not: behold, your God will come with vengeance, even God with a recompence; he will come and save you."

This weapon will draw the arrows of divine vengeance upon the enemy. When God introduces the mystery of vengeance your enemy and their offspring will suffer.

THE MYSTERY OF VENGEANCE

The weapon of divine vengeances does not know generational barriers. This weapon takes the Almighty to the field of battle. It is a weapon that makes God to arise and scatter His enemies. No wonder the Bible says. **Hebrew 10:31**

"It is a fearful thing to fall into the hands of the living God."

Invoke this weapon against the powers that have vowed not to let you go and God's vengeance will sweep them into the Red sea.

PRAYER POINTS

1. O God, arise in Your vengeance and avenge me of my adversaries, in the name of Jesus.
2. Let the spirit of the vengeance of the Lord arise in opposition and deal with the powers threatening my peace, in the name of Jesus.
3. O vengeance of the Lord, arise and cut off the tongue of the wicked fashioned against me, in the name of Jesus.
4. Let the vengeance of the Lord arise and defend my interest, in the name of Jesus.
5. Powers opposing my enlargement, receive the vengeance of the Lord, in the name of Jesus.
6. Oh heaven arise with the vengeance of the Lord and contend with those who contend against me, in the name of Jesus.
7. Power of the Lord, flow into every area of my life and let the vengeance of the Lord fight for me, in the name of Jesus.
8. Every opposition to my elevation, receive the vengeance of the Lord, in the name of Jesus.

WEAPON 68

HAMMER OF GOD

▶ USE THIS WEAPON WHEN YOU WANT GOD TO MANIFEST HIS AWESOME POWER.
▶ IT IS A POWERFUL OFFENSIVE WEAPON.
▶ IT IS A WEAPON OF THOROUGH AND TOTAL DELIVERANCE.
▶ THIS WEAPON WILL BRING YOU OUT OF SATANIC CAGES.
▶ IT WILL BULLDOZE AND CLEAR AWAY SATANIC ROAD-BLOCKS.

There are moments when God rises up in anger and makes the hammer of judgment to land upon the head of wicked powers that are challenging His authority. The hammer is an instrument of sudden judgment. When the hammer descends, the regime of the enemy is brought to an end. The hammer goes beyond a mere knock on the head.
The enemy who receives the hammer of the Almighty on his head will never live to tell the story. When the hammer lands on the head of witches and wizards, household wickedness, fetish priests, eaters of flesh and drinkers of blood and powers behind wicked arrows they are knocked down and they do repeated sommersaults and die.

A TRAGIC BLOW

The hammer of the Almighty is not a toy. The descent of its weight upon any satanic culprit will lead to instant tragedy. The weapon of divine hammer is described below. **Jer. 23:29**

> ***"Is not my word like as a fire? saith the LORD; and like a hammer that breaketh the rock in pieces?"***

Nahum 2:1

> ***"He that dasheth in pieces is come up before thy face: keep the munition, watch the way, make thy loins strong, fortify thy power mightily."***

God's hammer breaks, scatters and shatters. It will leave terrible casualties in the camp of the enemy. It dashes the head of the enemy in pieces in such a way that nothing can be gathered together again. This weapon is a befitting instrument for the stubborn heads of the enemy. Beloved if we had been making use of this type of weapon, it would have been impossible for a lot of God's children to be dribbled back and forth. This weapon is needed now more than at any time in the history of the world. Just one knock on the head of the enemy is what we need to win tough battles and obtain complete deliverance. We need hammer prayer points to hit the enemy's head on target. We need to locate the head of the enemy and break it to pieces without showing any form of mercy. Even when the head of the enemy can be likened to a rock, the hammer will break it to pieces. Now is the time to pick up the weapon of hammer from heaven's armoury and destroy the head of Goliath.

PRAYER POINTS

1. Father, use Your hammer to dispossess every strongman and every power holding tight to the instruments of my breakthroughs, in the name of Jesus.
2. Father, use Your hammer to shake down the power of the strong man that has stolen from me, in the name of Jesus.
3. By the hammer of the Holy Spirit, let every stronghold of the oppressor be dashed to pieces, in the name of Jesus.
4. By the hammer of the Lord, let every evil structure constructed against me be demolished, in the name of Jesus.
5. By the hammer of the Lord, I pull down the devices of the enemy, in the name of Jesus.
6. By the hammer of the Lord, I move to my place of destiny, in the name of Jesus.
7. By the hammer of the Lord, I disgrace every opposition, in the name of Jesus.
8. By the hammer of the Lord, I possess all my possessions, in the name of Jesus.
9. By the hammer of the Lord, I enter into my place of rest and remove every power blocking my way, in the name of Jesus.
10. By the hammer of the Lord, I enter into my place of celebration, in the name of Jesus.

WEAPON 69

THE SPIRIT OF JUDGEMENT AND BURNING

- ***THIS WEAPON CAN BE USED AT INSTANCES THAT BOTHER ON TOUCHING THE LORD'S ANOINTED.***
- ***THIS WEAPON WILL ENABLE YOU TO SUMMON ANGELS THAT HAVE NO MERCY.***
- ***YOU WILL NEED THIS WEAPON WHEN YOU WANT TO HANDLE BACK TO SENDER WARFARE.***
- ***USE IT WHEN YOU WANT TO TROUBLE YOUR TROUBLE.***
- ***IT IS A WEAPON YOU CAN USE WHEN YOU WANT THE ENEMY TO EXPERIENCE THE WRATH OF THE ALMIGHTY.***

The weapon we are considering here is a combination of two powerful weapons working harmoniously. The spirit of judgment is a strong weapon in itself, while the spirit of burning is another weapon. The moment the two are combined we will have a weapon that terrifies the enemy. The spirit of judgment is the spirit of vengeance. It is used when you know that you have had enough of satanic attacks. Here we are not just talking about the spirit of judgment but it is combined with what we call the spirit of burning. This weapon is used by God to address oppression, wickedness, injustice and all forms of uncommon wickedness emanating from the camp of the enemy.

AN INSTRUMENT OF FIRE

The spirit of burning judgment symbolizes the fire of God's wrath. It is an expression of the severity of God's anger. It is a threatening weapon when God unleashes the spirit of burning judgment upon the enemy, no one can determine the far-reaching consequences.
The spirit of judgment and burning is described below. **Isaiah 4:4**

> ***"When the Lord shall have washed away the filth of the daughters of Zion, and shall have purged the blood of Jerusalem from the midst thereof by the spirit of judgment, and by the spirit of burning."***

THE TARGET

The spirit of judgment and the spirit of burning have been reserved for those who touch the Lord's anointed, unrepentant enemies, household wickedness and the power of your father's house. One unique feature is that it displays the full wrath of the Almighty. The moment this weapon is in place, enemies will be dealt with, and dark agents will be forced to go into a mission of self destruction. There is no power of the enemy that can withstand the spirit of judgment and the spirit of burning. The combination of these two violent weapons will attack your attackers, make diviners mad and sentence satanic agents to the journey of no return. Wicked powers will be paid in their own coin. Destructive satanic agents will be destroyed; merciless powers will be mercilessly dealt with. The spirit of judgment and burning will take anti-breakthrough powers to the furnace of divine judgment.

THE EFFECT ON THE ENEMY

When you command the spirit of judgment and burning to locate wicked powers, you sentence them to utter destruction.

With the spirit of burning judgment your enemies are in trouble. The use of this weapon will activate your victory and cause power to change hands. Use this weapon today and you will move from the camp of victims to the camp of victors. You will attack your attackers with ease and your testimonies shall be glorious.

PRAYER POINTS

1. Every power that wants me to die, die in my place by the spirit of judgement and burning, in the name of Jesus.
2. Father, utilize the spirit of judgement and burning and burn to ashes every plantation of the enemy, in the name of Jesus.
3. Father, utilize the spirit of judgement and burning to swallow every power that has swallowed my destiny, in the name of Jesus.
4. Father, utilize the power of the spirit of judgement and burning to burn every serpent and scorpion assigned against me, in the name of Jesus.
5. Father, let the power of the spirit of judgement and burning be released to burn to ashes every plantation of darkness, in the name of Jesus.

WEAPON 70

THE INSTRUMENT OF DEATH

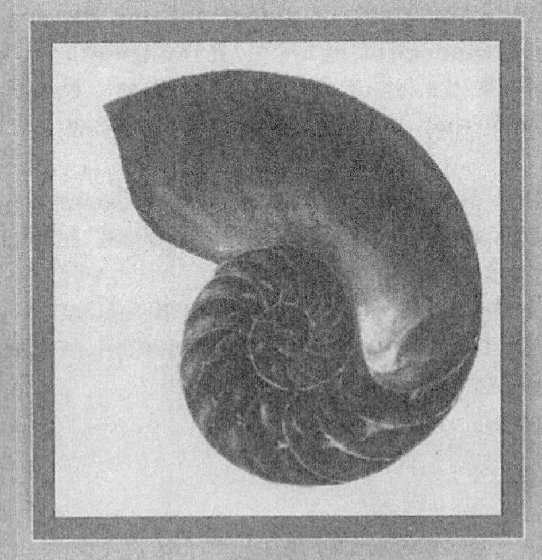

▶IT IS USEFUL WHEN YOU ARE CARRYING OUT AN OPERATION WIPE-OUT PROGRAMME.
▶ IT IS USEFUL WHEN YOU ARE TACKLING DEMONIC AGENTS.
▶ WITH THIS WEAPON THE SPIRIT OF DEATH AND HELL WILL BE BURIED.
▶IT WILL ENABLE YOU TO DISGRACE THE FORCES OF PHARAOH
▶ THIS IS AN INSTRUMENT OF DIVINE JUDGMENT.
▶ IT WILL ENABLE YOU TO TERMINATE THE AGENDA OF DARKNESS.

God has several instruments of death. He knows how to deal with your persecutors and oppressors. There are powers that do not give up unless they face the judgment of death. Beloved, he that must die must die if you have to move forward in life. You cannot experience total deliverance unless some powers die.

God has not established instruments of death in vain. Arrays of instruments of death are prepared by God waiting for you to dispatch them against wicked powers. An instrument of death is a weapon of termination. ***Psalm 7:13***

> ***"He hath also prepared for him the instruments of death; he ordaineth his arrows against the persecutors"***

OPERATION WIPE OUT

An instrument of death is a weapon for wiping out the powers of oppressors. An instrument of death has been prepared by God to deal with wicked powers. Beloved, some powers will not give up or stop their hot pursuit unless you throw instrument of death into their camp.

There are lots of instruments of death in the hand of the Almighty. When God kills the agenda of evil powers, instruments of death are in place. God can use instruments of death to kill the powers behind your oppression and suppression. When instruments of death locate demonic powers there will be tragic announcements in the camp of the enemy.

THE COMMAND

The power that will not allow you to fulfill your destiny must be commanded to die. You must learn how to dispatch multiple instruments of death into the camp of eaters of flesh and drinkers of blood. The powers that have turned you to a punching bag must be made to face instruments of death this is one weapon you must use if you want your deliverance to be total or final.

PRAYER POINTS

1. My Father, prepare the instruments of death to swallow every power planning my elimination, in the name of Jesus.
2. O God of Elijah, arise and prepare the instruments of death against my enemies, in the name of Jesus.
3. Father, employ Your instruments of death to stop every enemy that wants to stop me, in the name of Jesus.
4. Lord by Your power, I invoke the instrument of death against every evil voice speaking against me, in the name of Jesus.
5. I invoke the instrument of death against the voice of the grave speaking against me, in the name of Jesus.
6. I invoke the instrument of death against every power of the oppressor planning my elimination, in the name of Jesus.
7. Let the instruments of death from heaven visit the camp of my stubborn oppressors, in the name of Jesus.

WEAPON 71

VOICE OF GOD

▶IT IS A POWERFUL WEAPON OF DELIVERANCE.
▶ THIS WEAPON IS USEFUL WHEN YOU WANT TO EXPERIENCE VICTORY IN THE HUMAN COURT.
▶ USE THIS WEAPON WHEN YOU WANT GOD TO RAISE A VOICE FOR YOUR VICTORY AND DELIVERANCE.
▶ THIS WEAPON WILL SILENCE DEMONIC VOICES SPEAKING AGAINST YOUR DESTINY.
▶ THIS WEAPON WILL USHER YOU INTO YOUR GLORIOUS REALM.

One of the most powerful weapons that is available for use in our battles is the weapon of the voice of God. The voice of God is a voice of finality. The voice of God is a voice of deliverance. The voice of God is the voice of vengeance. The voice of God is loaded with fire.
When the voice of God sounds, evil ears will become deaf. The sound of the voice of God will spread disaster in the camp of your enemy. The voice of God will swallow the voice of bondage. The voice of God will render null and void the voice of failure and disgrace. When God speaks the earth shakes. When the Almighty speaks, demons tremble. When the voice of God thunders agents of darkness are struck down. The voice of God makes the enemy to go into repeated summersaults and die ultimately.

THE VOICE OF DELIVERANCE

The voice of God changes evil verdicts to declaration of victory. The voice of God makes diviners mad. The voice of God will make the voice of your enemies to pale into insignificance. The voice of God erases every handwriting of darkness. The voice of God turns defeat to victory. When the voice of God hits the cage of darkness your prison doors will become open. No power in hell, on earth or in the heavenlies can challenge the voice of the Almighty. The voice of God rings with a note of finality and echoes or reverberates your total deliverance. **Psalm 29:3-9**

> ***"The voice of the LORD is upon the waters: the God of glory thundereth: the LORD is upon many waters. The voice of the LORD is powerful; the voice of the LORD is full of majesty. The voice of the LORD breaketh the cedars; yea, the LORD breaketh the cedars of***

Lebanon. He maketh them also to skip like a calf; Lebanon and Sirion like a young unicorn. The voice of the LORD divideth the flames of fire. The voice of the LORD shaketh the wilderness; the LORD shaketh the wilderness of Kadesh. The voice of the LORD maketh the hinds to calve, and discovereth the forests: and in his temple doth every one speak of his glory."

One weapon that can make wars to cease is the weapon of the voice of God. Make use of these weapons today and total deliverance will be yours.

PRAYER POINT

1. Father, let Your voice open doors unto me, in the name of Jesus.
2. Let the voice of the Lord pass through the camp of my enemies and throw them into panic and confusion, in the name of Jesus.
3. Let the voice of the Lord rage against the camp of my enemies and confront every opposing power, in the name of Jesus.
4. Let the voice of the Lord eliminate every power speaking death to my situations, in the name of Jesus.
5. Let the voice of the Lord contend with any evil voice speaking against my destiny, in the name of Jesus.
6. I invoke the voice of God to scatter the camp of the oppressors, in the name of Jesus.
7. I invoke the voice of the Almighty to scatter the voice of witchcraft, in the name of Jesus.
8. O God release Your voice to scatter every power of enchanters and diviners working against me, in the name of Jesus.

WEAPON 72

PRAISE

▶ ***YOU NEED THIS WEAPON WHEN YOU WANT YOUR CELEBRATION TO BE COMPLETE.***

▶ ***USE THIS WEAPON WHEN YOU WANT TO MAGNETISE YOUR TESTIMONIES.***

▶ ***A POWERFUL WEAPON WHEN YOU ARE FIGHTING TOUGH BATTLES.***

▶ ***IT IS A WEAPON YOU CAN MAKE USE OF WHEN YOU WANT POWER TO CHANGE HANDS.***

▶ ***USE THIS WEAPON WHEN YOU WANT GOD TO ARISE AND FIGHT FOR YOU.***

This is, without doubt, one of the toughest weapons of spiritual warfare. The operation of this weapon is strange. The weapon of praises may appear simple but its operation is complex. It is one weapon that has dribbled and confused the enemy. Praise provokes the Most High God. When the Almighty is fully provoked He rises up as a man of war. If you want to invite God into your battles make use of the weapon of praises. Where the high praises of God is offered the devil is thrown into deep confusion.

The Bible makes it very clear that there is a type of praise that is an essential part of the instruments of warfare. ***Psalm 149:6***

"Let the high praises of God be in their mouth, and a twoedged sword in their hand;"

As we go into warfare you must be armed with the high praises of God in your mouth and the double-edged sword in your hand. This combination will unleash terror upon household wickedness and stubborn Pharaoh who has vowed not to let you go. This weapon is a subtle method for drawing God into your battle when you know that your power alone cannot handle some specific battles. As you fight with the sword you also summon angelic assistance through the praises of God in your mouth since the Bible has declared, ***Psalm 22:3***

"But thou art holy, O thou that inhabitest the praises of Israel.

Tough battles can be fought when you pick up the weapon of praises. Making a joyful noise unto the Lord will always launch an arrow into the camp of the enemy. ***Psalm 95:1-2***

"O come, let us sing unto the LORD: let us make a joyful noise to the rock of our salvation. Let us come before his presence with thanksgiving, and make a joyful noise unto him with psalms."

When your battle becomes tough, when you are struggling with confusion, when your strength is weak and hope appears lost, just sing the high praises of God and power will automatically change hands. Every warrior must know how to make use of the weapon of praises. When you offer extra ordinary praise unto God, the Almighty puts on His regalia as man of war. Woe betide that enemy that remains on the field of battle at that point.

Praise takes the battle to the next level. The mystery of praises is that when it is used as a weapon, the Almighty rises on his feet and each time our Commander in Chief decides to go to the war front Himself all manner of terrible weapons will automatically be moved to the battle field. The weapon of praises will cause power to change hands. The weapon of praises will place the camp of the enemy in jeopardy. Praises will ensure that there is monumental casualty among your stubborn pursuers.

The use of this weapon will make heads to roll among the rank and file of the power of the emptiers, the spirit of Herod, the power of household wickedness and the domain of ancestral powers. Praise is an irresistible weapon. Whenever this weapon is used, angels that have no mercy often descend upon wicked powers in high places. Put this weapon to use today and God will give you the head of your Goliath, the horses of Pharaoh and his riders.

PRAYER POINTS

1. My Father, let Your praises on my lips confuse my enemies, in the name of Jesus.
2. Oh Lord, let the power of Your high praises disgrace the enemy concerning my situation, in the name of Jesus.
3. Thou weapon of praises arise and silence every evil tongue speaking against my life, in the name of Jesus.
4. I invoke the mystery of divine praises against every power that has vowed that I will not sing my song and dance my dance, in the name of Jesus.
5. O Lord, let Your praises provoke my testimonies, in the name of Jesus.`

WEAPON 73

CONFUSION

- ***USE THIS WEAPON WHEN YOU WANT TO DEAL WITH SATANIC GANG-UP.***
- ***USE THIS WEAPON WHEN YOU ARE DEALING WITH HOUSEHOLD WICKEDNESS.***
- ***USE THIS WEAPON WHEN YOU WANT TO PUT AN END TO DEMONIC REBELLION.***
- ***THIS WEAPON WILL ENABLE YOU ARREST SATANIC AGENTS.***
- ***IT IS A WEAPON YOU CAN USE WHEN YOU WANT TO WREST YOUR DESTINY FROM THE HANDS OF STAR HUNTERS.***
- ***THIS WEAPON WILL DRIBBLE AND CONFUSE THE POWER OF THE EMPTIERS.***

God knows how to deal with the relentless foe. God knows how to handle boasting powers and wicked dark agents. It is interesting, however, that the methods which God will use will mesmerize the enemy. Often times, God's weapon can be likened to David's five smooth stones. Beloved, who would have thought that little pebbles could be used by God to bring down the lofty head of an enemy with amazing credentials like Goliath?

There are direct weapons and there are indirect weapons. While the enemy watches out for noticeable spiritual warfare weapons, little or no attention may be paid to indirect weapons. Yet, those indirect weapons may be as deadly as the obvious ones. The weapon of confusion is one of such subtle weapons.

A TOUGH WEAPON

When God wants to destroy the enemy, He uses the weapon of confusion. When the enemy receives the arrow of confusion, there will be loss of focus. This will enable you to jump out of the gate of bondage.

When Pharaoh received the arrow of confusion two things happened. Out of panic, he decided to let the children of Israel go. All of a sudden, the same arrow made him to change his mind. He decided to pursue Israel. Thus, when he got into the middle of the Red sea, tragedy struck. **Exodus 14:23-28**

> ***"And the Egyptians pursued, and went in after them to the midst of the sea, even all Pharaoh's horses, his chariots, and his horsemen. And it came to pass, that in the morning watch the LORD looked unto the***

> ***host of the Egyptians through the pillar of fire and of the cloud, and troubled the host of the Egyptians, And took off their chariot wheels, that they drave them heavily: so that the Egyptians said, Let us flee from the face of Israel; for the LORD fighteth for them against the Egyptians. And the LORD said unto Moses, Stretch out thine hand over the sea, that the waters may come again upon the Egyptians, upon their chariots, and upon their horsemen. And Moses stretched forth his hand over the sea, and the sea returned to his strength when the morning appeared; and the Egyptians fled against it; and the LORD overthrew the Egyptians in the midst of the sea. And the waters returned, and covered the chariots, and the horsemen, and all the host of Pharaoh that came into the sea after them; there remained not so much as one of them."***

TOTAL VICTORY

This weapon was also used when God wanted to subject the Philistines to resounding defeat. **1 Sam. 7:10**

> ***"And as Samuel was offering up the burnt offering, the Philistines drew near to battle against Israel: but the LORD thundered with a great thunder on that day upon the Philistines, and discomfited them; and they were smitten before Israel."***

The Lord thundered and there was confusion in the camp of the philistines.
God used the same weapon when He wanted to deal with the rebellion that took place during the building of the tower of Babel. **Gen. 11:7-9**

> ***"Go to, let us go down, and there confound their language, that they may not understand one another's speech. So the LORD scattered them abroad from thence upon the face of all the earth: and they left off to build the city. Therefore is the name of it called Babel; because the LORD did there confound the language of all the earth: and from thence did the LORD scatter them abroad upon the face of all the earth."***

You can use the weapon when you want to deal with the following problems.

1. Witchcraft attacks
2. The noise of boasting enemies
3. The agenda of territorial powers
4. The power of the emptiers
5. Household witchcraft
6. Demonic incantations
7. Network of enemies and attackers

PRAYER POINTS

1. My Father, send confusion to the camp of my enemies, in the name of Jesus.
2. Let confusion destroy my stubborn pursuers, in the name of Jesus.
3. Every whispering familiar spirit, be silenced by the confusion of the Lord, in the name of Jesus.
4. Every witch who speaks or mutters, be silenced by the confusion of the Lord, in the name of Jesus.
5. Opportunity wasters, I waste you by the confusion of the Lord, in the name of Jesus.
6. My Father, disappoint the devices of the crafty by the confusion of heaven, in the name of Jesus.

WEAPON

74

DRY WIND

SPIRITUAL WEAPON & DELIVERANCE GUIDE

- ***USE THIS WEAPON WHEN YOU WANT TO EXHIBIT HOLY ANGER.***
- ***USE THIS WEAPON WHEN YOU WANT TO SUFFOCATE WICKED AGENTS OF DARKNESS.***
- ***YOU MUST USE THIS WEAPON WHEN YOU HAVE DECIDED THAT POWER MUST CHANGE HANDS.***
- ***IT IS A WEAPON THAT MUST BE USED WHEN YOU WANT TO ARREST THE POWERS BEHIND YOUR BONDAGE.***
- ***YOU NEED THIS WEAPON WHEN YOU WANT TO DISGRACE POWERS THAT ARE WAITING FOR YOU AT THE COAST OF YOUR TESTIMONY.***
- ***USE THIS WEAPON WHEN YOU HAVE DISCOVERED THE SECRETS OF THE DARK KINGDOM.***
- ***YOU MUST USE THIS WEAPON WHEN YOU WANT THE ENEMY TO VOMIT YOUR BREAKTHROUGHS.***

God is sufficiently aware of the length which the enemy has gone in attacking His children. When God opens your eyes to the huge damage done by satanic agents you will be angry beyond description. The devil has done lots of damages in the lives of individuals, families, communities and nations.

Beloved, the field of humanity is littered with causalities. Many have died. Several destinies have been buried. Tragedies have become monumental and there are terrible losses every wherever. The powers that bite without remnant are on rampage. Bloodsuckers and flesh eaters have switched to a tough gear. Hence, the devil has recruited an innumerable company of wicked hands in order to perfect his vicious agenda. Unless we resort to the use of equally terrible weapons, move damages will be suffered.

We cannot afford to fold our hands.

AN AGGRESSIVE WEAPON

This is the time to increase our aggression and take our prayer temperature to a level that is dangerous or inimical to the kingdom of darkness. Beloved, we must go for the toughest weapons in God's armory. One of the outstanding weapons is the weapon of the dry wind. When this weapon is used, there will be disaster in the camp of the enemy. Lamentations and woe will fill the air. The tragedy that has been schemed for you will be heaped upon all wicked enemies assaulting your life and destiny.

The weapon of dry wind is a terrible one. **Jer. 4:11**

> ***"At that time shall it be said to this people and to Jerusalem, A dry wind of the high places in the wilderness toward the daughter of my people, not to fan, nor to cleanse,"***

SUFFOCATING VAPOURS

This kind of wind can be described as pestilential wind characterized by suffocating vapours and propelled by pillars of sand collected by the whirl wind. God uses this weapon when He wants to orchestrate a devastating invasion upon the arena of the enemy. The dry wind describes the hot and withering wind from the eastern desert. It conveys terrible desolations being a vehicle of divine judgment. Beloved the dry wind is terrific and destructive, blowing across sandy deserts. According to the name of this wind, it destroys. When the dry wind sweeps over the high places of the enemy, there will be terrible catastrophes. The weapon of the dry wind can be used to command the resources of the enemy to dry up. It can be used to blast and scorch the agenda of darkness. It is stormy and furious. When this weapon is used it will blow away everything that comes on its way. The dry wind, beloved, is far from being a peaceful wind. It is a weapon that portrays the extent of the anger of the Almighty.

WASTE THE WASTERS

This weapon will waste wasting powers. It will destroy destructive powers. When God releases the dry wind from His armoury you will experience victory. Wicked satanic agents will be wickedly dealt with by this uncommon weapon. This weapon will put an end to satanic rebellion. It will make powers that are stopping you from singing your song and dancing gloriously to fall down and die. Use this weapon today and your story will change.

PRAYER POINTS

1. Father, I provoke the dry wind against the enemy, in the name of Jesus.
2. Let the power of the dry wind arise and cause confusion in the camp of my enemies, in the name of Jesus.
3. Thou power of the dry wind, drive away every rain of sorrows,

in the name of Jesus.

4. Thou power of the dry wind, disgrace every plantation of darkness and blow them away, in the name of Jesus.
5. Thou power of the dry wind, quench the power of Satanic rain fighting against my destiny, in the name of Jesus.
6. Thou power of the dry wind, arrest every rain of darkness falling in the garden of my destiny, in the name of Jesus.
7. Oh dry wind, arise and confuse the camp of my enemies, in the name of Jesus.

WEAPON 75

THE WRATH OF GOD

SPIRITUAL WEAPON & DELIVERANCE GUIDE

▶ THIS IS A WEAPON OF VENGEANCE.
▶YOU CAN USE THIS WEAPON WHEN YOU ARE FIGHTING TOUGH AND REPEATED BATTLES.
▶YOU CAN USE THIS WEAPON AGAINST STUBBORN PURSUERS.
▶THIS WEAPON CAN BE USED WHEN YOU WANT TO CONFRONT FAMILY WITCHCRAFT.
▶ THIS WEAPON IS TO BE USED WHEN YOU WANT TO CONFRONT THE ENEMIES OF THE GOSPEL.
▶THIS WEAPON CAN BE USED TO DISGRACE STUBBORN PHARAOH.
▶THIS WEAPON CAN BE USED TO UNSEAT ANY EVIL KING TROUBLING YOUR DESTINY.

This is one of the toughest weapons of deliverance and spiritual warfare. It is a weapon that no power from the kingdom of darkness can withstand. When the battle gets hot and you are confronted by wicked enemies, you should simply go to the armoury of the Almighty and release the weapon of the wrath of God upon satanic agents. When God is furious, anything can happen. The Almighty shows his military might when His anger is provoked. His wrath is released in a manner that is simply indescribable. **Exodus 15:4-7**

> ***"Pharaoh's chariots and his host hath he cast into the sea: his chosen captains also are drowned in the Red sea. The depths have covered them: they sank into the bottom as a stone. Thy right hand, O LORD, is become glorious in power: thy right hand, O LORD, hath dashed in pieces the enemy. And in the greatness of thine excellency thou hast overthrown them that rose up against thee: thou sentest forth thy wrath, which consumed them as stubble."***

In the above passage, God cast Pharaoh and His chariots into the sea. When the weapon of the wrath of God is used, it can sentence your enemy to total burial in the grave or in the sea. From this passage we discover that God can decide to send forth His wrath which consumes in a devastating manner. When this weapon is unleashed upon the enemy there will be lots of troubles. **Num 11:33**

> ***"And while the flesh was yet between their teeth, ere it was chewed, the wrath of the LORD was kindled against the people, and the LORD***

smote the people with a very great plague."

When the wrath of God was kindled, He smote them with a great plague. You can invoke God's wrath upon stubborn powers. You can also execute the fierce wrath of God upon powers that have vowed that your destiny will remain buried in oblivion. **1Sam 28:18**

> ***"Because thou obeyedst not the voice of the LORD, nor executedst his fierce wrath upon Amalek, therefore hath the LORD done this thing unto thee this day."***

Beloved, you can command God's anger to consume the enemy. **Psalm 90:7**

> ***"For we are consumed by thine anger, and by thy wrath are we troubled."***

You can also ask the wrath of God to trouble those who trouble you. When you want to deal with powers that bite without remnant, you simply command your enemies to drink the wine of the wrath. **Rev 14:10**

> ***"The same shall drink of the wine of the wrath of God, which is poured out without mixture into the cup of his indignation; and he shall be tormented with fire and brimstone in the presence of the holy angels, and in the presence of the Lamb:"***

When these powers persist stubbornly, you can, therefore, go ahead and pour the wrath of God without mixture. When you command the enemy to drink from the cup of divine indignation the consequences are far reaching.
2 Chronicles 36:16-17

> ***"But they mocked the messengers of God, and despised his words, and misused his prophets, until the wrath of the LORD arose against his people, till there was no remedy. Therefore he brought upon them the king of the Chaldees, who slew their young men with the sword in the house of their sanctuary, and had no compassion upon young man or maiden, old man, or him that stooped for age: he gave them all into his hand".***

According to the above passage when the weapons of the wrath of God are unleashed upon the enemy, you will record unchallengeable victory. For example, you can pray saying "O thou wrath of God arise against the powers of my father's house and set me free". You can also pray "O God of war, Arise in your anger and deal with every witchcraft gang-up against my destiny. You can also invoke this weapon against hidden stubborn enemies by saying ***"O God, be angry with my enemies and have no compassion upon them".***

When the wrath of God is opened the enemy will stagger like a drunkard and consequently fall into the pit that was dug for you. The powers that have vowed saying, over their dead bodies will you sing your song and dance your dance, will meet their waterloo. Use this weapon today and a divine volcano will bury every power that is carrying out evil assignments against your life.

PRAYER POINTS

1. Father, arise in Your wrath and pursue my pursuer, in the name of Jesus.
2. Let the power of your wrath put every digger of holes against my life into their holes, in the name of Jesus.
3. O wrath of the most high God, arise and frustrate my enemies, in the name of Jesus.
4. Let the fire of divine wrath arrest my arresters and contend with those who contend with me, in the name of Jesus.
5. O God, arise in your wrath and put to shame every power of the oppressor, in the name of Jesus.
6. O wrath of the most high God, arise and possess my possessions for me, in the name of Jesus.

WEAPON 76

WASTERS

SPIRITUAL WEAPON & DELIVERANCE GUIDE

▶ *THIS WEAPON CAN BE USED WHEN YOU WANT TO WASTE THE WASTERS.*

▶ *YOU CAN USE THIS WEAPON WHEN YOU WANT TO SUBJECT PHARAOH AND HIS ARMY TO INSTANT BURIAL.*

▶ *YOU CAN USE THIS WEAPON TO ORDER THE POWER OF THE OCCULT TO SOMERSAULT AND DIE.*

▶ *THIS WEAPON COMES HANDY WHEN YOU WANT TO DEAL WITH ANCESTRAL WICKEDNESS.*

▶ *YOU CAN MAKE USE OF THIS WEAPON WHEN YOU WANT TO DEAL WITH POWERS THAT ARE BEHIND PROLONGED BATTLES*

▶ *THIS IS THE WEAPON TO USE WHEN YOU WANT DRINKERS OF BLOOD AND EATERS OF FLESH TO EAT THEIR OWN FLESH AND DRINK THEIR OWN BLOOD.*

▶ *THIS IS A WEAPON YOU CAN USE WHEN YOU ARE DEALING WITH TERRITORIAL POWERS.*

As long as Satan continues to create deadly weapons of destruction, the Almighty will continue to demonstrate His supremacy. **Proverb 16:4**

> ***"The LORD hath made all things for himself: yea, even the wicked for the day of evil."***

God has, in His armoury, the weapon of the waster. When this weapon is unleashed upon wicked wasting powers they are also wasted. There is a squad of the divine military force that has been given the assignment of wasting the wasters. They make use of the weapon of divine wastage. You can make use of this weapon when your destiny is under the threat of wastage by household wickedness and witchcraft destroyers. God wants you to summon divine wasters and invoke them to unleash terror upon ancestral wickedness. When you are in the midst of tough battles and you suddenly discover that evil powers have vowed that you will remain restless like the sea, you simply need to command an invasion of divine wasting powers upon demonic agents and evil emissaries.

This is the weapon to use when your destiny is being wasted fiercely and your energy is fast ebbing out. You need to use this weapon when you discover that your virtue, talents, and benefits are under the attack of the spirit of wastage.

You can take up these weapons by commanding the wasters to be wasted by the divine weapon that would swallow all the powers that are bent on wasting your destiny, until nothing of value is left. God has created this weapon to prove to all agents of darkness that, much as they delight in wasting human destinies, there are divine weapons of wastage in God's armoury. The role of this weapon is to waste wicked wasters. **Isaiah 54:16**

> ***"Behold, I have created the smith that bloweth the coals in the fire, and that bringeth forth an instrument for his work; and I have created the waster to destroy."***

Both the powers that waste and their weapons will be wasted when they come across the department that wastes in God's army. As long as divine weapons remain available for use, all weapons that are fashioned against you shall not prosper in the name of Jesus. **Isaiah 54:17**

> ***"No weapon that is formed against thee shall prosper; and every tongue that shall rise against thee in judgment thou shalt condemn. This is the heritage of the servants of the LORD, and their righteousness is of me, saith the LORD."***

This is the kind of thing that happens when the serpent of the magicians are swallowed by Moses' serpent. The satanic mission of wastage will be brought to an abrupt end when divine wasters descend upon them and reduce them to rubbles. This is the weapon to use when you want to confront terrible powers that are on a mission of total destruction. When enemies multiply and drinkers of blood and eaters of flesh increase, God can create an army of wasters to waste them. When you discover that the spirit of Pharaoh will not let you go, you can invoke the spirit of the waster to waste them. Some powers may not bow unless you invoke the weapon of the waster upon them. Use this weapon today and your stubborn Pharaoh will have no option than to let you go after both Pharaoh and his hosts are wasted in a watery grave.

PRAYER POINTS

1. Oh God arise and send Your wasters to waste every enemy of destiny, in the name of Jesus.
2. Oh God arise, and let the power of Your wasters descend upon the power of darkness and reduce them to rubbles, in the name of Jesus.
3. Oh God arise and let the wasters waste eaters of flesh and drinkers of blood, in the name of Jesus.
4. Wasters from heaven, waste every force of Goliath assigned against me, in the name of Jesus.
5. Wasters of God arise dislocate every stubborn power planted to waste my life, in the name of Jesus.
6. Let the wasters of God waste all the wasters assigned against me, in the name of Jesus.
7. By the power of the Holy Ghost, wasters of heaven arise and waste every company of the oppressor assigned to trouble me, in the name of Jesus.

WEAPON 77

VENGEANCE OF GOD

- ***THIS IS A WEAPON OF TERROR.***
- ***YOU CAN MAKE USE OF THIS WEAPON WHEN YOU WANT TO DEAL WITH LOCAL WITCHCRAFT.***
- ***USE THIS WEAPON WHEN YOU WANT TO FORCEFULLY FEED THE ENEMY WITH DIVINE POISON.***
- ***YOU CAN MAKE USE OF THIS WEAPON WHEN YOU ARE CONFRONTING POWERS THAT ARE INSULTING YOUR GOD.***
- ***YOU CAN USE THIS WEAPON WHEN YOU WANT TO PUT AN END TO THE ENEMY'S USELESS ASSIGNMENT.***
- ***IT IS A WEAPON TO BE USED BY SEASONED WARRIORS AND PRAYER ADDICTS.***
- ***YOU CAN MAKE USE OF THIS WEAPON WHEN YOU WANT TO PROVOKE GOD TO UNLEASH TERROR ON POWERS THAT ARE BENT ON TERMINATING YOUR LIFE OR YOUR DESTINY.***

Battles are inevitable. As long as there are opposing forces, we all continue to fight battles in various departments of life. Beloved, victory is not cheap. But, the victory that comes after conquest is sweet. Perhaps, you have discovered that you have lots of battles to fight, I put it to you, beloved, that it is simply because you have a colourful destiny like Joseph in the scriptures. Joseph was destined for high places. Hence, the journey of his life was punctuated by repeated battles. Since God had earmarked him for the highest point on the ladder of progress, he faced uncommon battles. If you have discovered that your battles are fierce, tough and persistent, you can decide to deal squarely with the enemy by converting your battles to God's battles. **1Sam 17:47**

> ***"And all this assembly shall know that the LORD saveth not with sword and spear: for the battle is the LORD'S, and he will give you into our hands." 2Cronicles 20:15***

And he said, Hearken ye, all Judah, and ye inhabitants of Jerusalem, and thou king Jehoshaphat, Thus saith the LORD unto you, Be not afraid nor dismayed by reason of this great multitude; for the battle is not yours, but God's.
God's manner of fighting battles differs from the way you will personally fight your own battles. When your battle becomes God's battles, one of the weapons God uses is the weapon of vengeance. God releases the weapon of vengeance

when He has surveyed the entire spectrum of the wickedness of the kingdom of darkness and he has decided, fully, to unleash His vengeance, fire for fire, upon them. When the weapon of divine vengeance is used, stubborn enemies will never live to tell the story. ***Isaiah 35:4***

> ***"Say to them that are of a fearful heart, Be strong, fear not: behold, your God will come with vengeance, even God with a recompence; he will come and save you."***

Even if you find yourself bound and tied in the enemy's cage you can invoke the weapon of God's vengeance. God will come with vengeance and a powerful recompense upon the enemy in order to rescue or save you.
The vengeance of God is the weapon to use when you are tired of being a captive of the terrible. It is an appropriate weapon for sending evil arrows back to sender. It is the most powerful weapon to use when you want to pursue, overtake and recover all. It is a powerful weapon to use when eaters of flesh and drinkers of blood are feasting on your destiny. It is the weapon to use when you want the enemy to vomit your swallowed blessings. It is a useful weapon when you are bent on giving enemies a raw deal which will subsequently force them to taste the same poison which they once offered you in order to steal your destiny. When the weapon of the vengeance of God is fully invoked upon satanic agents, you will simply stand still and witness the destruction of destructive powers. The vengeance of God is a terrific weapon. Once the weapon is activated, the devastation it will cause will be monumental. Whatever the enemy has done against your life and destiny, you can bring in the day of the Lord's vengeance. **Isaiah 34:8**

> ***"For it is the day of the LORD'S vengeance, and the year of recompences for the controversy of Zion".***

With the day of the Lord's vengeance, the enemy's days are numbered. When God starts with His vengeance you will begin to witness what it means to see God in action.

PRAYER POINTS

1. O God, arise in Your vengeance and avenge me of my adversaries, in the name of Jesus.
2. Let the spirit of the vengeance of the Lord arise in opposition and deal with the powers threatening my peace, in the name of Jesus.
3. O vengeance of the Lord, arise and cut off the tongue of the wicked fashioned against me, in the name of Jesus.
4. Let the vengeance of the Lord arise and defend my interest, in the name of Jesus.
5. Powers opposing my enlargement, receive the vengeance of the Lord, in the name of Jesus.
6. Oh heaven arise with the vengeance of the Lord and contend with those who contend against me, in the name of Jesus.
7. Power of the Lord, flow into every area of my life and let the vengeance of the Lord fight for me, in the name of Jesus.
8. Every opposition to my elevation, receive the vengeance of the Lord, in the name of Jesus.

WEAPON 78

WORMWOOD

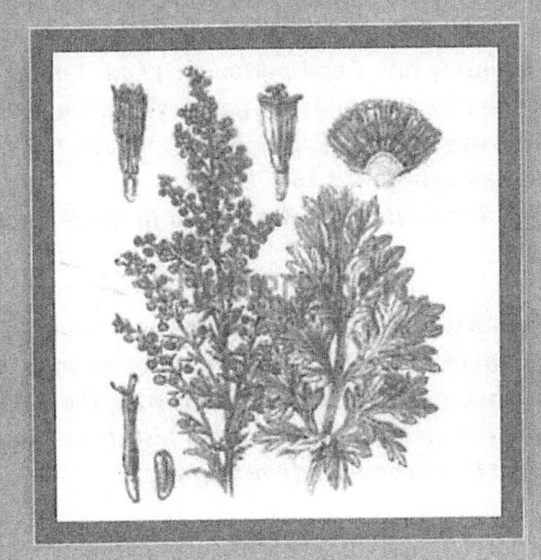

SPIRITUAL WEAPON & DELIVERANCE GUIDE

- ***THIS IS YOUR WEAPON OF DOMINION AND VICTORY.***
- ***YOU CAN MAKE USE OF THIS WEAPON WHEN YOU WANT TO PUNISH AND DISGRACE SATANIC AGENTS OR DEMONS SENT ON WICKED ASSIGNMENTS AGAINST YOU.***
- ***THIS WEAPON CAN BE USED TO DEAL WITH SATANIC OPPOSITION.***
- ***USE THIS WEAPON WHEN YOU WANT TO RULE IN THE MIDST OF YOUR ENEMIES.***
- ***YOU CAN MAKE USE OF THIS WEAPON WHEN YOU ARE CONFRONTED BY MULTIPLE ENEMIES.***
- ***YOU CAN MAKE USE OF THIS WEAPON TO SCATTER ANY FORM OF SATANIC GANG-UP.***
- ***USE THIS WEAPON WHEN YOU WANT THE ENEMY TO TASTE THE RAW POWER OF GOD.***

There are various classes of weapons. Some weapons are introduced when God is provoked and He is extremely angry with the enemy. Wormwood can be classified as one of the violent weapons that can be found in the armoury of God. God has created the weapon in order to put paid to the ugly uprisings coming from the kingdom of darkness. When you listen to stories of terrible ordeals which people are going through, you will understand why God has introduced a line of weapons that are very tough. To gain insight into the potency and uses of this weapon, it is necessary that we take a look into the depths of the connotations of the word wormwood. The word wormwood can only be compared in intensity with the word gall, it is extremely bitter, tough and harsh. Wormwood is an intensely bitter and poisonous plant. Consequently, it is a symbol for whatever is nauseating and destructive. When a weapon is described as having the qualities of wormwood, it shows that it has bitter properties and grave consequences. **Lamentations 3:15**

> ***"He hath filled me with bitterness, he hath made me drunken with wormwood."***

The Bible speaks of a root that bears gall and wormwood. **Deut 29:18**

> ***"Lest there should be among you man, or woman, or family, or tribe, whose heart turneth away this day from the LORD our God, to go and serve the gods of these nations; lest there should be among you a root that beareth gall and wormwood;"***

When this root is released into the enemy's camp, all the power that have ganged up against your life, progress and destiny will be forced to drink acidic, bitter, and deadly wormwood. **Jer 9:15**

> ***"Therefore thus saith the LORD of hosts, the God of Israel; Behold, I will feed them, even this people, with wormwood, and give them water of gall to drink."***

This weapon is useful when you have a raw deal from the hands of household wickedness and you want to fight back. You need this weapon when you want to turn things upside down in the enemy's camp. You need this weapon when you want to weaken the forces that are giving you a tough fight. You need this weapon when you want to inflict on the enemy, one devastating blow that will remain unforgettable. It is an appropriate weapon to use when you have had enough of bitter experiences and you want to silence the voice of oppression and put an end to shame and ignominy. The instrument can be used when you want to turn the tide and force eaters of flesh and drinkers of blood to eat their own flesh and drink their own blood. You can use this weapon when you want to sentence hidden wicked enemies to a biter end. **Proverb 5:4**

> ***But her end is bitter as wormwood, sharp as a two-edged sword.***

Unleashing the weapon of wormwood on the enemy can be likened to giving witches and wizards poison to drink. It is a weapon you can use when you want to give enemies of your destiny a large dose of the fierce wrath of the Almighty. Introducing the weapon of wormwood can be likened to taking a barrel of poison to the field of battle. This weapon will enable you to afflict the powers that afflict you. This is a weapon to be used by advanced students in the school of spiritual warfare.

PRAYER POINTS

1. Wormwood from heaven, locate every plantation of darkness in my life and uproot them, in the name of Jesus.
2. Wormwood from heaven, eat up every satanic seed planted in

the garden of my life, in the name of Jesus.

3. Let the commandment of the Lord go forth and deliver me from every plantation of the enemy using the weapon of the wormwood, in the name of Jesus.
4. Wormwood of the most high God invade every house of the strongman and pursue them out of their hiding places, in the name of Jesus.
5. I invoke the power of the wormwood of God to reposes and to reposition everything the enemy has stolen, in the name of Jesus.
6. Let the wormwood from heaven go forth in the thunder of thy power to send confusion into the camp of my enemies, in the name of Jesus.
7. I use the weapon of the wormwood to clear every blockage in my way, in the name of Jesus.

WEAPON 79

ROD OF IRON

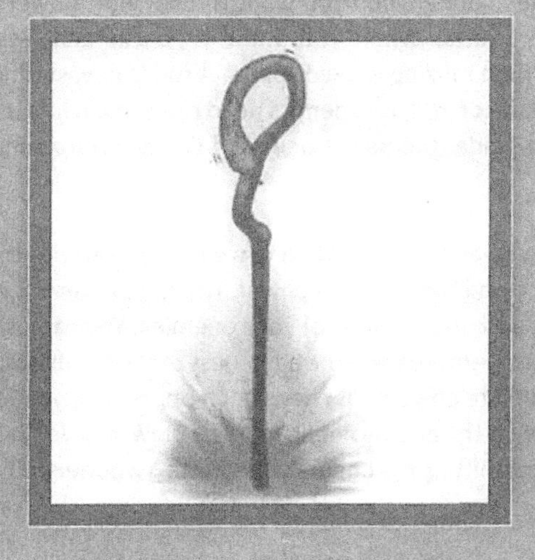

► *YOU CAN USE THIS WEAPON WHEN YOU WANT TO OVERPOWER SATANIC WICKEDNESS.*
► *USE THIS WEAPON WHEN YOU ARE SURROUNDED BY AN ARRAY OF WICKED FORCES.*
► *YOU CAN DISCHARGE THIS WEAPON AGAINST ANY FORM OF SATANIC INVASION.*
► *YOU CAN MAKE USE OF THIS WEAPON WHEN YOU WANT TO BURY POWERS THAT HAVE GATHERED TOGETHER TO BURY YOU.*
► *YOU CAN MAKE USE OF THIS WEAPON WHEN YOU WANT TO FIGHT STRATEGIC BATTLES.*
► *THE WEAPON OF GOD'S DAGGER CAN BE USED WHEN YOU WANT TO FINISH POWERS SENT ON A WICKED MISSION AGAINST YOU.*
► *YOU CAN MAKE USE OF THIS WEAPON WHEN YOU WANT TO DRIBBLE WICKED POWERS THAT ARE CLOSE TO YOU.*

The rod is an instrument for exercising dominion over the enemy. It is a weapon that can be used to tame obstinate, stubborn, relentless and rebellious foes. When the iron rod of God's anger descends heavily upon agents of darkness, they shall be completely devastated. You need to use the rod of iron when you want to deal with oppressors. The rod of iron denotes the severity of divine judgment, it is used when you want to shatter and scatter the enemy like a broken bottle that cannot be gathered together.
This weapon comes handy when you want to deal with powers that will not easily submit. It is used when you want to crush and destroy powers, principalities and high ranking wicked spirits. A rod is devastating enough, but when the rod is made of iron, no enemy's head can remain intact when hit. The enemy that comes under the heavy weight of the rod of iron shall be crushed and shattered.

The rod of iron is a weapon to use when you want to deal with the enemy with the use of the force and fury of God's power. The rod of iron is a weapon to use when you want to rule in the midst of your enemies. You can use this weapon when you want the enemy to taste the bitterness of the terrible power of God. It can be used to dislodge powers that have been oppressing you for quite a long time. It is useful when the enemy needs a deadly blow in order to stop troubling you. If you have been hitting the enemy's head with a wooden rod and nothing

has changed, you can introduce the rod of iron.
The rod of iron is a weapon that will make you an overcomer. It is your quickest way to the realm of victory and dominion over stubborn powers and oppressors. The rod of iron will give you the badge of conquest and earn you the title of an unconquerable warrior. This weapon is effective when you discover that there is an array of evil forces sent to destabilize you and swallow you up. It is the weapon to bring out when there is an evil gang-up against you and you are bent on celebrating the defeat of powers of darkness. Use this weapon today and the enemy will never be in doubt of the supremacy of the power of God.

PRAYER POINTS

1. Oh God, arise and dash my stubborn enemies to pieces with the rod of iron, in the name of Jesus.
2. Oh God, arise and put my enemies to shame with the rod of iron, in the name of Jesus.
3. Let the rod of iron arise and break every cauldron of darkness, in the name of Jesus.
4. Oh God, arise with Your rod of iron and pursue my pursuers back to the red sea, in the name of Jesus.
5. Oh rod of iron from heaven arise, pass through the camp of my enemies, in the name of Jesus.
6. O rod of iron, stamp, disgrace and defeat upon every power contesting my elevation and celebration, in the name of Jesus.
7. O rod of iron, dash in pieces every company of the wicked boasting against my God, in the name of Jesus.
8. O rod of iron, arise and smash to pieces every power mocking my prayer, in the name of Jesus.

WEAPON 80

DAGGER

▶ YOU CAN MAKE USE OF THIS WEAPON WHEN YOU ARE FIGHTING ANCESTRAL POWERS THAT HAVE CAUSED HAVOC IN YOUR ANCESTRY.

▶ YOU CAN MAKE USE OF THIS WEAPON WHEN YOU WANT TO EXTERMINATE, IN ONE FELL SWOOP, POWERS THAT WANT TO PUT YOU TO SHAME.

▶ YOU CAN USE THIS WEAPON WHEN YOU WANT YOUR ENEMY TO WITNESS THE FURY OF THE ALMIGHTY.

▶ THIS WEAPON CAN BE USED TO ATTACK THE ENEMY'S BASE AND SET IN MOTION, A PROGRAMME OF TOTAL ALIENATION.

▶ YOU CAN MAKE USE OF THIS WEAPON WHEN YOU WANT THE ENEMY TO FACE GOD'S IRRESISTIBLE WRATH.

▶ THIS IS A POWERFUL WEAPON FOR DEALING WITH ATTACKS FROM WITCH DOCTORS, OCCULT POWERS AND DEMONIC ARROWS.

▶ YOU CAN MAKE USE OF THIS WEAPON WHEN YOU WANT TO STOP SATANIC AGENTS FROM CARRYING OUT THEIR AGENDA.

▶ YOU CAN MAKE USE OF THIS WEAPON WHEN YOU WANT TO PERSECUTE THOSE WHO ARE PERSECUTING GOD'S CHILDREN.

The dagger is a short sword. It is a strategic weapon that can be used when victory becomes urgent and important. It is a weapon you can use when you want to confront enemies that are disturbing you. It is a weapon you can use when you want to disembowel demonic powers after the order of Ehud.

Judges 3:16

> ***"But Ehud made him a dagger which had two edges, of a cubit length; and he did gird it under his raiment upon his right thigh."***

You can use this weapon when you are dealing with powers that have come too close for comfort. It is a powerful weapon for strategic warfare. You can use this weapon to rip open the stomach of the enemy and paralyze wicked forces perpetually. This weapon is useful when you want to overpower environmental forces and powers that are closing in to the point of almost catching up with you. There is the weapon to use when unfriendly friends are at the verge of subjecting your destiny to untimely burial. It is a very powerful weapon and will lead you into divine rest. It can be used to terminate terminators and oppress oppressors.

You can use it when you want to attack the attackers of your destiny. It is a weapon to keep handy when you begin to sense an uprising of revolt and antagonism. Use it when familiar spirits and household witchcraft are trying to make your life restless. When you invoke the dagger of the Almighty against the powers that surround you, the dagger will hit them and make them to collapse. All deliverance ministers must learn how to make use of the dagger of divine judgment and retribution.

PRAYER POINTS

1. O dagger of the Lord, arise send confusion to the camp of my enemies, in the name of Jesus.
2. O heavens, bombard every evil gathering assigned against me with the dagger of the Lord, in the name of Jesus.
3. My Father, locate every hidden enemy of my soul with Your dagger, in the name of Jesus.
4. Where is the dagger of the God of Elijah? Pursue my pursuers, in the name of Jesus.
5. Every power shooting me from the dark, receive the dagger of the Lord, in Jesus' name.
6. O dagger of the Lord, arise in the thunder of Your power and paralyse my oppressors, in Jesus' name.
7. Drinkers of blood and eaters of flesh, hear the word of the Lord, receive the dagger of heaven, in the name of Jesus.
8. Dagger of the Lord, locate and destroy every enemy of my destiny, in the name of Jesus

WEAPON 81

DESTROYING STORMS

- *YOU CAN MAKE USE OF THIS WEAPON WHEN YOU ARE FIGHTING ENOUGH IS ENOUGH BATTLES.*
- *YOU CAN INVOKE THIS WEAPON AGAINST POWERS THAT ARE ON A SUICIDE MISSION.*
- *THIS IS A WEAPON TO BE USED WHEN YOU ARE DEALING WITH STUBBORN POWERS.*
- *YOU CAN USE THIS WEAPON WHEN YOU ARE DEALING WITH HIDDEN, WICKED ENEMIES.*
- *MAKE USE OF THIS WEAPON WHEN YOU WANT TO DISGRACE THE ENEMY OPENLY.*
- *YOU CAN MAKE USE OF THIS WEAPON WHEN YOU WANT TO ARREST WICKED FOUNDATIONAL POWERS.*
- *YOU CAN MAKE USE OF THIS WEAPON WHEN YOU WANT GOD TO DEAL DECISIVELY WITH ANY POWER THAT HAS DECLARED THAT YOU WILL NOT SING YOUR SONG AND DANCE YOUR DANCE.*
- *THIS IS A POWERFUL WEAPON OF UNCHALLENGEABLE VICTORY.*

There are weapons that can be used when you want to destabilize evil spies and demonic agents that are on a deadly assignment. Such powers may not budge when you make use of simple or ordinary weapons. You need a weapon that will produce far-reaching consequences. You need a weapon that can deal with a network of evil agents. You also need a weapon that can, in one fell-swoop, produce massive negative effects upon multiple enemies that are attacking you from several points.

You also need a weapon that can have blinding effect on powers that are sent to arrest and enslave you. You also need an instrument with which you can unleash divine judgment. This weapon of destroying storms is what stubborn enemies need if they must stop their evil activities.
This is the most effective weapon when you want to deal with ancestral forces that have become so fortified that they have obtained the keys for keeping you in the wicked cage of the enemy.

The destroying storm is one weapon you can use and you will capture Pharaoh and his hosts and consequently bury them in the sea of divine judgment. The destroying storm is one weapon that is cataclysmic. The moment it is released against the powers of your father's house there will be disaster. One primary function of the destroying storm is to completely exterminate every trace of oppression, domination, manipulation and satanic bondage. It flags off a storm that destroys the totality of the agenda of darkness. **Isaiah 28:2**

> ***"Behold, the Lord hath a mighty and strong one, which as a tempest of hail and a destroying storm, as a flood of mighty waters overflowing, shall cast down to the earth with the hand."***

The destroying storm functions as an unstoppable scourge of mighty waters. It will put to flight an entire company of forces of darkness. When it overflows, every power on its way is swept to a point of no-return. Beloved, God is a mighty warrior who has created the destroying storms in order to arrest, overpower, destabilize and destroy fetish arrows sent against your life and destiny.

When the destroying storm is at work, demons are scattered, witchcraft covens are turned upside down, and the powers of your father's house are paralysed.

When God releases a fierce stormy wind, the hands of wicked powers shall not perform their enterprise. The One behind the destroying storm is the "I am that I am", the Almighty. This weapon comes into operation when God wants to reveal His might and showcase His fierce wrath. This is one weapon that God releases and supervises when He wants to deal with the enemy in a devastating way. This is a weapon you can use when you want to break the backbone of the enemy. You can also use it when you want to inflict fatal wounds on the enemy. **Job 9:17**

> ***"For he breaketh me with a tempest, and multiplieth my wounds without cause."***

If you want to inflict leprosy upon the enemy you must invoke the devouring storms. To persecute your persecutor you need the weapon of the devouring storms. **Psalm 83:15**

> ***So persecute them with thy tempest, and make them afraid with thy storm.***

You can ask God to persecute your enemies with His destroying storm. Now is the time to make the enemy tremble. Use this weapon when you want to cause an alarm in the kingdom of darkness. You can subject the enemy to total instability, restlessness and impotence. Let the enemy taste the same horror which they inflict upon others.

PRAYER POINTS

1. Father, I invoke the weapon of destroying storm from the Lord against every power monitoring my destiny, in the name of Jesus.
2. Let destroying storm from the Lord pursue my pursuer, in the name of Jesus.
3. Let destroying storm from the Lord arrest my arresters, in the name of Jesus.
4. Let destroying storm from the Lord destroy my Goliath, in the name of Jesus.
5. Let destroying storm from the Lord scatter my oppressors, in the name of Jesus.
6. Let destroying storm from the Lord render blind, deaf and dumb every diviner divining against me, in the name of Jesus.
7. Let destroying storm from the Lord put to shame every operation of darkness, in the name of Jesus.

WEAPON

82

DESTROYER

► *YOU CAN MAKE USE OF THIS WEAPON WHEN YOU WANT TO DEAL WITH HOUSEHOLD WICKEDNESS.*

► *THIS WEAPON CAN BE USED WHEN YOU WANT GOD TO TURN THE TABLES AND GIVE YOU AN UNPRECEDENTED VICTORY.*

► *YOU CAN MAKE USE OF THIS WEAPON WHEN YOU WANT THE ENEMY TO TURN BACK.*

► *YOU CAN MAKE USE OF THIS WEAPON WHEN YOU WANT TO PUSH THE ENEMY INTO THE PIT OF TOTAL DEFEAT AND DESTRUCTION.*

► *YOU NEED THIS WEAPON WHEN YOU WANT YOUR STORY TO CHANGE.*

► *THIS IS A GREAT WEAPON TO USE WHEN YOU WANT TO EXPERIENCE THE TOTAL DEFEAT OF EVERY ENEMY OF YOUR DESTINY.*

► *YOU CAN USE THIS WEAPON WHEN YOU WANT TO HIT THE ENEMY ON TARGET.*

God is aware of the entire scope of the onslaught of evil powers. Hence, He has established certain weapons that will foster deliverance and enable His children to obtain victory when it matters most. What happens on the field of spiritual warfare can be likened to the ruthlessness that takes place during a wrestling tournament. God decides to give agents of darkness a dose of the bitterness, the horror, and the deadly pain which they inflict upon their victims.

There is a time to confront the enemy, fire for fire and subject the destroyers to utter destruction. Just as there are destroyers in the satanic kingdom God has stationed a team of divine destroyers in order to take captivity captive and imprison satanic warders. Destroyers can be dispatched from heaven and ordered to invade the enclaves of ancestral demons, witchcraft devourers, evil spies and eaters of flesh and drinkers of blood. When divine destroyers are invoked they will not rest until they have totally annihilated the company of evil destroyers.

You need this weapon when you have suffered for too long and you are at the verge of being reduced to a shadow of yourself by the powers of your father's house. You can invoke divine destroyers when you want to effect the exhuming of your buried virtues or glory. This weapon can be used when you want to possess your possessions and recover what demonic thieves or burglars have

stolen. You need to make use of this weapon when you want to silence voices that are bent on disgracing you.
This is the weapon to use when you want to arrest the evil tide of satanic plague. You can make use of this weapon when you want to arrest the tide of untimely death and instances of repeated accidents. When you dispatch the weapon of the destroyers, you will experience unchallengeable victory.
Exodus 12:23

> ***"For the LORD will pass through to smite the Egyptians; and when he seeth the blood upon the lintel, and on the two side posts, the LORD will pass over the door, and will not suffer the destroyer to come in unto your houses to smite you."*** **Exodus 22:12-13**

And if it be stolen from him, he shall make restitution unto the owner thereof. If it be torn in pieces, then let him bring it for witness, and he shall not make good that which was torn.
Beloved, you can command destroying angels to fall upon the camp of the powers that are destroying you and charge the angels not to spare any agent of darkness. **2 Sam 24:16**

> ***"And when the angel stretched out his hand upon Jerusalem to destroy it, the LORD repented him of the evil, and said to the angel that destroyed the people, It is enough: stay now thine hand. And the angel of the LORD was by the threshingplace of Araunah the Jebusite."***

Such angels must be commanded to slay unrepentant agents of darkness, witches and wizards and powers that bite without remnant. **Ezekiel 9:6**

Slay utterly old and young, both maids, and little children, and women: but come not near any man upon whom is the mark; and begin at my sanctuary. Then they began at the ancient men which were before the house.
Stubborn powers must be arrested and brought to book by sending destroying angels against them.

PRAYER POINTS

1. Let the power of the destroyer arise and swallow my swallowers, in the name of Jesus.
2. Thou power of the destroyer, arise and fight against every yoke of the enemy, in the name of Jesus.
3. Thou power of the destroyer, pursue my pursuers, in the name of Jesus.
4. Thou power of the destroyer, torment and oppress my oppressors, in the name of Jesus.
5. Thou power of the destroyer, eat into the bones and the marrows of wickedness, in the name of Jesus.
6. Thou power of the destroyer, move in Your mysterious power and disappoint the devices of the crafty, in the name of Jesus.

WEAPON

83

SPEAR

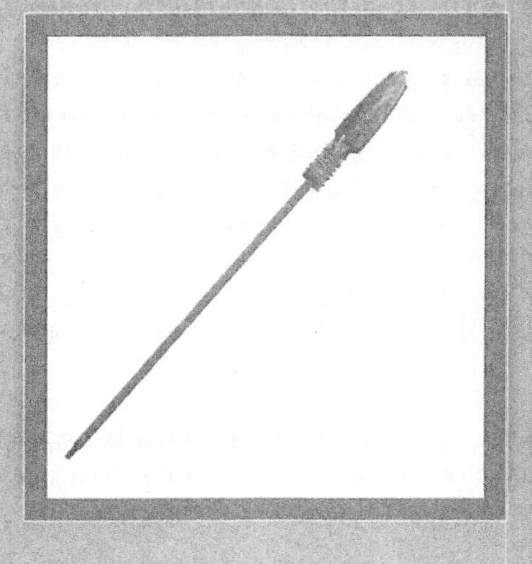

SPIRITUAL WEAPON & DELIVERANCE GUIDE

► *USE THIS WEAPON WHEN YOU WANT TO GIVE THE ENEMY A TECHNICAL KNOCKOUT.*
► *THIS IS A WEAPON TO USE WHEN YOU WANT GOD TO GIVE YOUR ENEMIES USELESS ASSIGNMENTS THAT WILL DIVERT THEM.*
► *THIS IS A WEAPON OF OFFENSIVE WARFARE.*
► *USE THIS WEAPON WHEN YOU NEED TO EXHIBIT VIOLENCE AND FORCE ON THE FIELD OF BATTLE.*
► *THIS IS A WEAPON TO USE WHEN YOU WANT TO EMBARRASS SATANIC AGENTS SENT TO EMBARRASS YOU.*
► *THIS IS A WEAPON TO USE WHEN YOU WANT THE ENEMY TO PANIC.*
► *THIS IS ONE POWERFUL WEAPON WHEN YOU WANT TO FRIGHTEN THE DEVIL AND HIS HOSTS.*

The spear is a strange weapon of spiritual warfare. It is also a weapon of uncommon victory. It is used when you want to invade the territory of the enemy. When there is an evil invasion and you want to defeat the enemy and conquer evil powers, in such a manner as to break wonderful records, just make use of the spear. When enemies surround you, you can stretch out the spear of the Lord towards the direction where you are being harassed.

Josh 8:18

> ***"And the LORD said unto Joshua, Stretch out the spear that is in thy hand toward Ai; for I will give it into thine hand. And Joshua stretched out the spear that he had in his hand toward the city."***

There is a divine spear in your hand; stubborn pursuers can only be conquered when you throw it. Even when an array of demons are trying to invade your life, just a single throw of the spear of God will earn you unchallengeable victory. You can command the spear of the Lord to locate household wickedness, evil spies, familiar spirits, witchcraft covens, environmental demons and territory spirits. No power from the pit of hell can survive the hot spear of the Lord.

Use this weapon when you want your enemies to turn back. Invoke the spear of the Lord in an aggressive shout and stubborn pursuers will either turn back or be slaughtered.

This is the weapon to use when you are ready to declare enough is enough. Use the weapon when you want to possess the gate of your enemies. It is a weapon

to use when you want the enemy to know that you can no longer tolerate the show of shame that has been unleashed upon your destiny.
This is your weapon of great victory. Use it today and you will continue to launch holy invasions upon the territory of anti-breakthrough powers.

PRAYER POINTS

1. O spear of the Lord, arise send confusion to the camp of my enemies, in the name of Jesus.
2. O heavens, bombard every evil gathering assigned against me with the spear of the Lord, in the name of Jesus.
3. My Father, locate every hidden enemy of my soul with Your spear, in the name of Jesus.
4. Where is the spear of the God of Elijah? Pursue my pursuers, in the name of Jesus.
5. Every power shooting me from the dark, receive the spear of the Lord, in Jesus name.
6. O spear of the Lord, arise in the thunder of your power and paralyse my oppressors, in Jesus name.
7. Drinkers of blood and eaters of flesh, hear the word of the Lord, receive the spear of heaven, in the name of Jesus.
8. Spear of the Lord, locate and destroy every enemy of my destiny, in the name of Jesus.

WEAPON

84

EAST WIND

- ***THIS WEAPON IS USED FOR ENOUGH IS ENOUGH BATTLES.***
- ***IT IS USED WHEN YOU WANT TO CONFRONT THE ENEMY OPENLY.***
- ***IT IS USED FOR ROOT OR FOUNDATIONAL BATTLES.***
- ***IT IS ADEQUATE AND EFFECTIVE WHEN YOU WANT TO CONFRONT STUBBORN PURSUERS.***
- ***IT IS AN EFFECTIVE WEAPON FOR FIGHTING GENERATIONAL BATTLES.***
- ***IT IS USED TO ROOT OUT TERRIBLE DEMONIC PRESENCE.***
- ***IT IS A USEFUL WEAPON WHEN YOU WANT TO COMBAT DEEPLY ENTRENCHED WITCHCRAFT POWERS.***

Strange and powerful weapons are seldom introduced into the field of battle. But when the battle gets hot the toughest weapons are brought out. Those who are involved in spiritual warfare as well as deliverance ministers know that there are ordinary weapons and there are extraordinary weapons. The enemy can only harass you when you are making use of simple or ordinary weapons.

The moment you introduce violent weapons, you will be amazed at the speed with which agents of darkness will begin to flee or withdraw from the race. When satanic spies and agents of the kingdom of darkness decide to turn you to a punching bag, you must rise gallantly and launch an offensive warfare which they will never forget.

Woe betide the satanic agent that tries to trouble you when you are armed with a lethal weapon of destruction. Other agents will never come near your vicinity when they see from afar the amount of casualty that litters the battle field. The best way to deal with the enemies that invade you like obnoxious house-flies is to spray a divine insecticide that will knock all of them down in a split second.

The weapon we are studying here is the weapon of the east wind. The east wind is a mighty wind that is witnessed when something violent is about to take place. **Ex. 10:13-15**

> ***"And Moses stretched forth his rod over the land of Egypt, and the LORD brought an east wind upon the land all that day, and all that night; and when it was morning, the east wind brought the locusts.***

And the locusts went up over all the land of Egypt, and rested in all the coasts of Egypt: very grievous were they; before them there were no such locusts as they, neither after them shall be such. For they covered the face of the whole earth, so that the land was darkened; and they did eat every herb of the land, and all the fruit of the trees which the hail had left: and there remained not any green thing in the trees, or in the herbs of the field, through all the land of Egypt."

When God introduces the east wind His goal is to embarrass, and throw your enemies into a panic. Pharaoh, the stubborn despot, was the victim of the terror which the east wind unleashes. The east wind was a weapon that was used all day and all night. It brought an army of locusts that darkened the land of Egypt.

This is a weapon you can use when you want to oppress your oppressors. If you want the powers that have vowed that your destiny will remain buried to experience violent oppression and grievous pain just invoke the east wind. This is a weapon to use when a witchdoctor had been contracted to use divination against you. You simply raise a prayer point by commanding the east wind of the Almighty to visit both the home and shrines of the witchdoctor.

You can also command the east wind to blow an army of powerful locusts into the house of satanic agents that are plotting your death or calamity through fetish means. When the east wind descends it will blind evil spies, slay your stubborn pursuers, paralyze the powers of your father's house and arrest agents of darkness assigned against your destiny.
You need to invoke the east wind of the Almighty. Let the wind blow with all its fury. Let it carry poisonous locusts that will sting those who have gathered in witchcraft covens.

PRAYER POINTS

1. Thou east wind of deliverance, arise from your abode and scatter the camp of my enemies, in the name of Jesus.
2. East wind of deliverance, blow and cause confusion in the

camp of my oppressors, in the name of Jesus.

3. East wind of deliverance cause deliverance to happen in every situation concerning me, in the name of Jesus.
4. East wind of deliverance, attack every plantation of darkness assigned against me, in the name of Jesus.
5. Oh east wind of deliverance, go to the north, south, east and west and shake down every wickedness positioned against me, in the name of Jesus.
6. Thou east wind of deliverance, move in the amazing name of Jesus and cause great deliverance to happen in my body, soul and spirit, in the name of Jesus.
7. East wind of deliverance move and contend with those that contend with me, in Jesus' name.

WEAPON 85

THUNDER OF GOD

▶ THIS PRAYER PROGRAMME IS TO BE USED WHEN WITCHCRAFT BIRDS ARE ON RAMPAGE.

▶ YOU CAN USE THIS WEAPON WHEN YOU WANT POWERS THAT TROUBLE YOUR DESTINY TO BE LOCKED UP IN A CAGE.

▶ THIS WEAPON IS YOUR KEY TO UNCHALLENGEABLE BREAKTHROUGHS.

▶ THIS WEAPON MUST BE USED BY PRAYER WARRIORS AND DELIVERANCE MINISTERS.

▶ YOU NEED THIS WEAPON WHEN YOU ARE CONFRONTED BY SITUATIONS OR CIRCUMSTANCES THAT REQUIRE ACIDIC PRAYERS.

▶ USE THIS WEAPON WHEN ENEMIES MULTIPLY AND SATANIC HARASSMENT IS ON THE INCREASE.

▶ THIS IS THE WEAPON TO USE WHEN WITCHES AND WIZARDS ARE DISTURBING YOU.

In the physical realm thunder is visible to the eyes, the loud noise felt by the ear and when thunder strikes the extent is noticed from one end of the sky to another.

The thunder of God is a weapon of dreadful judgment. When you use the weapon of thunder you are unleashing, upon the enemy, the visitation of terror. **Isaiah 29:6**

> ***"Thou shalt be visited of the LORD of hosts with thunder, and with earthquake, and great noise, with storm and tempest, and the flame of devouring fire."***

The weapon of thunder is used when God wants to lay bare His holy arm. **Isaiah 52:10**

> ***"The LORD hath made bare his holy arm in the eyes of all the nations; and all the ends of the earth shall see the salvation of our God."***

You need to make use of the weapon when mocking powers are asking "where is thy God?"

God introduces the use of the weapon of thunder and lightning when He wants the enemies of His children to tremble. **Exod. 19:16**

> ***"And it came to pass on the third day in the morning, that there were thunders and lightnings, and a thick cloud upon the mount, and the voice of the trumpet exceeding loud; so that all the people that was in the camp trembled."***

You can use this weapon when stubborn pursuers and unrepentant Pharaoh need to witness the raw power of God. When you use this weapon the kingdom of darkness will be shaken. You can also use the weapon when you want to drive satanic agents far away from your vicinity. **Exod. 20:18**

> ***"And all the people saw the thunderings, and the lightenings, and the noise of the trumpet, and the mountain smoking: and when the people saw it, they removed, and stood afar off."***

This type of weapon is useful in a neighbourhood where there are nagging witchcraft attacks. When you invoke the thunder of the Almighty witches and wizards will be arrested. Beloved, you can command the thunder of God to strike any power militating against the fulfilment of your destiny.
Territorial intercessors and deliverance ministers can invoke this weapon whenever heavy demonic presence is felt in a particular locality. This is a weapon to use when you are not ready to tolerate any form of demonic harassment.

PRAYER POINTS

1. O thunder of God, arise, strike terror and fear into the camp of my enemies, in the name of Jesus.
2. O God arise by the weapon of Your thunder and scatter every conspiracy against my life, in the name of Jesus.
3. O God arise and let the weapon of Your thunder move into the camp of my pursuers, in the name of Jesus.
4. O thunder of God arise, go into the waters, into the forest and into the mountains and destroy every stronghold mounted against me, in the name of Jesus.
5. O thunder of God, move in an uncommon way and empower me to possess my possessions, in the name of Jesus.
6. O thunder of God, move in your fire and in your rage and pursue

my pursuers, in the name of Jesus.

7. Let the thunder of the Lord begin to strike fear and terror to the camp of my stubborn pursuers and into the camp of my unrepentant enemy, in the name of Jesus.

WEAPON 86

CAGE

▶ ***THIS PRAYER PROGRAMME IS TO BE USED WHEN WITCHCRAFT BIRDS ARE ON RAMPAGE.***

▶ ***YOU CAN USE THIS WEAPON WHEN YOU WANT POWERS THAT TROUBLE YOUR DESTINY TO BE LOCKED UP IN A CAGE.***

▶ ***THIS WEAPON IS YOUR KEY TO UNCHALLENGEABLE BREAKTHROUGHS.***

▶ ***THIS WEAPON MUST BE USED BY PRAYER WARRIORS AND DELIVERANCE MINISTERS.***

▶ ***YOU NEED THIS WEAPON WHEN YOU ARE CONFRONTED BY SITUATIONS OR CIRCUMSTANCES THAT REQUIRE ACIDIC PRAYERS.***

▶ ***USE THIS WEAPON WHEN ENEMIES MULTIPLY AND SATANIC HARASSMENT IS ON THE INCREASE.***

▶ ***THIS IS THE WEAPON TO USE WHEN WITCHES AND WIZARDS ARE DISTURBING YOU.***

In an era where satanic birds are on rampage, we need a weapon that would trap them. Activities of witchcraft are on the increase. Nowadays, witches fly in the day as well as in the night. Birds of darkness are being empowered by the forces of witchcraft to perpetrate untold damage in families, communities and several work places.

These birds are on the increase as a result of the inability of God's children and prayer warriors to use a weapon that has been tailor made to arrest and cage these wicked satanic powers. What we are looking at in this section is what is called a trap cage. Just as fowlers put birds in a cage, in order to attract other birds which they will consequently trap, God wants us to invoke the weapon of the trap cage to go out to wherever evil birds are flying and trap them. ***Isaiah 5:27***

> ***"None shall be weary nor stumble among them; none shall slumber nor sleep; neither shall the girdle of their loins be loosed, nor the latchet of their shoes be broken:"***

There is a time to shoot birds down. There is also a time to fire divine arrows at them. However, there is a time to make use of acidic prayers that metamorphose into a huge cage which will magnetize, arrest and trap a large company of evil birds that are flying either in the day or in the night.

Here in lies a great strategy; when you are dealing with multiple witchcraft attacks, time, energy and weapons might be wasted if you begin to deal with them one by one. For example if you get to a particular community where there are over one thousand witchcraft birds; facing each witchcraft bird and saying fall down and die might be elementary. But a mature prayer warrior would simply declare in a violent prayer point saying *"O the cage of the Almighty open, and magnetize every evil bird in this community and be closed against them.*

When you take such a prayer point you will use one stone to kill several birds. You need the weapon of the cage of the Almighty when you face multiple satanic attacks and there is an invasion of destructive evil birds. This weapon will catch and deal with more birds that can be dealt with by making individual efforts when you are surrounded by birds that fly around you, under you, and above you. It is a strange weapon to use when you get to the arena of tough battles. This kind of cage will make you a threat to the kingdom of darkness. Use this weapon today and you will experience unchallengeable victory.

PRAYER POINTS

1. My Father, attack my attackers with the cage of fire, in the name of Jesus.
2. O heavens, fish out every strange power in charge of my case by your cage, in the name of Jesus.
3. O heavens, command your cage to possess my possessions, in the name of Jesus.
4. My Father, use Your cage of fire to restore my stolen stars, in the name of Jesus.
5. O cage of the Lord, hear the word of the Lord, pursue my pursuers, in the name of Jesus.
6. Holy Ghost and blood of Jesus defend me by Your cage of fire, in the name of Jesus.
7. O Lord, dispatch Your violent angels with their cage to disgrace my disgrace, in the name of Jesus.

WEAPON 87

THE BEES OF THE LORD TO STING

- *THIS IS A STRATEGIC WEAPON TO USE WHEN THERE IS ANY FORM OF SATANIC GANG UP.*
- *THIS WEAPON WILL PUT YOUR ENEMIES TO FLIGHT.*
- *IT WILL CONFRONT AND SILENCE STUBBORN PURSUERS.*
- *THIS IS THE WEAPON TO USE WHEN MISCHIEVOUS ENEMIES ARE GIVING YOU SLEEPLESS NIGHTS.*
- *YOU NEED THIS WEAPON WHEN YOU ARE DRIBBLED TO A POINT OF CONFUSION BY AGENTS OF DARKNESS.*
- *YOU NEED TO USE THIS WEAPON WHEN YOU SENSE THE INVASION OF MULTIPLE SATANIC AGENTS.*
- *YOU NEED TO MAKE USE OF THIS WEAPON WHEN YOU WANT GOD TO SOUND AN ALARM AND CAUSE PANIC IN THE KINGDOM OF DARKNESS.*
- *MAKE USE OF THIS WEAPON WHEN YOU WANT TO MAKE A PERMANENT MARK ON THE BODIES OF YOUR ENEMIES.*

Some battles of life can be described as completely confusing and extremely tough. **Isaiah 7:18-19**

> ***"And it shall come to pass in that day, that the LORD shall hiss for the fly that is in the uttermost part of the rivers of Egypt, and for the bee that is in the land of Assyria. And they shall come, and shall rest all of them in the desolate valleys, and in the holes of the rocks, and upon all thorns, and upon all bushes."***

Isaiah 5:26

> ***"And he will lift up an ensign to the nations from far, and will hiss unto them from the end of the earth: and, behold, they shall come with speed swiftly:"***

The bee of the Lord is a weapon that can be used to deal with fierce and mischievous enemies. The bees of the Lord to sting can be used when you are under the attack of Beelzebub spirits. It can be used when you can feel the sting of the powers of darkness in your life.

This weapon can be used when the insects of death have surrounded you and you need to fight back. This is a powerful weapon to use when you need to scatter the company of aggressive enemies. The bees of God to sting are used when you want to wage war against witchcraft covens.

You need this weapon when there is an evil gang up against you. You can use it in your community or workplace when satanic agents are brewing an evil plot in order to subject you to severe setbacks, or attack you with a disease that will drain your entire resources. You need this weapon when you want to deal a deadly blow upon the enemy.

When you invoke the bees of the Lord to sting stubborn pursuers and wicked satanic agents will receive fatal blows and severe stings that will make them know that you are too hot to handle.

PRAYER POINTS

1. Father, let the bees of the Lord begin to sting every power of Beelzebub assigned to trouble me, in the name of Jesus.
2. Let the bees of the Lord capture and destroy every insect of death assigned to fight my life, in the name of Jesus.
3. Let the bees of the Lord be released to scatter the company of every aggressive enemy working against me, in the name of Jesus.
4. Let the bees of the Lord be used to scatter every witchcraft coven assigned against my life, in the name of Jesus.
5. Let the bees of the Lord arise and put into confusion and terror every evil gang up against my life, in the name of Jesus.
6. Let the bees of the Lord be released to disgrace every satanic agent consulting oracles against me, in the name of Jesus.
7. Let the bees of the Lord pick out every environmental enemy and put them to shame, in the name of Jesus.

WEAPON 88

THE BLAST OF GOD

▶ ***THIS IS A TOUGH WEAPON TO USE WHEN YOU WANT TO DESTABILIZE TOUGH ENEMIES.***

▶ ***THIS WEAPON CAN BE LIKENED TO THROWING AN EXPLOSIVE BOMB INTO THE CAMP OF YOUR ENEMIES.***

▶ ***USE THIS WEAPON AGAINST LOCATIONS OR PLACES WHERE YOUR NAME IS MENTIONED FOR EVIL.***

▶ ***YOU CAN MAKE USE OF THIS WEAPON WHEN YOU WANT TO WITHDRAW THE PEACE OF YOUR ENEMIES.***

▶ ***YOU CAN INVOKE THE BLAST OF GOD UPON EVERY POWER TOYING WITH YOUR DESTINY.***

▶ ***USE THIS WEAPON WHEN YOU WANT TO INVOKE THE REBUKE OF THE ALMIGHTY UPON DEMONIC POWERS.***

▶ ***YOU NEED THIS WEAPON WHEN YOU WANT TO PUT AN END TO CYCLICAL BATTLES.***

The blast of God is used when you want your enemies to hear terrifying rumours that will send them packing. It is the right weapon to use when you want your enemies to beat a hasty retreat or when you want your enemies to turn back and flee in panic.

You need this weapon when you want to send enemies back to where they came from. It can be used when you want to cause the enemy to fall by his own sword. It is also used when you want to withdraw the peace of your enemy. As a matter of fact, it is one of the strongest back-to-sender weapons

1 Sam 18:15

> ***"Wherefore when Saul saw that he behaved himself very wisely, he was afraid of him."***

You need this weapon when you want to rebuke the enemy. When the blast of God hits the enemy, the enemy will step aside and allow you to move on and fulfil your destiny.

PRAYER POINTS

1. O blast of God, arise, strike terror and fear into the camp of my enemies, in the name of Jesus.
2. O God arise by the weapon of Your blast and scatter every conspiracy against my life, in the name of Jesus.
3. O God arise and let the weapon of Your blast move into the camp of my pursuers, in the name of Jesus.
4. O blast of God arise, go into the waters, into the forest and into the mountains and destroy every stronghold mounted against me, in the name of Jesus.

5. O blast of God, move in an uncommon way and empower me to possess my possessions, in the name of Jesus.
6. O blast of God, move in your fire and in your rage and pursue my pursuers, in the name of Jesus.
7. Let the blast of the Lord begin to strike fear and terror to the camp of my stubborn pursuers and into the camp of my unrepentant enemy, in the name of Jesus.

WEAPON

89

BLINDNESS

- ***USE THIS WEAPON WHEN YOU WANT TO ACTIVATE THE MANIFESTATIONS OF THE POWER OF GOD IN YOUR LIFE.***
- ***IT IS A WEAPON TO BE USED WHEN YOU NOTICE A GATHERING OF DEMONS OR SATANIC AGENTS THAT ARE READY TO ATTACK YOU.***
- ***THIS IS THE WEAPON TO USE WHEN YOU WANT TO DIVERT ENEMIES AND GIVE THEM USELESS ASSIGNMENTS.***
- ***YOU CAN MAKE USE OF THIS WEAPON WHEN YOU WANT TO BLIND EVIL SPIES.***
- ***USE THIS WEAPON WHEN YOU WANT TO TERMINATE THE AGENDA OF THE KINGDOM OF DARKNESS.***
- ***THIS IS THE BEST WEAPON FOR TACKLING EXTREMELY WICKED ENEMIES.***
- ***YOU CAN USE THIS WEAPON TO TERRORIZE THE ENEMIES OF YOUR DESTINY.***

The weapon of blindness is used when you want to deal with witchcraft eyes monitoring you. It is the right weapon to use when aggressive enemies are trying to locate you in order to carry out their evil assignment. You need this weapon when evil wise men are searching for your star. It is used when there is an array of enemies grouping together to terminate your existence. It is the right weapon to use when you are going through automatic failure mechanism. It is a very powerful weapon to use when you are surrounded by physical forces seeking to terminate your life. This weapon will deal with the enemy with devastating accuracy. The weapon of blindness is used to deal with those who were sent to arrest Elisha. **2Kings 6:17-22**

> ***"And Elisha prayed, and said, LORD, I pray thee, open his eyes, that he may see. And the LORD opened the eyes of the young man; and he saw: and, behold, the mountain was full of horses and chariots of fire round about Elisha. And when they came down to him, Elisha prayed unto the LORD, and said, Smite this people, I pray thee, with blindness. And he smote them with blindness according to the word of Elisha. And Elisha said unto them, This is not the way, neither is this the city: follow me, and I will bring you to the man whom ye seek. But he led them to Samaria. And it came to pass, when they were come into Samaria, that Elisha said, LORD, open the eyes of these men, that they may see. And the LORD opened their eyes, and they saw; and, behold, they were in the midst of Samaria. And the king of Israel said unto Elisha, when he saw them, My father, shall I smite them? shall I smite them? And he answered, Thou shalt not smite them: wouldest thou***

smite those whom thou hast taken captive with thy sword and with thy bow? set bread and water before them, that they may eat and drink, and go to their master."

When you discover that some enemies have gathered to attack you, simply invoke the weapon of blindness. **Zech. 12:4**

> ***"In that day, saith the LORD, I will smite every horse with astonishment, and his rider with madness: and I will open mine eyes upon the house of Judah, and will smite every horse of the people with blindness."***

Use this weapon when you want to disgrace your enemies and when you want to give them a useless assignment. You can also use this weapon when you want to send your enemies on a mission of self-destruction.

PRAYER POINTS

1. Oh blindness, arise and trouble every warfare waged against my life, in the name of Jesus.
2. Blindness from the Lord, march in your fury to pursue my pursuers, in the name of Jesus.
3. Father, let blindness be released upon every evil gathering summoned to trouble me, in the name of Jesus.
4. Father, let blindness be released upon every hindrance to securing my portion in the land of the living, in the name of Jesus.
5. Every cleverly concealed warfare assigned against me be scattered by the blindness from the Lord, in the name of Jesus.
6. Every storm of darkness assigned against me, let the blindness from the Lord scatter the tempest, in the name of Jesus.
7. Oh God arise with Your blindness and scatter every wicked association designed against my life, in the name of Jesus.

WEAPON 90

BOILS

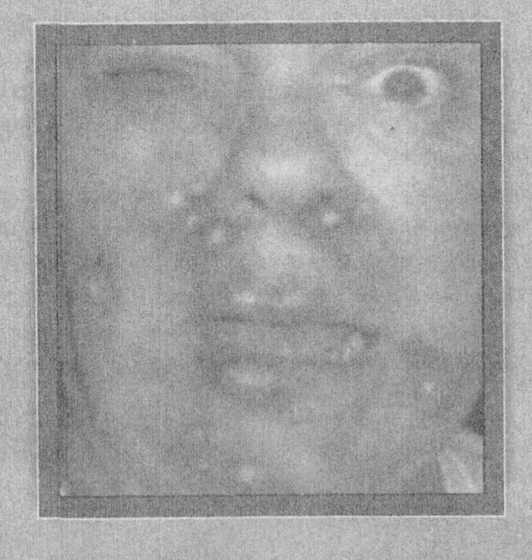

▶ *THIS WEAPON IS TO BE USED TO DESTROY WICKED ENVIRONMENTAL POWERS.*

▶ *YOU CAN PROGRAMME THIS WEAPON AGAINST THOSE WHO ARE PLANNING EVIL AGAINST YOU.*

▶ *IT IS A WEAPON TO BE USED TO TACKLE OCCULT POWERS.*

▶ *THIS IS THE RIGHT WEAPON TO USE DURING INSTANCES OF POWER ENCOUNTER.*

▶ *YOU CAN COMMAND THIS WEAPON TO DESTABILIZE WITCH DOCTORS AND FETISH PRIESTS WHO ARE ENGAGED IN FETISH PLANS IN ORDER TO SWALLOW YOUR DESTINY.*

▶ *WHEN THERE ARE POWERS THAT ARE BENT ON MAKING YOU RESTLESS THROUGHOUT YOUR EXISTENCE, YOU CAN INVOKE THIS WEAPON AGAINST THEM.*

▶ *THIS WEAPON WILL ENABLE YOU TO TROUBLE YOUR TROUBLE.*

The weapon of boils has been divinely established to enable you to destabilize and mesmerize occult and magical powers. The weapon of boils enables you to spray spiritual insecticides upon annoying forces. It can be used when magicians, sorcerers and evil diviners are after you. This weapon has the capacity to frustrate witchdoctors, fetish priests and those who operate with the spirit of divination.

It is a weapon you can use when you urgently need an environmental shield. You can sprinkle the weapon towards the direction of wicked satanic agents, household witchcraft and blood thirsty demons. **Exod. 9:9-11**

> ***"And it shall become small dust in all the land of Egypt, and shall be a boil breaking forth with blains upon man, and upon beast, throughout all the land of Egypt. And they took ashes of the furnace, and stood before Pharaoh; and Moses sprinkled it up toward heaven; and it became a boil breaking forth with blains upon man, and upon beast. And the magicians could not stand before Moses because of the boils; for the boil was upon the magicians, and upon all the Egyptians."***

Beloved, there are certain prayer points that you can make use of when you want to inflict painful boils upon stubborn pursuers, environmental demons and powers that are sent to spy on you. You can command the breaking forth of painful boils upon those who are planning to carry out evil agenda on your life and destiny.

PRAYER POINTS

1. Father, after the order of Moses, I sprinkle boils upon every sorcerer assigned against me, in the name of Jesus.
2. I provoke the weapon of the boils to pursue every environmental demon working against my destiny, in the name of Jesus.
3. I invoke the weapon of the boils to break forth with painful boils upon those who are practising magic against me, in the name of Jesus.
4. I invoke the weapon of the boils to disgrace every stubborn power militating against my life, in the name of Jesus.

WEAPON 91

BOW OF STEEL

► *USE THIS WEAPON WHEN YOU ARE ON A PROGRAMME OF NO ESCAPE FOR THE ENEMY.*
► *THIS WEAPON WILL MAKE RESISTANT POWERS TO BOW.*
► *THIS WEAPON WILL SWALLOW THE ENEMY'S WICKED WEAPONS.*
► *USE THIS WEAPON WHEN YOUR GOAL IS DECISIVE VICTORY.*
► *YOU CAN USE THIS WEAPON TO DESTROY ANCESTRAL GATES OF IRON.*
► *THIS WEAPON IS NEEDED WHEN THE ONLY PRAYER STRATEGY THAT IS NEEDED IS OPERATION JEHU.*
► *USE THIS WHEN YOU WANT TO REDUCE THE CAMP OF THE ENEMY TO RUBBLES.*

The bow of steel is the weapon to use when you are dealing with a stubborn enemy. It can be likened to a powerful missile that can rip through walls, break metals to pieces and shatter a whole building to pieces. ***Job 20:24***

> ***"He shall flee from the iron weapon, and the bow of steel shall strike him through."***

This weapon is reserved for enemies that have defied a class of ordinary weapons. You can resort to the use of the bow of steel when you want to confront highly resistant powers. The bow of steel is the weapon to use when thick darkness surrounds your vision. It is the appropriate weapon to use when you are battling with ancestral gates of brass and bars of iron. It is the weapon you can make use of when you need to strike through the territory of darkness. You need bow of steel prayer points when you want to send a devastating blow to the camp of the enemy. **Isaiah 24:1**

> ***"Behold, the LORD maketh the earth empty, and maketh it waste, and turneth it upside down, and scattereth abroad the inhabitants thereof."***

This is a weapon you can make use of when you do not want the enemy to escape. You can use this weapon when evil powers seem to have escaped other weapons. Use it when you want to capture and destroy the power that constitutes the strength of the enemy.

You can use this weapon when you want to invoke death sentence on the powers that are dribbling you on the field of battle. **Prov. 7:23**

> ***"Till a dart strike through his liver; as a bird hasteth to the snare, and knoweth not that it is for his life."***

The bow of steel is one weapon the enemy cannot resist. Use this weapon today, and your victory will became a reference point in your generation.

PRAYER POINTS

1. **Father, release Your bow and steel to strike through every camp of the enemy, in the name of Jesus.**
2. **Father release Your bow and steel to put to shame every demonic presence, in the name of Jesus.**
3. **I invoke the weapon of bow and steel to win every battle of my life, in the name of Jesus.**
4. **I invoke the weapon of bow and steel to break down ancestral gates of brass and bars of iron, in the name of Jesus.**
5. **I invoke the weapon of bow and steel to scatter the camp of the enemy, in the name of Jesus.**
6. **I invoke the weapon of bow and steel to return to the sender every arrow of the enemy, in the name of Jesus.**
7. **Let the bow and steel from heaven arise in their rage and anger and scatter every camp of the oppressor, in the name of Jesus.**

WEAPON

92

THE BREAD OF ADVERSITY

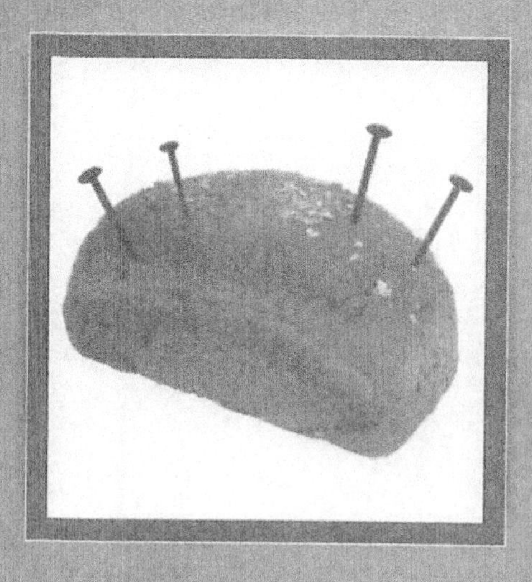

► *USE THIS WEAPON WHEN YOU WANT TO STARVE THE ENEMY TO DEATH.*
► *YOU CAN RAISE THIS WEAPON AGAINST POWERS THAT ARE AGAINST YOUR STAFF OF BREAD.*
► *USE THIS WEAPON WHEN YOU NEED TO DIVERT THE ENEMY'S ATTENTION.*
► *YOU CAN USE THIS WEAPON TO SCATTER WICKED GANG UPS AGAINST YOUR LIFE.*
► *THIS IS THE WEAPON TO USE WHEN YOU WANT TO DEAL WITH HOUSEHOLD WICKEDNESS.*
► *YOU CAN MAKE USE OF THIS WEAPON WHEN YOU WANT TO GET RID OF SATANIC HINDRANCES.*
► *THIS IS THE WEAPON TO USE WHEN YOU WANT TO SEND EVIL ARROWS BACK TO SENDER*
► *USE THIS WEAPON WHEN YOU WANT TO DESTROY THE JOY AND PEACE OF YOUR ENEMIES.*

One of the violent weapons you can use against stubborn enemies is the weapon of the bread of adversity. You can invoke the bread of adversity upon enemies in order to keep them occupied with problems and consequently divert their attention. When you command the enemy to eat the bread of adversity, the enemy will become pre-occupied with sorrow and would have no time to trouble you henceforth. **Psalm 127:2**

> ***"It is vain for you to rise up early, to sit up late, to eat the bread of sorrows: for so he giveth his beloved sleep."***

Some enemies will not give up until you pray that the bread of adversity be given to them. You can also compound their situation by adding the water of affliction to their diet. **Isaiah 30:20**

> ***"And though the Lord give you the bread of adversity, and the water of affliction, yet shall not thy teachers be removed into a corner any more, but thine eyes shall see thy teachers:"***

It is the right weapon to use when you are surrounded by powers that are hungry for blood. Use this weapon if you discover that you are surrounded by people who eat from you and are trying to destroy you. It is a weapon you can use when there is a terrible gang-up or deadly rebellion against your star. It is to be used when there are powers broadcasting your name for evil.

This is a weapon to use when you want to confront powers that are militating against your own staff of bread.

PRAYER POINTS

1. My Father, feed my stubborn enemies with the bread of adversity, in the name of Jesus.
2. My Father, let my enemies consume the bread of adversity, in the name of Jesus.
3. Every rage of adversity against me, I feed you with the bread of adversity, in the name of Jesus.
4. Every opportunity waster, I feed you with the bread of adversity, in the name of Jesus.
5. Let the power of God force feed my enemies with the bread of adversity, in the name of Jesus.
6. Let every terrible gang up and rebellion against my star receive the bread of adversity, in the name of Jesus.
7. Every confrontation against my staff of bread, receive the bread of adversity, in the name of Jesus.

WEAPON

93

BREATH OF GOD

► *THIS IS THE WEAPON TO USE WHEN YOU WANT TO SECURE YOUR EMPLOYMENT.*
► *MAKE USE OF THIS WEAPON WHEN YOU WANT YOUR PROSPERITY OR WEALTH TO REMAIN TAMPER-PROOF.*
► *USE THIS WEAPON WHEN YOU ARE DEALING WITH STUBBORN DEMONIC POWERS.*
► *YOU MUST INVOKE THIS WEAPON WHEN YOU ARE DEALING WITH ENEMIES THAT ARE WEAKENING YOUR STRENGTH.*
► *THIS IS A WEAPON OF DIVINE JUDGMENT AGAINST WICKED POWERS.*
► *MAKE USE OF THIS WEAPON WHEN YOU WANT TO SANITIZE YOUR DWELLING PLACE.*
► *THIS IS ONE WEAPON THAT WILL PUT AN END TO THE ACTIVITIES OF MOCKING POWERS.*

Job 37:10

> ***"By the breath of God frost is given: and the breadth of the waters is straitened."***

This weapon is required when you need prayers that slay the wicked."

Isaiah 11:4

> ***"But with righteousness shall he judge the poor, and reprove with equity for the meek of the earth: and he shall smite the earth with the rod of his mouth, and with the breath of his lips shall he slay the wicked."***

It is to be used when there is a thick cloud of antagonism to be dissolved through prayer. It is to be used when you want to become a terror to the kingdom of darkness. It can also be used you when you want the tide of evil to turn. It is earmarked for seasons when you are facing enemies more powerful than you, and you desire to scatter them. For example a dangerous prayer warrior can pray by saying ***"Oh breath of God, arise in your fury and scatter my oppressors".***

PRAYER POINTS

1. Father, You are a consuming fire, arise in Your full breath and trouble every troubler of my life, in the name of Jesus.
2. Oh breath of God, be released upon every satanic prophet troubling my life, in the name of Jesus.
3. Where is the Lord God of Elijah? Arise in Your breath and fight for me, in the name of Jesus.
4. Breath of God arise, burn to ashes every plantation of

darkness, in the name of Jesus.

5. Oh breath of God, arise and shake down every citadel of darkness and burn every citadel of darkness to ashes, in the name of Jesus.
6. By fire by force, let my portion be released, in the name of Jesus.
7. Oh God that answereth by fire, answer my prayers by fire, in the name of Jesus.
8. Oh God, arise in Your judgement, torment my tormentors, in the name of Jesus.
9. Every rage of the enemy, be quenched by the power of God, in the name of Jesus.
10. O breath of God arise, burn to ashes every coven of darkness, in the name of Jesus.

WEAPON 94

BRILLIANT LIGHT

► *USE THIS WEAPON WHEN YOU ARE SURROUNDED BY DARKNESS.*
► *IT IS A WEAPON TO USE WHEN YOU SENSE THE PRESENCE OF FOUL DEMONS.*
► *USE IT WHEN YOU NEED TO DISPEL THICK DARKNESS.*
► *USE THIS WEAPON WHEN YOU ARE IN THE MIDST OF BATTLES, ESPECIALLY WHEN YOU WANT GOD TO HAVE THE UPPER HAND.*
► *MAKE USE OF THIS WEAPON WHEN YOU WANT EVERY STRANGER TO COME OUT OF HIDING AND BE DISGRACED.*
► *THIS IS A VERY POWERFUL WEAPON TO USE AGAINST SPIRITUAL TERRORISTS AND PERSECUTORS.*
► *YOU CAN MAKE USE OF THIS WEAPON WHEN YOU WANT TO COMPLETELY DESTABILIZE THE FORCES OF THE ENEMY.*

There is no greater weapon for dealing with the kingdom of darkness than using the weapon of brilliant light. **Acts 22:6**

> ***"And it came to pass, that, as I made my journey, and was come nigh unto Damascus about noon, suddenly there shone from heaven a great light round about me."***

This weapon can be used when stubborn pursuers are after you. There are lots of weapons we have left unused. If today's believers have used the weapon of brilliant light some persecutors and terrorists could have been blindfolded and arrested. Disciples like Annanias who could pray made the weapon of brilliant light a formidable one. This weapon can be invoked when you want to show that God is God. It can also be invoked to disperse darkness.

It is also a weapon a child of God can invoke when the prince of this world has darkened the hearts of people and consequently made them resistant to the gospel. It can be invoked as a protective measure when there is a high spate of satanic attacks. This weapon can be used to harass the enemy of the saints.

PRAYER POINTS

1. Every stubborn pursuer, persecuting my star, let the light of God blind you, in the name of Jesus.
2. O heaven, release your light to disperse every darkness surrounding me, in the name of Jesus.
3. O light of God arise and illuminate my environment and disperse darkness, in the name of Jesus.
4. O heavens, arise with the light of God and put to shame every power assigned to put me to shame, in the name of Jesus.

WEAPON

95

BRIMSTONE AND THE FIRE OF GOD

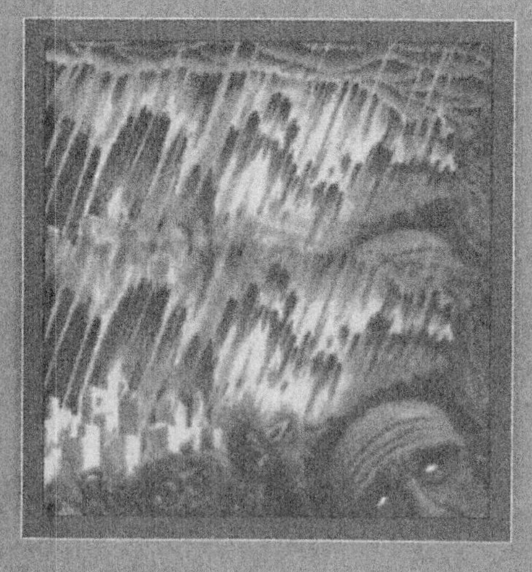

▶THIS WEAPON HAS BEEN CARVED OUT FOR HIGH LEVEL SPIRITUAL WARFARE.
▶ IT IS A BATTLE CRY TO BE RAISED WHEN YOU WANT TO SILENCE THE ENEMY.
▶ THIS WEAPON IS APPROPRIATE WHEN YOU WANT TO DESTROY THE DESTROYER.
▶ IT IS A FITTING WEAPON FOR CONFRONTING WITCHES AND WIZARDS THAT ARE CARRYING OUT DEADLY ATTACKS.
▶ YOU CAN USE THIS WEAPON TO DESTROY THE STRONGMAN OF FAMILY DESTRUCTION.
▶ THIS WEAPON CAN BE USED WHEN YOU NEED FIRE ON THE FIELD OF BATTLE.
▶ YOU CAN MAKE USE OF THIS WEAPON WHEN YOU NEED TO DISGRACE EVERY POWER CHALLENGING GOD IN YOUR LIFE.

Raise this battle cry when you want the Ancient of Days to protect His interest in your life. This is the weapon to use when you want to wipe off the company of wicked spies. **Ezekiel 38:22**

> ***"And I will plead against him with pestilence and with blood; and I will rain upon him, and upon his bands, and upon the many people that are with him, an overflowing rain, and great hailstones, fire, and brimstone."***

You can also invoke this weapon upon the enemy when you want to set their territory on fire. **Isaiah 34:9**

> ***"And the streams thereof shall be turned into pitch, and the dust thereof into brimstone, and the land thereof shall become burning pitch."***

This is the right weapon to use when you want to destroy demonic destroyers. **Luke 17:29**

> ***"But the same day that Lot went out of Sodom it rained fire and brimstone from heaven, and destroyed them all."***

This weapon can be invoked when you battle occultism, witchcraft covens and evil associations. It is a weapon you can use against eaters of flesh and drinkers of blood. It can also be used against strongmen of family destruction. They are useful weapons when you want to battle agents of Satan that are on assignment against you.

PRAYER POINTS

1. Father, You are a consuming fire, arise in Your fire and trouble every troubler of my life, in the name of Jesus.
2. O brimstone and fire of God, be released upon every satanic prophet troubling my life, in the name of Jesus.
3. Where is the Lord God of Elijah? Arise in Your fire and fight for me, in the name of Jesus.
4. Brimstone and fire of God arise, burn to ashes every plantation of darkness, in the name of Jesus.
5. O brimstone and fire of God, arise and shake down every citadel of darkness and burn them to ashes, in the name of Jesus.
6. By fire by force, let my portion be released, in the name of Jesus.
7. O God that answereth by fire, answer my prayers by fire, in the name of Jesus.
8. O God, arise in Your fire of judgement, torment my tormentors, in the name of Jesus.
9. Every rage of the enemy, be quenched by the brimstone and fire of God in the name of Jesus.

WEAPON

96

BROOM OF DESTRUCTION

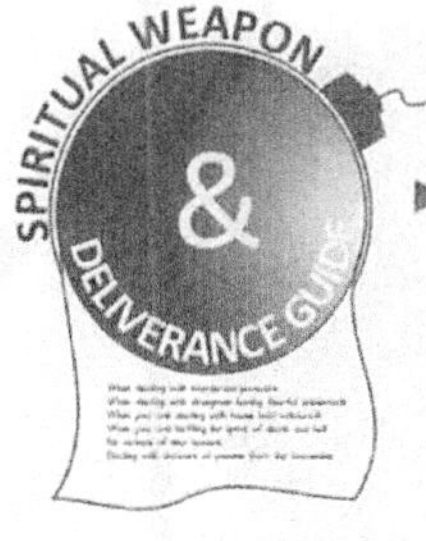

- ***THIS WEAPON CAN BE USED TO WIPE OFF SHAME AND DISGRACE.***
- ***IT CAN BE USED TO SWEEP AWAY EVERY PRESENCE OF THE STRONG MAN.***
- ***IT CAN BE USED WHEN YOU WANT TO SWEEP AWAY THE REBELLION OF DARK POWERS.***
- ***YOU NEED THIS WEAPON WHEN YOU NEED TO DEAL WITH SPIRITUAL POLLUTION.***
- ***IT IS A POWERFUL SANITIZER OR CLEANSER.***
- ***YOU NEED THIS WEAPON WHEN YOU WANT TO FUMIGATE YOUR IMMEDIATE ENVIRONMENT.***
- ***YOU NEED TO USE THIS WEAPON WHEN YOU WANT TO DEAL A DEATH BLOW ON AGENTS OF DESTRUCTION.***

Like the name sounds, it is a weapon you can use to wipe the enemy clean and make their power and whatever they stand for to become history. You can use this weapon when you need to deal with a cloud of satanic hatred around you. It is a clean up weapon; a sort of spiritual detergent to sanitize our environment from demonic infiltration. This weapon must be invoked when you are determined to sweep away the strong man assigned against you to trouble your star. **Isaiah 14:23**

> ***"I will also make it a possession for the bittern, and pools of water: and I will sweep it with the besom of destruction, saith the LORD of hosts."***

This weapon can also be referred to as the besom of destruction. The word besom stands for a broom or brush used for sweeping something away. When the broom descends on the enemy, the totality of rebellion, satanic arrows, and demonic campaign of calumny will be swept away. The camp of the enemy would be emptied. **Isaiah 34:11**

> ***"But the cormorant and the bittern shall possess it; the owl also and the raven shall dwell in it: and he shall stretch out upon it the line of confusion, and the stones of emptiness."***

It is a powerful weapon for dealing with spiritual defilement and pollution. It is very useful in missionary work when darkness has already overshadowed the land and demonic powers hold sway. In that instance, the weapon to use is the broom of destruction. Evil spirits may continue to ravage a community until you invoke the broom of destruction to descend upon them.

PRAYER POINTS

1. O God, arise and use Your broom of destruction to sweep away everything troubling my destiny, in the name of Jesus.
2. O God, arise and sweep away every demonic campaign against my life with Your broom of destruction, in the name of Jesus.
3. O God arise and use Your broom of destruction to sweep away every defilement and pollution working against my life, in the name of Jesus.
4. O broom of destruction from heaven, arise sweep away every evil gang up against me, in the name of Jesus.
5. I invoke the weapon of the broom of God to sweep away every evil word assigned against my life, in the name of Jesus.
6. I invoke the weapon of the broom of God to sweep away every incantation and every evil word spoken against my life, in the name of Jesus.
7. I invoke the weapon of the broom of destruction to sweep away every demonic presence in my environment, in my marriage, in my career and in my destiny, in the name of Jesus.

WEAPON 97

CANKERWORM

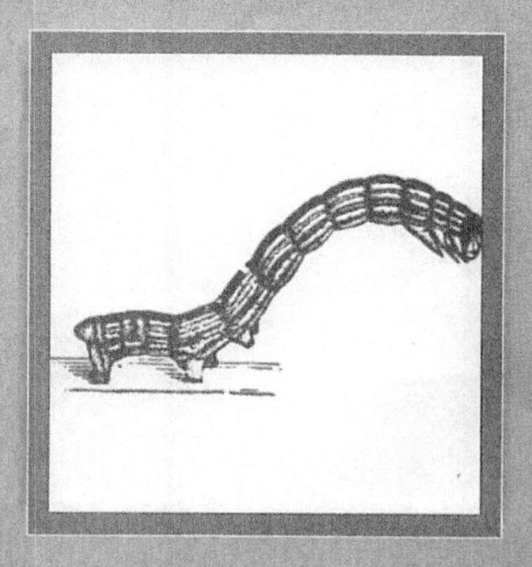

▶YOU CAN MAKE USE OF THIS WEAPON WHEN YOU WANT TO CARRY OUT AN OFFENSIVE AIRSTRIKE AGAINST THE ENEMY.
▶ THIS WEAPON WILL ENABLE YOU TO TAKE THE BATTLE TO THE REALM OF THE HEAVENLIES.
▶ THIS IS A WEAPON YOU CAN USE WHEN YOU WANT GOD TO LIFT UP YOUR HEAD AS A WARRIOR.
▶ THIS IS THE WEAPON TO USE WHEN YOU WANT POWER TO CHANGE HANDS.
▶YOU CAN MAKE USE OF THIS WEAPON WHEN YOU WANT THE ENEMY TO HAVE A TASTE OF THE RAW POWER OF GOD.
▶ USE THIS WEAPON WHEN YOU WANT TO ACHIEVE UNCHALLENGEABLE VICTORY.
▶YOU CAN MAKE USE OF THIS WEAPON TO ELIMINATE EVERY ENEMY OF YOUR DESTINY.

The canker worm is a powerful weapon. This weapon is needed when you want to send divine solders to eat up the strength of the enemy and his weapons of war. It is a weapon that totally devours the entire fabric of the forces of darkness. It is a weapon of the Almighty to devour the backbone of demonic invaders.

Prayers using the cankerworm are powerful prayers. It can be invoked to stop the activities of violent satanic agents. It can also be used to waste the enemy. Specifically, this weapon can be used to melt away the financial power of any power trying to use money to torment you. With this weapon you will bring the enemy down to his knees.

This weapon can be used when you want to clear away the residue of satanic arrows and left over weapons of darkness. It is a weapon that will enable you to totally damage the stronghold of darkness. It is a weapon you can use when you want to confiscate the weapons of satanic solders. **Joel 1:4**

> ***"That which the palmerworm hath left hath the locust eaten; and that which the locust hath left hath the cankerworm eaten; and that which the cankerworm hath left hath the caterpiller eaten."***

When this weapon is used, they function in the companies of divine caterpillars and divine locusts. **Deut. 28:38**

> ***"The LORD shall smite thee with madness, and blindness, and astonishment of heart:"***

Isaiah 33:4

> ***"And your spoil shall be gathered like the gathering of the caterpiller: as the running to and fro of locusts shall he run upon them."***

Joel 2:25

> ***"And I will restore to you the years that the locust hath eaten, the cankerworm, and the caterpiller, and the palmerworm, my great army which I sent among you."***

The cankerworm, the caterpillar and locust constitute a powerful squad in the army of the Lord. When you invoke this weapon you will succeed in grinding enemies and their territories to powder.

PRAYER POINTS

1. Cankerworm from heaven, locate every plantation of darkness in my life and uproot them, in the name of Jesus.
2. Cankerworm from heaven, eat up every satanic seed planted in the garden of my life, in the name of Jesus.
3. Let the commandment of the Lord go forth and deliver me from every plantation of the enemy using the weapon of the cankerworm, in the name of Jesus.
4. Cankerworm of the Most High God, invade every house of the strongman and pursue them out of their hiding places, in the name of Jesus.
5. I invoke the power of the cankerworm of God to repossess and to reposition everything the enemy has stolen, in the name of Jesus.
6. Let the cankerworm from heaven go forth in the thunder of thy power to send confusion into the camp of my enemies, in the name of Jesus.
7. I use the weapon of the cankerworm to clear every blockage in my way, in the name of Jesus.

WEAPON

98

CHARIOT OF GOD

▶ USE THIS WEAPON WHEN YOU WANT TO FIGHT ENEMIES AND DEFEAT THEM

▶ YOU NEED TO MAKE USE OF THIS WEAPON WHEN YOU NEED TO ANNOUNCE THE DEFEAT OF POWERS OF DARKNESS.

▶ MAKE USE OF THIS WEAPON WHEN YOU WANT TO INFLICT SUDDEN AND FATAL WOUNDS ON THE ENEMY.

▶ MAKE USE OF THIS WEAPON WHEN YOU WANT TO WITNESS THE POWER OF THE GOD OF VENGEANCE.

▶ YOU CAN MAKE USE OF THIS WEAPON WHEN YOU WANT TO OBTAIN COMPLETE DELIVERANCE.

▶ THIS IS THE WEAPON TO USE WHEN YOU WANT TO INVADE THE TERRITORY OF THE ENEMY.

▶IT IS YOUR BEST WEAPON WHEN YOU WANT TO EXPERIENCE TOTAL VICTORY.

Spiritual warfare is real. God has given us lots of practical weapons to enable us experience His raw power, either on the deliverance field or in the realm of spiritual warfare. One of such weapons is the weapon of the chariot of God. God is aware of all the angles and technicalities of war. Hence, he has created sufficient weapons to enable us dribble the enemy and score unchallengeable goals. There comes a time on the field of battle when God comes with his chariot like a whirlwind. When this happens the enemy is confused and locked on the horns of a dilemma. **Isaiah 66:15**

> ***"For, behold, the LORD will come with fire, and with his chariots like a whirlwind, to render his anger with fury, and his rebuke with flames of fire."***

God has chariots in the sky. He conveys them on the wings of the wind. **Psalm 104:3**

> ***"Who layeth the beams of his chambers in the waters: who maketh the clouds his chariot: who walketh upon the wings of the wind:"***

There is a powerful link between ground battles and air strikes according to the scriptures. **Amos 9:6**

> ***"It is he that buildeth his stories in the heaven, and hath founded his troop in the earth; he that calleth for the waters of the sea, and***

> ***poureth them out upon the face of the earth: The LORD is his name."***

The chariots of God have been created in order to help you take the battle to a realm where the devil cannot win. The chariots of God ride on the crest of the wings of the wind. **Psalm 18:10**

> ***"And he rode upon a cherub, and did fly: yea, he did fly upon the wings of the wind."***

The chariot of God can stand as ground armoured tanks. It can be used during ground warfare though it descends from heaven. This weapon can be invoked when you want the power of God to catapult you above the enemy. It is the weapon to invoke when you want to defeat frustration, disappointment and stagnation. It can be invoked when you want a change of level, or when you need a divine lift that will embarrass the enemy. It is the weapon to invoke when the forces of Syria and Pharaoh are arrayed against you. This weapon will make power to change hands and sentence your enemy to shame and divine embarrassment.

PRAYER POINTS

1. O God, arise with Your chariot, like a whirlwind and blow away every camp of the oppressor, in the name of Jesus.
2. O God arise with Your chariot of fire and pursue all my spiritual pursuers, in the name of Jesus.
3. Every warfare in the heavenlies, on the earth and in the sea, let the chariot of God pursue them and eliminate them, in the name of Jesus.
4. Let the chariot of God catapult me above my enemies, in the name of Jesus.
5. Let the chariot of God defeat every frustration, disappointment and stagnation in my life, in the name of Jesus.
6. Let the chariot of God enforce power to change hands from the hands of wickedness to my hands, in the name of Jesus.

WEAPON

99

ARROW OF GOD

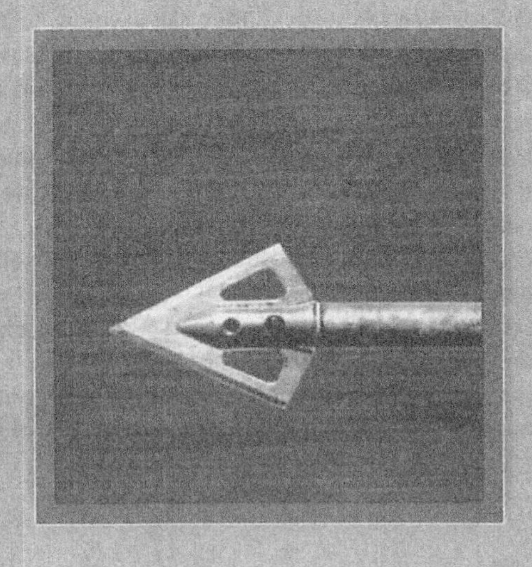

▶USE THIS WEAPON WHEN YOU WANT TO ADDRESS THE ROOTS OF YOUR PROBLEMS.

▶ USE THIS WEAPON WHEN YOU ARE DEALING WITH SATANIC BARRIERS.

▶YOU CAN MAKE USE OF THIS WEAPON WHEN YOU ARE ON A MISSION OF TOTAL EXTERMINATION OF DEMONIC COBWEBS.

▶THIS IS AN APPROPRIATE WEAPON TO USE WHEN YOU WANT TO MOVE FORWARD BY FIRE.

▶ YOU MUST USE THIS WEAPON TO BREAK THROUGH FROM THE SHACKLES OF BONDAGE.

▶ THIS IS THE WEAPON TO USE WHEN YOU WANT TO DISGRACE POWERS THAT ARE SPONSORED TO DISGRACE YOU.

▶ YOU CAN MAKE USE OF THIS WEAPON WHEN YOU WANT TO GO INTO SESSIONS OF AGGRESSIVE WARFARE.

Arrow of God constitutes one of the most formidable weapons of spiritual warfare. It has been divinely designed to enable you inflict deadly blows upon stubborn enemies. You need this weapon when you want to take life's battles to a realm where you will win decisive battles with ease.
The arrows of God are not a weak weapon by any standard. It is a potent weapon that will move you out of the cage of familiar powers. It is the right weapon to use when you are tired of being tired or sick of being sick, The arrow of God is a weapon you can use when you are surrounded by aggressive enemies. It is the weapon to use when agents of death are after you.

This weapon is powerful and effective when you have satanic arrows fired against you from afar and there is a need to fight back. This is a powerful weapon to use when you want to inflict fatal wounds on the enemy. It is also needed when you want to win decisive and swift victory over the enemy.

"And the LORD shall be seen over them, and his arrow shall go forth as the lightning: and the Lord GOD shall blow the trumpet, and shall go with whirlwinds of the south." - Zech 9:14

Here we are told that the spirit of invading the territory of the enemy can be likened to the speed of lightening. This weapon comes handy when you want to enjoy blessings from the Lord without unnecessary hindrance from the quarters of the power of the emptiers. You need the weapon when you want to obtain total deliverance.

"And he said, Open the window eastward. And he opened it. Then Elisha said, Shoot. And he shot. And he said, The arrow of the LORD'S deliverance, and the arrow of deliverance from Syria: for thou shalt smite the Syrians in Aphek, till thou have consumed them." - 2 Kings 13:17

This is the weapon to use when you want the God of the suddenly to descend upon the enemy and scatter evil powers.

"But God shall shoot at them with an arrow; suddenly shall they be wounded." - Psalms 64:7

God has promised to shoot and wound your enemies suddenly. You must use this weapon when you want the God of vengeance to arise and defend His interest in your life. While God uses His divine arrows to set you free and launches you into the realm of complete deliverance, God will, in another breath inject the poison of powerful arrows into the bodies of enemies that have vowed that your destiny will never be fulfilled. This is the type of arrows that Pharaoh and his hosts and their horses received and they perished in the Red Sea.

PRAYER POINTS

1. O arrow of the Lord, arise send confusion to the camp of my enemies, in the name of Jesus.
2. O God, bombard every evil gathering assigned against me with the arrow of the Lord, in the name of Jesus.
3. My Father, locate every hidden enemy of my soul with your arrow, in the name of Jesus.
4. Where is the arrow of the God of Elijah? Pursue my pursuers, in the name of Jesus.
5. Every power shooting me from the dark, receive the arrow of the Lord, in Jesus' name.
6. O arrow of the Lord, arise in the thunder of your power and paralyse my oppressors, in Jesus' name.
7. Drinkers of blood and eaters of flesh, hear the word of the Lord, receive the arrow of heaven, in the name of Jesus.
8. Arrow of the Lord, locate and destroy every enemy of my destiny, in the name of Jesus.

WEAPON

100

AXE OF GOD

▶ THIS IS ONE OF THE TOUGHEST WEAPONS TO USE ON THE FIELD OF BATTLE.

▶ THIS IS A STRANGE WEAPON TO USE WHEN YOU WANT TO OVERPOWER THE ENEMY.

▶ THIS IS THE WEAPON TO USE WHEN DEADLY WEAPONS ARE NEEDED DURING TOUGH BATTLES.

▶ TO DEAL WITH POWERS THAT BITE WITHOUT REMNANTS, YOU NEED TO USE THIS WEAPON.

▶ MAKE USE OF THIS WEAPON WHEN YOU NEED TO INJECT POISON IN THE BODY OF THE ENEMY.

▶ YOU NEED TO USE THIS WEAPON WHEN YOU WANT TO KILL EVERY POWER THAT WANTS TO KILL YOU.

▶ THIS IS THE WEAPON TO USE WHEN YOU ARE FIGHTING AGAINST THE POWERS OF YOUR FATHER'S HOUSE.

This is one of the most powerful weapons of spiritual warfare. It comes handy when you want to obtain your deliverance and come out of the cage of darkness. This weapon could be better understood when you consider what axes are used for. In a situation where the knife or cutlass fails, you resort to the use of axes. Consequently, you use the axe when you have deep rooted problems that need to be cut down. There are certain problems in the area of deliverance and life's battles that have become strongly entrenched. Such problems can only be tackled and solved when you use the weapon of the axe of God.

This is the weapon to use when satanic trees block your way and you face major hindrances on your way to the top. When you want to move forward by fire, you must use the weapon of the axe of God. It is the right weapon to use when you suddenly find yourself in an iron cage and you need to break loose and enjoy your liberty.

You need this weapon when you need to demolish and pull down the enemy's fortified strongholds. This is an important weapon to use when there is a satanic establishment against your progress and you need to clear the way. Resistant enemies and stubborn pursuers can be dealt with using this formidable weapon. This is not an ordinary weapon, it is a weapon of total extermination. It is useful when you want to embark on what I term as operation "Wipe out".

"And now also the axe is laid unto the root of the trees: therefore every tree which bringeth not forth good fruit is hewn down, and cast

> ***into the fire." Matthew 3:10***
>
> ***"And now also the axe is laid unto the root of the trees: every tree therefore which bringeth not forth good fruit is hewn down, and cast into the fire." - Luke 3:9***

When the axe hits the tree, the result is that evil trees are hewn down and cast into fire. Evil trees are not only uprooted, they are burnt to ashes when the weapon of the axe of God is in operation. Laying the axe at the root of a tree denotes that the tree is to be cut down. It is a weapon of finality or total destruction. With this weapon you would deal with satanic onslaughts from the roots.

> ***"Thou art my battle axe and weapons of war: for with thee will I break in pieces the nations, and with thee will I destroy kingdoms;"- Jer 51:20***

It is an aggressive weapon of war. It breaks in pieces and destroys totally, every stubborn stronghold that is militating against you from the kingdom of darkness. You need this weapon when you want to kill satanic arrows. It is a weapon of force. You can use it when you want to take military action against violent demonic powers. It is a weapon of speedy action against stubborn enemies. The phrase; "And now, the axe ..." Reiterates the fact that it is a weapon that functions with urgency and dispatch.

> ***"When thou shalt besiege a city a long time, in making war against it to take it, thou shalt not destroy the trees thereof by forcing an axe against them: for thou mayest eat of them, and thou shalt not cut them down (for the tree of the field is man's life) to employ them in the siege:" - Deut 20:19***

Now it is the time to lay a siege against the powers that have laid siege against you. You must command the axe of God to fall as a destructive force against wicked powers. The force of the axe will make the enemy to submit and surrender.

PRAYER POINTS

1. O heavens, release the axe of God to enforce the release of every good thing stolen from me, in the name of Jesus.
2. Every destiny robber assigned against my life, I come against you with the axe of God, in the name of Jesus.
3. Let the mystery of the axe of God defend my portion, in the name of Jesus.
4. I invoke the power of the axe of God to arrest my arrester, in the name of Jesus.
5. In the heavenlies, on earth, in the water, let the axe of God recover my stolen possession, in the name of Jesus.
6. Axe of God from heaven, confuse every coven assigned against my destiny, in the name of Jesus.
7. Power of the axe of God, arise in your mysterious power and scatter my oppressors, in the name of Jesus.

WEAPON 101

RELEASING THE BREAKER

- ***WHEN YOU ARE DEALING WITH EXTREMELY WICKED POWERS.***
- ***WHEN YOU WANT TO PUT AN END TO THE ACTIVITIES OF ASTRAL POWERS.***
- ***IT CAN BE USED TO TACKLE THE ROD OF THE WICKED.***
- ***YOU NEED THIS WEAPON WHEN YOU WANT TO BREAK THE HANDS OF THE WICKED.***
- ***IT IS A POTENT WEAPON FOR DEALING WITH OPPRESSORS AND STUBBORN PURSUERS.***
- ***IT WILL TACKLE BLOOD SUCKING DEMONS AND STUBBORN WITCHCRAFT.***

When spiritual warfare gets heated up, tough weapons are needed. When these weapons are brought to the field of battle, there shall be great consequences in the camp of the enemy. Tough weapons are used in the day of tough battles. When you release the breakers against the ranks of the enemy they shall be scattered and their bones shall be broken to pieces. The weapon of the breaker is used when God wants to break the rod of every power militating against you. It is used when God wants to break the teeth of every wicked lion assigned against your life. It also comes in handy when God wants to break in pieces every wicked oppressor. Use this weapon today and your stubborn enemies shall be broken to devastating pieces. The power of the Most High shall come like strong acid and grind to pieces every weapon of the kingdom of darkness.

Micah 2:12-13
I will surely assemble, O Jacob, all of thee; I will surely gather the remnant of Israel; I will put them together as the sheep of Bozrah, as the flock in the midst of their fold: they shall make great noise by reason of the multitude of men. The breaker is come up before them: they have broken up, and have passed through the gate, and are gone out by it: and their king shall pass before them, and the LORD on the head of them.

Deuteronomy 7:5
But thus shall ye deal with them; ye shall destroy their altars, and break down their images, and cut down their groves, and burn their graven images with fire.